NAILED!

NAILED!

THE IMPROBABLE RISE AND SPECTACULAR FALL OF
LENNY DYKSTRA

CHRISTOPHER FRANKIE

RUNNING PRESS
PHILADELPHIA · LONDON

ISBN 978-0-7624-4799-2

Library of Congress Control Number: 2013930105

E-book ISBN 978-0-7624-4828-9

9 8 7 6 5 4 3 2 1
Digit on the right indicates the number of this printing

Design by Joshua McDonnell
Edited by Geoffrey Stone
Typography: Akzidenz, Bembo

Running Press Book Publishers
2300 Chestnut Street
Philadelphia, PA 19103-4371

Visit us on the web!
www.runningpress.com

FOR EVERYONE WHO HELPED ME TELL THIS
AMAZING AND COMPLICATED STORY. I COULDN'T
HAVE DONE IT WITHOUT YOU.

CONTENTS

PREFACE

In 1986, as a nine-year-old Mets fan, I only dreamed of getting a phone call from Lenny "Nails" Dykstra. By late 2008, I dreaded it. My childhood hero had become my boss, and for a very long nine months I witnessed his devastating real-life, late-inning collapse.

But *Nailed!* isn't just about the nosedive—it's a view from inside the cockpit of Dykstra's meteoric ascent, his battle to stay airborne, and the violent internal turbulence that ultimately tore the wings from the plane years before the fuselage hit the ground.

It's also an entertainingly forensic account of Dykstra, the embodiment of the "Little Engine That Could," from his fight out of "the middle" beginning at birth in 1963 to his court appearances, incarceration, and convictions in 2012.

This true American tragedy recounts how one of the most memorable sports icons of my generation sold his soul with the help of some unscrupulous characters and, little by little, how dangerously close I came to losing mine without even knowing it. *Nailed!* details the two Lenny Dykstras I came to know—good Lenny and bad Lenny—and how the distance between those extremes grew wider than the Grand Canyon.

My small part in this crazy tale began in 2008 when I resigned from my job as managing editor at Money-Media, a unit of the *Financial Times*, to accept a job working *with* Dykstra through an established company. I quickly ended up working *for* Dykstra directly in his all-consuming, 24/7 world as his personal ghostwriter, editor, New York office manager, and right-hand man.

Ex-NBA star Charles Barkley once told the world, "I am not a role model," and as an adult I knew Dykstra wasn't either—at least outside the lines. His outrageous behavior and steroid abuse were no secret. I knew he was no Boy Scout when I took the job, but I also knew there was more to the man known as Nails than his public image suggested. He had reinvented himself not once, but twice—first as a car wash kingpin and then again as a stock market savant and sidekick to Jim Cramer, the biggest name in Wall Street entertainment.

I respected his resilience, determination, and uncanny ability to break through barriers and sniff out a buck. He had made more money after he retired from Major League Baseball than he ever did slipping on the stirrups, and the sky seemed to be the limit. Working for him was a risk, but one with a potentially huge payoff. I knew I would never forgive myself if I passed up this once-in-a-lifetime adventure.

However, I didn't quite comprehend at the time what I was getting myself into and how difficult it would be to escape. For many months I was stuck—no really good options and no clear way out. I did eventually "get out" when I walked away from Dykstra and the substantial debt he owed me in late 2008. It was clear Dykstra was a sinking ship, and much more than his being a financial wreck, I knew he was heading for trouble—real trouble—and I was powerless to do anything about it.

The redeeming qualities that first made me trust him were buried beneath severe, toxic paranoia, apparent substance abuse, reckless abandon, and a complete detachment from reality. It was only a matter of time, I suspected, before he would end up in jail . . . or worse.

That's why my decision to write this book was not an easy one. I had told Dykstra anecdotes to friends and family over countless dinners, drinks, and car rides. The reaction was always laughter, astonishment, uncomfortable squirming, or a combination of all three. Those stories were fun to tell and retell. Then there were the others. Because I knew Dykstra personally and because parts of this story were incredibly sad, I was conflicted.

Plus, I knew if I were to write this book—and do it right—I would have to face some uncomfortable subjects. Many of my decisions and actions would be printed on these pages for all to judge. More than a few people would be unhappy with their portrayal in this book. And at certain points I would also have to publicly defend Lenny Dykstra at a time when it's extremely unpopular to do so.

But in the end, I knew this story would be told, and I had to be the one to tell it if it were to be complete. My unique experience and insider's perspective made me one of the only people on the planet who knew the intricacies of this surprisingly complex story about an unusual and deceptively intelligent fallen star. I wanted to humanize Dykstra beyond the cartoon character created in the press. Plus, I wanted the whole story to be told—not just the narrative created by reporters and television show producers who labeled Dykstra a golden god in 2008 only to rebrand him as a buffoon and the devil incarnate a few months later. The truth, of course, is somewhere in between and much more nuanced.

To tell that story, I knew I couldn't just tell my story. I turned to my journalistic roots to meticulously craft and document the pages that follow.

Rather than just a firsthand account, *Nailed!* is a well-researched, fact-based story that provides you, the reader, with my insights plus the benefit of additional perspectives that I didn't have at the time in order to paint a fuller picture of the events unfolding around me and Dykstra.

To do that, I interviewed more than seventy-five of Dykstra's teammates, coaches, employees, reporters, law enforcement officials, victims, friends, and family. I reviewed thousands of court documents, e-mails, news articles, text messages, and videos. I also relied on my personal experience and on entries in an electronic journal I updated sporadically in 2008.

In this tale, fact truly is stranger than fiction. Life is a journey. Enjoy the read.

BACK TO THE MIDDLE

It all seems so surreal now. The multimillion-dollar palace on the mountaintop. The luxurious private jets. And most of all, working side by side with my childhood hero, legend Lenny "Nails" Dykstra, pulling all-nighters fueled by $70 ice cream sundaes, Twizzlers, and root beer.

But that's ancient history. Since my abrupt departure from Team Dykstra, life is way more relaxed. No more 3 a.m. phone calls or 115-hour workweeks. Instead, in many ways, I've returned to "the middle"—that gray area between winners and losers that Dykstra so despises.

I was sitting on my parents' couch as raindrops the size of quarters ricocheted off the sliding-glass-door windows and exploded on the back deck. That's when I got *THE* phone call. I didn't recognize the number, but I instantly knew it was HIM.

"Chris . . . it's Lenny," his gruff voice rang out, echoing in my ear. My eyes widened, and a wave of anxiety rushed through my veins. I had been considering writing *Nailed* for months and had done some preliminary research for it. It was only a matter of time before Dykstra got wind of my work and called to confront me—or threaten me, as he had before. Yet there was no anger in his voice and no mention of our falling out. My anxiety melted away, and suddenly I was transported back to better times when Nails had been on top of the world and he and I had been pals.

Prior to that call, we hadn't spoken in months. In the interim, Dykstra told *New York Post* reporter Keith Kelly that I was "delusional" and claimed, of all things, that I owed him money. Over some beers the night that article came out in the *Post*, my friends and I had a few good laughs at the absurdity of Dykstra's quotes, but part of me was hurt. I had gone to bat for the guy time and again and walked away bumped and battered.

But for forty minutes on a cold, soggy day in May 2009, it felt as if the last six months had never occurred. In reality, Dykstra was facing the deepest count of his life and the odds were clearly stacked against him. The only one who didn't seem to comprehend the gravity of the situation was Dykstra. What had once started out as an innovative, promising, and exciting new era for the mighty Nails had devolved into a full-on circus, with Dykstra in the center ring cracking the whip at whoever walked by.

It was hard to feel sorry for the guy after all the lousy things he had done to so many people. But thinking back to the all-nighters we had spent working together, how he had opened up his gorgeous $18 million mansion to me and my girlfriend, Rhea, and how he had always made a point of asking about my family, I couldn't help but feel sad for the guy and how far he'd fallen. It was as if the game were over, but he was still standing in the batter's box waiting for the next pitch as the grounds crew shut down the stadium's lights.

I told him I had seen the news articles. I asked if he was okay. "I don't read the papers," he shot back. "I know that they wrote some stuff that's been pretty bad, like talking to all the criminals. All that stuff's bullshit, dude," he said, his voice growing louder and angrier. He then bounced from topic to topic, forwarding e-mail conversations to me and telling me about folks on his list of traitors—onetime friends, fellow superstars, employees or business associates who had betrayed him somehow.

As I sat there bewildered that I was on the phone again with Dykstra, he told me about former employees who were bashing him in the press or had taken him to court. "Oh yeah, dude, they're scumbags, dude," he said. "People are just piling on trying to get free money." He said he "smoked" all the people challenging him and "gassed" employees who were whining. "You know all the stories. You know what's true and what's not true. They can take their jabs now, but you know what? It's short term."

In the days leading to our conversation, Dykstra felt he had taken quite a few kicks to the teeth—ones he hadn't seen coming. He said a former business partner was "hijacking" a newsletter the two had partnered on and was replacing him with "some guy with a ponytail." One of TheStreet.com's top execs, Wall Street heavy hitter Jim Cramer, "completely cowered out" on him, while a second bigwig used "being a fag to not get fired," Dykstra said.

Phone calls like this were commonplace when I worked for Dykstra, and before long I was elbow-deep in a new one. Talking to Dykstra was both entertaining and exhausting all at once, I had found, because the conversation would change direction all of a sudden and without notice, like a base runner caught in a rundown. His speech was often hard to understand, complicated by a severe lack of sleep, a slight lisp, and years of life in the fast lane.

Finally, after about thirty minutes of winding, aimless conversation, Dykstra turned to the reason for the call. "You know I wanted to call you because, hey, everybody's gotta eat," he said with his patented slow-motion chuckle. His mood suddenly turned jovial, and I could tell he was putting on his best charm. I didn't mind; I actually enjoyed the show. "We all gotta make a living, and you know my business better than anybody."

He urged me to come back to work for him again, telling me there was a lot of money to be made. It sounded good, but I knew Dykstra just didn't have the bullets to pay everyone he owed. He was facing a mountain of bills and was in denial. "I have that mansion, okay, and it's got four separate houses on it," he said, suggesting that Rhea and I move cross-country to California and come live with him. I wasn't sure what to say. It was a kind gesture from Dykstra, who, in all honesty, couldn't offer me much money at that time.

But he had to find a way to turn the money spigot back on quickly, and I was a known entity. I had already ghostwritten for him, helped create one of his business lines, and played an integral role in another. And I had staying power. I had lasted longer than any other editor and had provided a degree of stability in his otherwise chaotic world.

"I know you know this stuff cold, and I'm gonna do this regardless," he said of relaunching his newsletter business. I didn't doubt he would keep on fighting to stay in the game. Quitting was not in his nature. But asking me to run it? Was he serious? Almost nothing that came out of Dykstra's mouth surprised me, but after all that had happened, I was stunned.

"Look, the things that happened with me and you weren't so much between you and I," he said, in the closest thing to an apology anyone could expect from Dykstra. Business pressures had been getting to him back when we had last worked together, and he said that he understood the source of my frustrations. "Me and you never really fought," he said.

"So think about what I'm talking about. I'm one of them guys that goes forward. I don't believe in going backward. I try and go forward, and I try and learn from things," Dykstra said. "If there's things that I can do better, then I try and do them better. You know, I don't dwell on the past. I don't live in that kind of world. It doesn't do anyone any good. So think about it, and me and you will talk tomorrow." And just like that, Nails was back!

CHAPTER 1

LITTLE LENNY LESWICK

Long before he was Lenny Dykstra, New York Mets and Philadelphia Phillies pint-sized folk hero, he was Leonard Kyle Leswick, the middle child of three boys living in an overcramped apartment in Southern California. His dad walked out on the family when Lenny was just a toddler, leaving the boys and their mom struggling to fend for themselves.

"Jerry Leswick was our blood father—he played pro golf for a while," says Brian Dykstra, Lenny's older brother. By the time Jerry was twenty-two years old, he had a wife and three kids—Lenny, Brian, and their younger brother, Kevin. "He and my mom were having problems, and he left my mom with three boys by herself."

At about the same time, the boys' mom, Marilyn, met a man named Dennis Dykstra while they were both working at the Pacific Telephone Company. "My mom was a blonde knockout bombshell back then," Brian says. "He was like Kris Kristofferson with muscles."

Dennis and Marilyn bonded. She confided in Dennis, a recent divorcé and the father of three young girls, about her troubles with Jerry. Crying, she would tell Dennis how Brian and Lenny would wait in vain at the curb outside their apartment all day for Jerry to pick them up and take them to a ballgame as he had promised.

"The boys really believed that he was coming, and he never came," says Danna Dykstra-Coy, Dennis's oldest daughter. "He would do this to them a lot. Dad said it just broke his heart."

Once Marilyn and Dennis's relationship grew more serious, they decided to introduce the children to each other during a fun-filled night out at Chris & Pitt's Barbeque. The Leswick boys dressed in matching suits—black slacks with blue jackets and ties. Brian was five years old, Lenny was four, and Kevin was one and a half. With the exception of Johna, who was the same age as Lenny, Dennis's girls were a bit older than the boys. Danna was age nine and Brenda, eight.

"The boys were so nervous," Danna recalls. "They put their hands out, and they shook our hands and said how nice it was to meet us. We immediately clicked." Brian compared the newly formed clan to the Brady Bunch. "My mom had three boys and she was by herself, and my dad had three daughters." The group later rode in the back of Dennis's pea-green Volkswagen bus yelling out the windows at cars passing by and singing the song "the Dykstra Bunch."

Marilyn and Dennis eventually married, and the three boys and their mom packed up everything they owned and moved into Dennis's pea-green-colored house on Crosby Avenue in Garden Grove, a working-class suburb in Orange County, California. The move was a big step up for the boys. Even though they shared a bedroom, the house had a basketball hoop outside and a Ping-Pong table in the garage, both luxuries Brian and Lenny had only dreamed of while living in their apartment.

"For the boys, the move was just amazing because they came out of poverty," Danna says. "It was like a castle to them. They moved into our house, they got our dad—it's like they took our life, and yet there was no resentment. We just loved them to pieces, and they loved us."

Dennis spent countless hours in the yard pitching a baseball to the boys or teaching them how to throw a football. Inside the house, he was the strong father figure they had never had. "Dennis was really the driving force for all the kids in the family, but especially the boys and especially Lenny," says Dan Drake, who coached all three boys in high school baseball and taught Lenny in driver's education and health class. Lenny later became a teacher's assistant under Drake. "Growing up with those boys, if you fought one, you fought all three. It was just that type of family."

When Dennis formally adopted the boys, he and Marilyn sat them down for a serious talk. "He said, 'You don't have to call me dad, you can call me Dennis, but I'm going to be your father. I'm going to raise you,'" Brian recalls. Marilyn and Dennis then asked the boys to take on the Dykstra name, which they did, symbolically ending the Leswick part of their lives.

———

In Garden Grove, sports were one way to combat boredom. Another was mischief, which Lenny Dykstra was drawn to like a mosquito to the mysterious purple light of a bug zapper. Dennis called him "Weird Leonard," a nickname he proudly earned.

Although the neighborhood kids flocked to the Dykstra house in the 1970s to compete in every game imaginable, one kid had a particularly hard time gaining acceptance from the group. A plump Dutch boy who lived down the block assumed that because Dykstra was a Dutch surname, he and the Dykstras would become the best of friends. Instead, Lenny and Brenda, Dennis's middle daughter, would do "torturous stuff" to the boy.

"He was kind of a goof, and he would follow us around," Brenda explains. "We would say we didn't want to hang out with him. He came in our yard one too many times, so we tied him to a tree and took a shovel and threw poop at him. We had a goofy family."

As Lenny grew older, his hijinks expanded beyond hurling turds. In his teenage years, one of his favorite activities was to make what he called "fire extinguisher runs."

Danna recalls one afternoon when Lenny commandeered her Mustang. Lenny, who was about fifteen years old at the time, hopped in the passenger seat and said, "Let's go. . . . Just drive where I tell you to drive." The first stop was a local gas station, where Lenny swiped the shop's fire extinguisher before darting to his getaway car. The duo then drove to Disneyland. "Back then people still dressed up to go to Disneyland," Danna recalls. "There were older ladies that had dresses on, and Lenny would just start spraying them and knocking them down from the passenger side of the car." As the duo sped away, Lenny let out a goofy laugh and decided to douse some nearby bikers for good measure.

"That was one of his favorite things to do when he was bored," Danna recalls. When Lenny wasn't targeting bikers or old ladies, he was spraying transgender hookers on Sunset Boulevard, according to Brenda.

Lenny generally stayed out of trouble in school, except for one incident in which he chucked a half-eaten apple at the principal's head. The incident got him suspended from the baseball team briefly and earned him the moniker Apple Core, which eventually gave way to the more popular Nails nickname.

However, that's not to say the wheels in Lenny's mind weren't spinning constantly. He wasn't all that interested in books and didn't really care about being popular, but perhaps foreshadowing his future on Wall Street, he knew how to make a quick buck.

Despite having his lunch money, he would often pretend he was short on cash. Dykstra would roam the hallways and the cafeteria telling the other students he needed just a quarter so that he wouldn't go hungry during lunchtime. He would then repeat the same spiel over and over, collecting quarters from dozens of kids. "He'd collect so many quarters that at the end of the day, he'd go, 'Dude, I've got ten extra dollars today,'" Brenda recalls. "This was in the 1970s."

That minor mischief paled in comparison to Dykstra and his pals sneaking onto the field at Angels Stadium to horse around. During his sophomore year, Dykstra and his crew decided they would break onto the field on Christmas Day. Security was sure to be light on the holiday, they thought.

"Back then it was easier to jump the fence at Angels Stadium," Danna says. They hopped over the left field fence and ran onto the field. Dykstra imagined himself alongside his idols, Fred Lynn and Rod Carew of the Angels. The boys pitched from the mound, ran the bases, and stood at the edge of the infield launching high, arching fly balls to the warning track so that Lenny could practice making leaping catches and crashing into the outfield wall.

"They would have the security lights on, and some way those knuckleheads would be down there on the baseball field taking batting practice on the main diamond," Drake says. That is . . . until they got caught.

"Out of nowhere, there was this helicopter over us, and there's this guy on the bullhorn: 'PUT DOWN THE BATS, AND WAIT FOR THE POLICE TO ARRIVE,'" Dykstra told *Esquire* in a likely embellishment of the event.[1] "I just climbed the fence and bolted, dude. And nobody was gonna catch me—no fucking way."

Another version of that story involves Dykstra and his friends being detained by stadium security. "Lenny got picked up and put in a holding place at the police department," Danna says. "Dad had to go pick him up."

Lenny's obsession with the Angels didn't end with sneaking onto the field. He wanted to meet his idol, Rod Carew, the Angels second baseman, in the worst way. However, his pursuit almost landed him in juvenile hall, according to his brother Brian.

Dykstra would wait for Carew after Angels games and follow behind him in his first car, a Volkswagen he and Dennis restored together. "Rod Carew told the cops someone was following him, and the police came to our house a couple of times and told Lenny he couldn't wait after games for Rod Carew," Brian says. "He did it for like two years straight. Rod Carew didn't know it was some kid named Lenny Dykstra."

Carew's impact on Dykstra stretched beyond the bat and the ball. Lenny read that Carew believed chewing tobacco helped him see the ball better. The theory was that a wad of tobacco in his cheek helped stretch the skin around the eye, keeping it open wide and preventing it from twitching. So, wanting to be like his idol, Dykstra started lining his cheek with dip. By the big leagues, it would become part of his trademark look and what he called "the show."

Although playing gags and chasing stars were fun and games, Dykstra was dead serious about being a professional athlete, and he wasn't shy about letting everyone know it. "He would go up to the senior quarterback and the studs of the school when he was a freshman and tell them he was going to be this famous ballplayer," Danna says. "One time they took him and they dumped him in the dumpster because they were so sick of him because he was a little pest."

When other students drank beer or smoked dope at parties, Dykstra would walk around with a glass of orange juice in hand for the short time he actually stayed at the soiree. It didn't matter that he was a lowly freshman; he would question the popular seniors about their vices.

Brenda says that during high school Dykstra would pick her up from parties and usually stop in just long enough to berate the star athletes. "He'd lecture them, and then he would go the whole way home throwing oranges at people's windshields," she says.

Dykstra was also very protective of the girls. In high school he would scan the yearbook and pick out the guys he felt his stepsisters should date. He was very upset when one of his friends asked Danna to dinner.

She went on the date at an upscale surf-and-turf restaurant, and as Danna and her date were conversing, they noticed something odd. "We were talking about Lenny and how Lenny was very concerned about the date," Danna says. "We were looking out the window, and all of a sudden we saw Lenny hiding in the bushes watching us."

Brenda did date one guy Dykstra picked out for her and eventually had a child with him. Her pregnancy, at age nineteen, caused conflict within her family because she was not married, Brenda says. However, it also showed her another, more caring side of Lenny.

After her daughter was born, Brenda was having a hard time making ends meet. She needed baby formula and diapers. Although Lenny was just a kid and didn't have much money, he did what he could to help, even if his actions were "kind of shady."

"He found this truck that did deliveries all over the county, and he followed them to know their routes and how long they were in the houses," Brenda says. "While they were inside making their deliveries, he'd go and steal baby formula and diapers. I thought that was precious. Good or bad, he always had my back."

CHAPTER 2

DYKSTRA DNA

Lenny Dykstra isn't well spoken. He doesn't come from money. He didn't have powerful connections. He wasn't naturally blessed with big muscles, great height, or any of the physical attributes that are usually a gateway to success at the highest levels of competitive sports or life. In short, Dykstra wasn't part of what he calls the "lucky sperm club."

However, athletics are in his genes. Three of his uncles on his biological father's side—Pete Leswick, Jack "Newsy" Leswick, and Tony Leswick—played in the National Hockey League. Pete skated in just a handful of games for the Boston Bruins and New York Americans,[1] while Newsy played in thirty-seven games for the Stanley Cup champion 1933–34 Chicago Blackhawks before being found dead in the Assiniboine River in western Canada. Some suspected foul play, but the Winnipeg coroner ruled that Newsy, who was found without his wallet or any items of value, had died either through accident or suicide.[2]

Tony, in contrast, was a mainstay in the lineups of the New York Rangers and Detroit Redwings in the late 1940s and early 1950s. He was by far the most successful of the trio. Best known for his overtime, game-winning goal in Game 7 of the 1954 Stanley Cup finals against the Montreal Canadiens, Tony also won the Stanley Cup, hockey's championship trophy, as part of the 1952 and 1955 Redwings.

At just five feet six inches tall and 160 pounds, Tony was nicknamed Mighty Mouse because of his small stature and pesky ways on the ice.[3] Dykstra surely inherited some of those traits, but applied them to different sports. Although he broke tackles as a tailback on the Garden Grove High School football team and could dart up and down the basketball court, blowing past defenders and making shots, the baseball diamond was where Dykstra shined the brightest.

Baseball wasn't just a game for Dykstra—it was his ticket out of a boring, average, middle-class existence in "Garbage Grove," as he called it. His first year in high school, Dykstra became the only freshman ever to play varsity baseball under coach Dan Drake. "He took an eighteen-year-old's job as a fifteen-year-old," says Brian Dykstra, who played catcher on that same team.

By his sophomore season, the undersized Dykstra was dominating the team. "He had the best instincts I've ever seen," says Drake, who has been a pro scout for decades.[4] "On the baseball field, I've never had another athlete or seen another athlete do what he does in all the years of coaching, teaching, and of being a professional scout."

Dykstra's defense was phenomenal. In the outfield, he would dive headfirst to make a catch or launch a laser beam of a throw to home plate to nail a runner trying to score. On the base paths, he would constantly apply devastating pressure to the opposing teams, daring defenses to try and stop him. They rarely did. He ran so hard that players on the other teams would get nervous and rush a throw or make errors, Drake says. They knew they had to be perfect to beat him, and even then it often wasn't enough.

"I've never seen anybody, black or white, run the bases as well as Lenny, especially at the high school level," Drake says. "If he got to third base, you knew he was going to score somehow, someway." If his teammates didn't get a hit to drive him in, sometimes he just stole home, an incredibly difficult and rare feat.

Dykstra became such a nuisance to opponents that one rival high school team resorted to creating trick plays just to deal with the onslaught. One such play—an elaborate version of the hidden ball trick—was designed as a counterattack to Dykstra's apparent invincibility.

Once Dykstra reached first base, the opposition's goal was to create confusion about what was actually going on in the field. When the pitcher threw the ball toward home plate, Dykstra took off running in an attempt to steal second base. The batter, Dykstra's teammate, swung but unfortunately missed. However, everyone on the opposing team pretended the batter hit a pop-up to the second baseman. Players in the opposing dugout even clanked two bats together to replicate the sound of a ball hitting the bat.

The second baseman looked toward the sky as if locating the ball and shouted, "I got it." Dykstra knew that if any fielder caught a pop-up, the rules said he could not advance to second base. Believing the ruse, Dykstra darted back toward first base, hoping to be standing safely on the base when the opposing player caught the pop-up.

However, while the second baseman was putting on the acting performance of his life, the catcher quietly threw the ball to the first baseman, who was waiting to tag Dykstra out when he returned to the base. "Lenny was just fuming, but he wasn't more upset than I was," Drake says. "That was the one and only time he got thrown out."

Trick plays aside, nothing was going to stop Dykstra from success. In fact, he dumped his girlfriend, Gabby, a friend of the family, right before baseball season his senior year, according to Brian Dykstra. He said to her, "'I'm sorry, we're done, it's baseball time. Nothing is going to stand in my way—no chicks, nobody.'"

His all-encompassing passion to achieve his baseball dreams spilled over into every aspect of his life. While Brian and a lot of the other kids took off after three hours of varsity baseball practice to go home and watch television, drink, or chase girls, Lenny and his pal Fairchild would stay behind to run drills. "They would be taking soft toss in the dark," Brian says. Lenny would later say he had only one friend growing up and that's because he needed someone to play catch with. He was referring to Fairchild.

After leaving the ball field hours after practice was officially over, Lenny would run home, shovel dinner into his mouth, and race back out the door to his job at Bob's Batting Cage, where he worked the 7:30 to 9:30 p.m. shift.

"Me and my buddies would pull up to the batting cages, and there would be a line of people trying to get tokens," Brian says. Instead of helping customers, Lenny would be anchored in one of the batting cages with the machine cranked up to 90 miles per hour. He would take one-armed swings at the pitches whipping in. "People were in amazement," Brian says. But when customers needed help, Lenny would tell them to "kiss my ass."

His workouts and baseball education weren't limited to conventional drills. During class, he carried around Ping-Pong balls and stared at them all day so that when it came time to play in a game, the baseball would look gigantic in comparison and be easier to hit. At practice, he would stuff one cheek with beans or corn kernels and spit them, one by one, into the air and whack them with the bat. The drill was designed to improve his hand-eye coordination, but also make the baseball look as big as a softball.

However, he was best known for his showdowns with mechanical pitching machines. They were both reckless and awe-inspiring at the same time—the ultimate game of chicken between man and machine.

"As he worked out in the batting cage, he kept getting closer and closer to the pitching machine because he wanted to work on a faster pitch," says Myron Pines, a scout for the New York Mets at the time Dykstra was drafted by the organization. For most batters, the machines are placed about 60 feet away from the batter. "One time he was only about 15 feet away from the machine, and I had to run in there and yell at him to get out," Pines says. "I was afraid he was going to get killed by the ball. He just couldn't wait to face better competition or faster speeds."

He was truly a baseball rat—he played two or three games a day for various leagues and was on several teams at the same time. "He didn't want to just play in the big leagues; he wanted to be a star," says Pines, who was a longtime scout and a coach on Dykstra's scout team. "We used to laugh that if you invited Lenny to come out and play with you, you would have to make sure he didn't drive by another field because if he saw a baseball game there, he would stop and play for those people."

Although Dykstra exuded confidence and a cocksure swagger throughout most of his playing days, he took his lumps too. During a scout game late one January, Dykstra struck out five times. He was devastated. Several other players were older and were using that game as a tune-up for spring training the following month with professional baseball clubs.

After the game, Coach Pines gave Dykstra a lift home. "He was crying in the car," Pines recalls. "He said, 'I can't play and I can't hit.'" He told Dykstra it was important to bounce back from failure, and Dykstra didn't disappoint. "The next game he got two or three hits—one of them was a home run off a signed professional pitcher."

———————

No matter how hard Dykstra worked, though, one issue that never seemed to go away was his small stature. At a workout with the Mets prior to the 1981 amateur baseball draft, the camp was filled with future major leaguers, including home run hitter Cecil Fielder, pitcher Eric Plunk, outfielder Darrin Jackson, and utility player David Cochrane. Dykstra wasn't even on the radar of some of the team's executives.

As the workout was about to begin, Dykstra walked in with his glove in hand. Harry Minor, one of the team's cross-checkers in the scouting department, thought he was the batboy and asked Dykstra to gather the bats. Dykstra shot back, "'I'm here to play, man. . . . I'm Lenny Dykstra, and I'm the best player you're going to see today." He then proceeded to turn some heads, running faster than any of the other players and showcasing the best arm of the lot of outfielders.

It didn't matter. The day of the draft Dykstra watched as team after team passed up a chance to pick him in the first round. His hometown Angels took

Dick Schofield. His future Mets teammates Ron Darling and Kevin McReynolds were also taken in the first round by the Texas Rangers and San Diego Padres, respectively. Then the second, third, fourth, and fifth rounds came and went, and Dykstra was still left out in the cold.

Joe McIlvaine, the Mets' new scouting director at the time, says he was originally prepared to take Dykstra in the third round of the draft. He liked the way Dykstra "was like a hockey player in a baseball uniform. He was very, very aggressive on the field."

However, in the days leading to the draft, his staff urged him to wait because there was almost no competition for Dykstra—only one other club seemed interested in him. Instead, they said, in the early rounds he should pick players who were garnering interest from opposing clubs. There was little risk in waiting to pick Dykstra later.

"In the second round we took John Christensen," McIlvaine recalls. "In the fourth round we took David Cochrane. He really wasn't as good as Lenny, but a lot of times in the draft it's the market that's out there. If you can wait longer, you wait longer." The seventh, eighth, and ninth rounds came and went, and Dykstra remained undrafted.

"We waited and waited and got to about the twelfth round and took a pitcher only one guy had seen out of junior college in Texas named Roger Clemens," McIlvaine says. "He was our twelfth pick."

Finally, in the thirteenth round and after more than three hundred other players had been taken, the Mets picked Dykstra. "He just vowed at that time, 'I'm going to make everybody sorry they ever drafted me this late,'" Coach Drake recalls. Upset with the Mets, Dykstra told the club he was going to pass on playing in its organization. "He was pissed," Brian Dykstra says. In fact, Dykstra had already signed a letter of intent to play college ball for the Sun Devils at Arizona State.

"He thought he should have gotten drafted sooner, and he should have gotten drafted sooner," Pines says. "We told him, 'Hey Lenny, we got you sooner than anybody else did, so we liked you better than anybody. We kept talking to him and telling him, 'We really like you, but this is part of the business. Because of your size, they're a little skeptical. They don't think you can make it, but we think you can.' Back then the little kids had to prove they could play. The big player had to prove he couldn't."

If he were to sign, Dykstra wasn't about to accept the typical contract offered to a low-round draft pick . . . and he had a list of demands. He wanted to skip the rookie league, where most draftees go to play their first season. "Lenny said, 'If you don't send me to A-ball, I'm not signing because I'm too good for the rookie league," McIlvaine recalls.

The Mets had never done that before. The organization didn't want to put him in a situation he couldn't handle, but Dykstra insisted and McIlvaine relented. "We had a low A-ball club in Shelby, North Carolina. He did all right the first year, and the second year we had to have him repeat there." His third year in the minor leagues he was promoted to the Lynchburg Mets, where he stole 105 bases and won MVP of the Carolina League.

Years later, after a successful big league career, Dykstra changed a lot of people's perspectives about the relationship between size and big league viability. "Lenny kind of broke open the door for smaller players—especially in the outfield," Pines says. Several major league teams have changed their thinking and now use Dykstra as the measuring stick for their undersized prospects, he says. "Now, if you can play, size doesn't matter."

CHAPTER 3

THE TINIEST MET

When I was nine years old, the mighty New York Mets won the 1986 World Series and Lenny Dykstra was my all-time favorite player . . . my hero. Wiry and reckless, #4 would dive headfirst into a wall to make a catch or belly flop into second base to avoid a tag. It appeared his sole purpose was to get his uniform as filthy as possible while ensuring a Mets victory.

The man behind the dirty uniform was about as cool as they came—at least to this third-grader. He used words like "dude" and "bro" during interviews and had his own peculiar Southern California lingo, which included a unique interpretation of the word "nails." In addition to being his nickname, nails was a colorful slang expression Dykstra used to indicate that he liked something. In the 1980s, when others might have said something was "cool" or "mint," Dykstra said it was "nails."

But most importantly, to the chagrin of my best friend, Erik, a diehard Yankees fan, Dykstra helped the Mets wrestle control of New York away from the Bronx Bombers. The Yankees, who have racked up a record number of championships since the dawn of baseball's existence, were no longer at the front and center of America's pastime. Although a solid group of players in the mid- to late 1980s, the Yankees were a sleepy bunch compared to their cross-borough neighbors.

The Mets were arrogant, brash, and electric. They got into brawls on the field and in bars. Meanwhile, the Yankees players feuded publicly with owner George Steinbrenner about his facial hair policy. Yawn!

The Mets had gritty players with catchy nicknames like Mex and Doc and Straw and Nails. The Yankees had . . . Donnie Baseball—a quiet leader with an impressive batting average and an extremely lame nickname. No longer "the other team" in New York, the Mets owned the city, the state, and the surrounding suburbs.

From very early on in 1986—Dykstra's first full season in the big leagues—it became apparent that the Mets were a force to be reckoned with. They steamrolled through the National League, amassing an impressive 108 wins and a gaudy 21.5 game lead over the second place Philadelphia Phillies by season's end.

Dykstra's on-the-field hustle endeared him to fans. At only twenty-three years old, he appeared to be a throwback to an earlier time when players played hard all the time and treated the opposition as enemy combatants. He used to tell his teammates that they were going to go into the other team's yard to "take their money and fuck their women."[1]

Dykstra usually sported a mischievous grin while tossing his body all over the field. He was like a big kid, and fans immediately took to him. They cheered for him. They embraced him. They bought replica Mets jerseys with his name and number on the back.

Some fans wanted even more. One obsessed woman showed up at Shea Stadium dressed in a bridal gown on at least two separate occasions and holding a sign proposing marriage. She also followed the team to Wrigley Field in Chicago for their matchup against the Cubs.[2]

However, Dykstra was already off the market. He met his future wife, Terri, when he was playing in her hometown for the Class-AA Jackson Mets, part of the New York Mets minor league system in Jackson, Mississippi. In 1985, while Dykstra was living in Port Washington on the North Shore of Long Island and playing for the New York Mets, he married Terri, the young blonde with the Mississippi twang whom he had met at a bank.

Shortly after the marriage proposal from the crazy fan in the wedding dress, a pair of young, ponytailed girls furnished a sign at Shea displaying a big heart and reading "Adopt us Lenny."[3] One thing was clear: New York loved Nails.

When they weren't being solicited by fans, or dominating the National League, the Mets were busy tearing up the town. With the Mets preparing to square off in the playoffs against the Houston Astros, Dykstra and Mets relief pitcher Roger McDowell dropped by the MTV studios to promote "Let's Go Mets," a four-minute music video featuring the team and celebrities such as shock jock Howard Stern and New York City mayor Ed Koch.

At MTV, video jockey Martha Quinn playfully asked the guys about baseball, music, and the wedding-dress stalker.

Dykstra raised some eyebrows with his growing confidence both on and off the field.

Quinn wanted to know if the guys could be in a band, what kind of a band it would be. "I'd like to be in a band like Huey Lewis and the News," Dykstra said with a head bob.[4] "I like the Rolling Stones too. Yeah, but I like you better, though." The trio laughed, Quinn slightly surprised at his advances.

Then the conversation turned to baseball as Dykstra lightheartedly bragged that he did whatever was necessary to win, prompting the following exchange:

> **Dykstra:** I even cheat a little sometimes . . . if that's what it takes.
> **Quinn:** What, what, what? I feel like Howard Cosell. What do you mean exactly, Mr. Dykstra? [she says in her best nasal-toned impersonation].
> **Dykstra:** I'm a good cheater.
> **Quinn:** Should you be saying this?
> **Dykstra:** Sure, they'll never know.

It was that kind of catch-me-if-you-can attitude that captured New York's collective attention and made opponents hate little Lenny Dykstra and the New York Mets. For Dykstra, nothing was off limits to try and gain an edge. In his 1987 book *Nails*, Dykstra wrote that during football games he used to love "giving cheap shots. . . . I used to tackle the ballcarrier, then get on the bottom of the pile and twist his ankle. Make him hurt."

I don't recall the exact day I became a fan of Nails—it was probably early during that magical season. However, it was during the 1986 postseason that the scrappy twenty-three-year-old rookie vaulted himself from promising newcomer to New York sports folk hero for the ages.

During the playoffs, when most of the Mets' big bats were suffering from a severe power outage, he had more hits than any other Met. Despite his lack of power during the regular season, he tied slugger Darryl Strawberry, whom he called "Awesome Strawsome," with the team lead in postseason home runs: 3. He also had the highest batting average of any of the regulars in the lineup, hitting a solid .300.

At every turn, Dykstra seemed to read the situation correctly, providing exactly the right spark at precisely the right time. On October 11, 1986, a Saturday afternoon at Shea Stadium, Dykstra stepped to the plate in the ninth inning of Game 3 of the National League Championship Series with the outcome hanging in the balance.

The Mets were trailing and in serious danger of falling behind 2–1 in the best-of-seven series. Unhittable, unstoppable hurler Mike Scott had blanked the Mets in Game 1, and because they were about to face him again in Game 4, a loss in Game 3 would have been devastating.

Dykstra hadn't started Game 3, but he was in a position to end it. Veteran Mookie Wilson opened the game in center field, and rookie Kevin Mitchell got the nod in left field.

"The tag against Lenny early on was that he was not an everyday player, meaning he was only going to play against right-handed pitchers where Mookie Wilson would play center against left-handed pitchers," said Gary Carter, a Hall of Fame catcher and teammate of Dykstra on the Mets. "I think nobody really believed he could be an everyday player because he was little and he had the crouched-down-type stance. He was always kind of vulnerable to left-handed pitching."

With a wad of tobacco in his bulging cheek and the game on the line, Dykstra faced off against Dave Smith, the Astros' seasoned, All-Star right-handed reliever. He knew the situation called for something big.

Shea Stadium was not a hospitable environment for any opposing player, but especially not for the thirty-one-year-old Smith. Earlier in the season, a fan in the upper deck had pissed over the railing and down onto Smith in the visitors' bullpen several stories below.[5] Now, in the biggest game of the season, players on both benches felt momentum tilting in the Mets' favor. The Astros had already blown a 4–0 lead earlier in the game and were now desperately clinging to a 5–4 advantage.

The Shea Stadium crowd roared as "the tiniest Met," as some reporters dubbed him, dug in.

Smith reared back and fired a forkball, a pitch that is supposed to have a dramatic tumbling or dropping motion, toward home plate. Only it didn't fork, and with a sweeping, one-armed stroke, Lenny laced the pitch into the cool October air. The crowd rose to its feet as the ball sailed into the Mets' bullpen beyond the right field fence for a home run. Lenny and teammate Wally Backman, who was on second base, leaped for joy as they rounded the bases, hooting and hollering. Game over. Final score: Mets 6, Astros 5.

"The last time I hit a home run in the bottom of the ninth to win a game was in Strat-o-Matic Baseball against my brother Kevin a couple of years ago," Dykstra told reporters following the game. "Don't get used to this. You're not going to see too many like that from me."[6]

Dykstra wasn't known for hitting home runs. In fact, the coaches discouraged him from swinging for the fences, advice he was not about to take. "Last year I was choking way up on the bat, but this winter I decided that I could go ahead and hold the bat like a man," he told *Sports Illustrated*.[7] On that occasion, the coaches didn't mind.

That rousing come-from-behind victory was just the first hill in the death-defying roller-coaster ride the 1986 Mets would embark upon that postseason. And it was just the beginning of the Lenny Dykstra Show.

Fast-forward to Game 6 against the Astros. The Mets were leading the best-of-seven series against the Astros 3–2, just one victory away from advancing to the World Series. However, by the ninth inning, the Mets' anemic offense hadn't mustered a single run and trailed in the game 3 runs to 0.

With the dominant Mike Scott looming on the horizon, scheduled to pitch a potentially deciding Game 7 for the Astros, the Mets needed to put the series away in Game 6. Scott, whom the Mets had accused of illegally scuffing the baseball, had allowed just one run while striking out nineteen Mets over eighteen innings in Games 1 and 4—both Astros victories.[8]

Bob Knepper, a left-handed pitcher, started Game 6 for Houston, so Dykstra was again relegated to the bench. Just as in Game 3, he was called on to pinch-hit late in the game. He proceeded to rip a triple to center field off a tired Knepper, jump-starting the Mets' offense and scoring the team's first run. The Mets drove in two more runs that inning, tying the score and sending the game into extra innings. "If I don't hit that triple, we don't win the World Series," Dykstra later told me proudly.

After the Mets briefly took the lead in the fourteenth inning and the Astros countered with a run of their own, the teams squared off in the decisive sixteenth inning. The exhausted Mets pushed two more runs across the plate, giving them a 6–4 lead by the time Dykstra got to take his cuts. His second hit of the night, however, would be just as important as the first. With Backman on third base, Dykstra singled to right field, driving in the Mets' final run of the night, giving the team a 7–4 advantage.

The Astros battled back, tightening the score to 7–6. With the potential tying and winning runs on base, Mets relief pitcher Jesse Orosco repelled the attack, striking out the "dangerous" Kevin Bass on a curveball to end the game and the series and send the Mets to their first World Series appearance in thirteen years.

"Lenny was kind of an inspiration to us—here he is, a little guy, and he got the reputation as Nails because he played the game hard," Carter said. "He may not have been an everyday player in '86, but when he was called upon, he came through. He was very instrumental in us winning that championship."

Dykstra's performance against the Astros was clutch, but it wouldn't have meant a damn thing if the Mets lost to the Red Sox in the World Series. However, less than a week after knocking off the Astros, the Mets were once again staring down the barrel of a loaded shotgun. Despite being the most heavily favored team in the World Series since 1950, with 12:5 odds in some places,[9] they had dropped the first two games at Shea Stadium, surrendering home-field advantage.

The Mets desperately needed to avoid a crippling loss in Game 3. Coming back from a 2–0 deficit was hard enough, but winning four games in a row after losing the first three in the World Series has never happened. EVER!

Dykstra knew the lifeless Mets needed a shot in the arm to prompt them to get back up off the deck and keep fighting. A quick pop to the jaw of Boston's pitcher Dennis "Oil Can" Boyd was in order, he thought.

Oil Can, a six feet one inch, 156-pound right-hander, was an emotional guy. He had been institutionalized earlier in the year for a psychological evaluation after he went nuts when he wasn't selected to the American League's All-Star squad.[10] Boyd was also a bit cocky, but most of all, he was hittable. To Dykstra he was dead meat. Lenny knew the Mets needed to bend the momentum in their favor.

So on Oil Can's third pitch, Dykstra swung for the fences. He made solid contact, spinning Oil Can around and sending the ball soaring toward the short porch in right field. As the crowd gasped, the ball landed in the stands near the right field foul pole. Home run, 1–0 Mets!

"That was one of the few times I actually tried to hit a home run and did," Dykstra later told WFAN's Mike Francesa.[11] "Usually when you try and hit one, you pop up."

The hit set the tone for the Mets and breathed new life into their sluggish offense. They scored three more times that first inning, jumping out to a quick 4–0 lead. When the final out of the game was recorded, the scoreboard read Mets 7, Red Sox 1. Dykstra had four hits in five at bats, with an RBI and two runs scored. "We had something to prove to ourselves, to the Boston Red Sox and the rest of baseball," Dykstra told reporters after the game. "We didn't win 108 games for nothing."[12]

The very next night, Dykstra struck again. Although the game is largely remembered for Carter's two home runs, Dykstra helped put the score out of reach. With the Mets ahead 3–0 in the seventh inning, he took a pitch from Boston reliever Steve Crawford deep for a two-run home run. Boston right fielder Dwight Evans got his glove on the ball but wasn't able to hold on to it. As Dykstra rounded the base paths, the only noise that could be heard from the crowd of approximately 34,000 was the Mets wives cheering from the third-base grandstand. The Mets cruised to a 6–2 victory, evening the series at two games apiece and wiping away the Sox's advantage.

The sudden power surge from Dykstra frustrated the Sox and surprised some newspapers, which referred to him as "Babe Dykstra," an obvious reference to Babe Ruth, the most famous home run hitter in history. The Red Sox's Evans questioned whether Dykstra and the Mets were corking their bats, an illegal enhancement that makes the ball go farther when hit.

"That ball Dykstra hit carried back toward center field," Evans told reporters. "It went a little further than it should have. They oughta check that kid's bat. And a couple of others too."[13] Mets manager Davey Johnson simply said Lenny was "in another zone," noting that he was a "strong little guy."[14]

Lenny cooled off a bit after that, striking out with a runner on and two outs in the ninth inning to end Game 5, a 4–2 loss. In Game 6, Lenny took a back-seat to one of the most memorable moments in World Series history: Mookie Wilson's slow-rolling ground ball that went between the legs of veteran Boston first baseman Bill Buckner, capping one of the most improbable comebacks in the history of sports.

However, the Mets wasted the momentum, quickly surrendering three runs in the second inning of the decisive Game 7 to fall behind 3–0. Left-handed starter Bruce Hurst, who had stymied the Mets in winning Games 1 and 5, made quick work of the Mets' batting order during the first five innings of Game 7. Finally in the sixth, the Mets broke through for three runs, tying the score at 3.

Lenny, who had been riding the pine all game, was brought in after Hurst was removed in the seventh inning. Batting second in the inning, Lenny was right in the thick of a critical three-run rally that put the Mets ahead for good. Victory!

Days later, New York threw the Mets the largest ticker tape parade in the city's history to that point. An estimated 2.2 million fans crammed Lower Broadway's Canyon of Heroes in Manhattan to catch a glimpse of their newly crowned world champions. They screamed, they cheered for their Mets, and they chanted, "Len-ny! Len-ny" at an ear-splitting decibel.[15]

CHAPTER 4

RUSTY NAILS

Despite the quick start to Dykstra's career, by the end of the decade it appeared that his best days were behind him. He had clearly captured the hearts of New York baseball fans, but he hadn't fully won over his coach. Mets manager Davey Johnson firmly believed that, despite Dykstra's postseason heroics, he just didn't have the skills to be an everyday player.

Dykstra, however, entered spring training in 1987 believing he had earned a starting role, setting the stage for years of turmoil in center field at Shea Stadium. It was like night and day compared to a year earlier, when Dykstra had been the new kid in town. He had entered spring training in 1986 as the "other" center fielder behind veteran Mookie Wilson, whom General Manager Frank Cashen later characterized as the "heart and soul of the ball club from the rebuilding years to the world championship."[1]

Taking Mookie's job wasn't going to be easy, but Dykstra was used to uphill battles. He walked around with a chip on his shoulder and a desire to prove people wrong. "He was tiny. He was thin. He was not someone that you knew was going to be a big league player when you looked at him or even when you first saw him play," says Barry Lyons, a former Mets catcher who first met Dykstra while playing for the minor league affiliate in Shelby. "I remember showing up in Shelby midseason after the draft and this little dude was driving a Porsche. My first impression was 'what the hell is he doing here?'"

However, after playing together, Lyons was struck by Dykstra's enthusiasm for the game. "Guys want to win, but Lenny had a passion that was off the charts. He proved himself every day. He was the kind of guy you loved him if he was on your team, but you hated him if he was on the opposite team."

Dykstra sought out "the action," a term he used that was as relevant to his lifestyle as to his playing career, Lyons says. "He liked to be in the middle of 'the action,' being in the middle of it, being in the spotlight. That's what motivated him and allowed him to be as successful a baseball player as he became. His drive to do the best and be the best led him to things that unfortunately he is probably paying the consequences for today."

Entering the spring of 1986, the Mets' championship season, Dykstra had had only a little taste of the action in the big leagues. He had barely played half a season with the New York Mets, filling in for Wilson, who was out of the lineup with a shoulder injury during part of the 1985 season. Then, everything changed in a split second when Wilson suffered a gruesome injury to his right eye while running drills during spring training of 1986. That opened the door for Dykstra.

By the spring of 1987, however, just a few months after the Mets' championship, Dykstra's spot in the starting lineup was already in jeopardy. Despite getting a pay increase from $92,500 to $202,500;[2] authoring his own book, *Nails*; and becoming one of the heroes of the previous postseason, Dykstra struggled at the plate during spring training. Mookie, on the other hand, smacked the ball around on a regular basis.

Making matters worse for Dykstra was the fact that the Mets imported slugger Kevin McReynolds from the San Diego Padres during the off-season to be their everyday left fielder. Although that wasn't Dykstra's position, it changed the dynamics of the team, making the outfield more crowded with experienced players (McReynolds was making $625,000 a year).[3] Down the stretch run in 1986, Wilson had often played left field. That position now belonged to McReynolds.

Just a few weeks before opening day in 1987, manager Johnson told reporters that Wilson had the upper hand in the battle for center field. "If the season were to open today, Mookie Wilson would be my regular centerfielder," he told a reporter for the *New York Times*. "Lenny oughta get his stuff together. Maybe he was thinking about all the banquets and worrying about selling too many posters."[4] In the end, the platoon was back in effect.

"A lot of teams would have killed just to have one of them," says pitcher Terry Leach, who won eleven games while losing just one for the 1987 Mets. "Here we are, we have both of 'em. Lenny wanted to play more, and Mookie wanted to play more. People that love the game like they do want to be out there all the time."

For me, 1987 was truly awesome. My parents had purchased season tickets at Shea Stadium for the first time, meaning I would get to go to almost every home game the Mets played. We had four seats in the loge section, the blue seats in the second tier. We sat near the right field foul pole overlooking Darryl Strawberry, just a few feet from the stadium's edge leading down to the Mets' bullpen.

On our way to the game each night, my sister would sit in the front seat of our gray Oldsmobile with my mom, while I would do my homework in the back as we fought our way through rush hour traffic on the Long Island Expressway. We would make a quick stop-off in Queens to pick up my dad after his shift delivering packages for UPS and then head to Shea. The traffic backed up for what seemed like miles as we approached the gigantic bluish-purple stadium. When we finally saw the junkyards down the road from Shea, we knew we were close.

For the next several years, Shea would become a second home to me. On the way back from games, I would often fall asleep in the car while Mets radio announcer Bob Murphy did the "Happy Recap." We'd get home close to eleven at night and then repeat the same scenario the next day.

While I was loving the seats and being at Shea, Dykstra was experiencing some growing pains. By midseason that year, Nails was complaining that he was "rusting away on the bench" and urged the Mets to "trade someone soon" to resolve the outfield platoon. He meant Wilson. "I don't want to be traded. I want to play in New York, and I stress the word play," he told reporters.[5]

"It was like a yo-yo situation," says Tom Romano, a clubhouse attendant with the Mets from 1986 to 1988. "They would announce Lenny was the starting center fielder, and two weeks would go by and he wouldn't hit a lefty or two, and they were back to the platoon. Then Mookie would get hot and Lenny would sit on the bench, only getting an at bat here or there or making an appearance as a pinch runner."

Despite winning 92 games that year, the Mets' season was a colossal failure filled with on- and off-the-field turmoil. The Mets didn't make the playoffs, finishing in second place behind the St. Louis Cardinals.

That season was a personal disappointment for Dykstra as well. He played in 15 fewer games than in 1986, getting into 132 out of 162 games. He also saw his batting average dip slightly. He was going backward, not forward.

Following the subpar 1987 season, Dykstra set out to get bigger. "It's a strong man's game, and I wanted to be stronger," he said at the time.[6] He added twenty pounds during the off-season, showing up to spring training in 1988 looking like Popeye, according to Davey Johnson, who was not thrilled with the development.

"Me and Davey didn't really get along," Dykstra later told WFAN's Mike Francesa.[7] "Davey was a good manager because he had good players—let's put it that way." Johnson often became frustrated with Dykstra's obsession with hitting home runs and wanted the speedster to work on pumping out line drives and ground balls. He thought Dykstra should focus on getting on base and leave the slugging to the big boys. "Davey didn't like that Lenny always wanted to hit for power," Romano says.

By the midway point of the 1988 season, despite the team being in first place, Dykstra wanted out of New York. At the Hershey Hotel he told Romano, "I have to get out of here. I have to play every day to make the glue." Romano says he was shocked. Up until that point, Romano was still a kid and thought it was all about "team, team, team." He didn't really think about how the platoon affected Dykstra financially. "His whole thing was 'I have to play full time if I'm going to make any money.' He didn't care who he went to; he wanted to play."

Heading into the last month of the regular season, Wilson had taken hold of the center field spot. Dykstra's batting average fell for the second straight year, and he got into fewer games. Much to Dykstra's disappointment, Mookie had the upper hand as the Mets faced off against the Los Angeles Dodgers in the 1988 National League Championship Series. Mookie started three of the first four games and struggled. Dykstra started the final three games.

Although he was unable to provide the same kind of theatrics he had in 1986, Dykstra did produce gaudy numbers. He grabbed six hits in fourteen at bats—a beefy .429 average during the series. He smacked three doubles and a home run, worked four walks, and scored six times. In comparison, Mookie got just two hits, batting .154, with no extra base hits.

"Lenny really believed he was the best player on the field when he was on it. He walked around like he was six feet five inches," says Romano, recalling a conversation he and another attendant had with Lenny in the clubhouse before Game 5 of the 1988 playoffs at Shea. "He says, 'Dude, I'm going deep today. I'm going yard.' We kind of chuckled. He said, 'You don't understand; the red light is on. I'm a big-game fucking player.' He went out and hit a three-run home run."

Joe McIlvaine, the Mets' assistant general manager that year, says that Dykstra had a knack for coming up big when it counted most. "He lived for stuff like that. There are players that are like that. Reggie Jackson was along those lines too. When it really counts, they really want to shine, and Lenny was clearly in that mode."

Despite being heavily favored over the hobbled Dodgers, the Mets lost that series in the seventh and deciding game. Opposing pitcher Orel Hershiser, who ended the regular season with a record-breaking consecutive fifty-nine scoreless innings, shut down the Mets' offense.[8] Most fans considered the season a massive disappointment. I surely did.

After the season, the Mets picked up a $1 million dollar option on Wilson's contract, while Dykstra was awarded a $575,000 salary for the 1989 season via arbitration.[9] That represented a $270,000 raise for Dykstra and meant that the "Mook-stra" platoon, as many had dubbed it, was about to enter its third full season—fourth if Wilson's injury-shortened 1986 season is included.

Dykstra wanted out, even if it meant going to a losing franchise. He asked to be traded during the 1988–89 off-season, and the trade rumors plastered the pages of the daily newspapers.

The Mets were close to sending Dykstra to the basement-dwelling Atlanta Braves as part of a package for perennial All-Star outfielder Dale Murphy, according to several news reports. Other papers said the Mets and the Red Sox were working on a trade that would send Dykstra and pitcher Sid Fernandez to the Sox for outfielder Ellis Burks.

The Padres reportedly dangled catcher Sandy Alomar Jr. for Dykstra and third baseman Howard Johnson, while the crosstown Yankees even tried to pry Dykstra from the Mets organization.

McIlvaine says that a lot of the trade rumors were simply made up or were stories planted in the press, but that the team entertained moving Dykstra because of Davey Johnson.

"For two years, he came and lobbied us to try and trade Dykstra," McIlvaine says, adding that the team's front office had a "little dispute" with Johnson. "Davey wanted us to solve his problem. He had four or five really good outfielders, and he had to decide how to get them playing time. He thought the answer was to trade somebody."

As the 1989 season wore on and the trade rumors continued to swirl, the platoon began to negatively affect Dykstra's production.

Finally, on Father's Day, June 18, 1989—one day after my twelfth birthday—Dykstra and pitcher Roger McDowell were summoned to Johnson's office. Mel Stottlemyer and some of the team's coaching staff were there as well as members of the front office. "We were in there together and told together that we'd been traded," McDowell says. "For both of us it was a surprise."

I heard the news from my best friend, Erik, the Yankees fan. He called me gloating that the Mets had traded away my favorite player. I was in shock. In return for Dykstra and McDowell, the Mets got Juan Samuel, a player who had some pop in his bat but who struck out once every four times at bat.

"I was upset," Dykstra later said of the trade during an interview with Mike Francesa on WFAN.[10] "The Mets are in my heart. They'll always be. That's where I won the World Series. . . . But the bottom line is I had to be an every-day player. . . . I told them I need to play every day and if you don't give me a chance to play every day, trade me because I want to play. I'm here to play baseball, not sit on the bench."

Once the deal was complete, Johnson was "the happiest guy on the planet," McIlvaine says. However, there were others who questioned the trade. "There were a lot of people that didn't want to do it. The scouts, other people in the organization, and some of the fans were not enamored of it."

In New York, the deal was treated like front-page news and met with a massive backlash by fans unhappy with the direction management was taking the team. Fans felt that the Mets' brass was dismantling the heart and soul of that '86 team with a string of questionable transactions.

Fans weren't the only ones left scratching their heads. "I didn't really understand that deal at that time at all," says Barry Lyons, a catcher on that 1989 Mets team. "Looking back today, I still don't understand it. It bewildered pretty much everyone." Lyons says that on the bus ride home from Philadelphia, McIlvaine came to the back of the bus to try and justify the trade. Lyons, who had come up through the ranks with both Dykstra and McDowell, says McIlvaine told him the deal was made to "jump-start the offense."

When Dykstra and McDowell returned to Shea Stadium on the opposing Phillies a week later, they received a roaring, standing ovation. "They just never gave me a chance," Dykstra said of the Mets at the time. "I don't care what they say, I only started two games in a row at the most. I had some great years here, but I'm glad they're over."[11]

The trade turned out to be one of the worst in Mets history as Samuel, who had played second base most of his major league career, struggled defensively in center field, his new position. He batted a putrid .228 with the Mets that season. With Samuel roaming the outfield in Flushing, the Mets traded Wilson to Toronto.

Fans booed Samuel mercilessly—in part because he had replaced two fan favorites. His car was even broken into twice. When the season ended, a disgruntled Samuel asked to be traded and the Mets sent him packing—to the Los Angeles Dodgers—during the off-season.

Dykstra did even worse, hitting .179 in his final 196 at bats with the Phillies. Cracking the lineup every day was Dykstra's goal, but when he finally got his chance, he floundered. It was by far the worst season of his career. Phillies general manager Lee Thomas said at the time that it was a "tough year" for Dykstra. Terri was pregnant with the couple's first child together.[12] "The adjustment [to impending fatherhood] was difficult, especially when we continued to struggle," Thomas said.[13]

Tommy Herr, Dykstra's teammate, told a radio program that Nails gave up on the season and liked the nightlife a little too much. He said Dykstra had developed bad work habits while platooning in New York. There was even speculation that Dykstra couldn't or wouldn't perform on a losing club and that he wanted to be traded again—this time to a better club.

His hometown California Angels and Los Angeles Dodgers were mentioned as potential suitors. The Phillies even reportedly offered Dykstra back to the Mets. They replied, "No thanks."

CHAPTER 5

ONE FOR THE ROAD

Dykstra's stint in New York is often described as teetering on the brink of out of control. If so, then the only way to describe his stay in Philadelphia is completely and utterly friggin' unhinged. The highs were exhilarating, but the lows were potentially backbreaking and included links to illegal gambling and steroids. He even reportedly threatened to beat up Pennsylvania state senator Earl Baker when the politician asked him to curb the steady flow of four-letter words spewing from his mouth while the two men dined separately at the same suburban restaurant.[1]

However, fresh off a pitiful 1989 season, Dykstra experienced a rebirth. He put on thirty pounds during the off-season, and his muscles looked as if they would pop out of his skin at any moment. He attributed the increased muscle mass to really "good vitamins," an open joke about steroids.

"He walked with a swagger because he wanted to stand out and he wasn't going to stand out because he was small," says Kirk Radomski, a former Mets batboy and clubhouse hand from 1985 to 1995. Radomski is widely known as one of the star witnesses in former senator George Mitchell's investigation into steroid abuse in Major League Baseball. He says that Dykstra was the first of several big league ballplayers whom he helped get steroids.

"I dealt with him. He was one of my clients. I helped him with training. I helped him get his anabolic steroids," Radomski says, noting that he was friends with Dykstra and that the two kept in touch after Dykstra was traded to Philadelphia. However, before Dykstra sought out Radomski's help, he reportedly received steroids from another source—steroids he didn't know how to use.

He bulked up quickly and then would lose the muscle mass just as fast because he had no clue what he was doing or taking. Radomski says he first suspected Dykstra was taking the juice when he saw him arrive at spring training much heavier one year. Instead of trying to hide the fact that he was taking the drugs, he flaunted it.

"He wanted to be noticed," Radomski says. "He didn't care." That's when Dykstra and Radomski started talking about the proper way to use steroids and which types of steroids to use. There are many different kinds. "I tried to teach the kid about something, but to him he thought more was always better with everything," Radomski says. "If one cup of coffee was good, he wanted ten."

Once on the ball field, Lenny proceeded to tear the cover off the ball the first part of the 1990 season. He wielded such a hot bat that his batting average was above .400 into June as he tried to chase down a nearly impossible feat. The last player to hit above that mark for a full season had been Ted Williams in 1941.

Dykstra was also named to his first of three All-Star games that year and launched himself into a new stratosphere. No longer a part-time player, his batting average skyrocketed well beyond that of any of his teammates. He was once again well on his way to being one of the best leadoff hitters in baseball and showing all his detractors that he wasn't done yet.

"Once he got between the white lines, he was hell on wheels," says Bill Conlin, a now-infamous Philly sports columnist who would later go on to play a significant role in one of Dykstra's postbaseball endeavors. "He would have run through hell in a gasoline suit."

Dykstra also lived just as hard off the field as he did on it, according to Conlin. And that hard living didn't include a hint of social etiquette. Conlin says he penned a rather unflattering piece about Dykstra for the *Delaware Valley Magazine* toward the end of his playing career. The article broadly hinted that Lenny was taking steroids, which were not banned by baseball at the time, and painted Dykstra as a bit of a Neanderthal.

The backdrop for the article was Dykstra, a current Phillies star, playing tennis with Richie Ashburn, one of the most beloved figures in Philadelphia sports history. Ashburn played for the Phillies from 1948 to 1959 and later became a broadcaster for the team until his sudden death in 1997. The two men were playing on a tennis court near Ashburn's home, Conlin says. At the time, Dykstra was on the court "dropping the f-bomb and the mf-bomb and the cocksucker-bomb," Conlin recalls. He was also losing bet after bet to Ashburn, dropping some serious money and becoming a "cottage industry" for the elderly announcer.

There was a pair of women on the court next to Lenny cringing every time he came out with a string of curses. "On one of the line changes, Ashburn walks over to the women and says, 'Ladies, I know the language you're hearing from my opponent is foul and indefensible, but I have to tell you he suffers from Tourette's syndrome.'" It wasn't true, but the women felt sorry for Lenny. From that point on, he had a license to curse with impunity, not that it mattered. "Another time, right in the middle of the match, he walked to the corner of the court and took a leak."

After his flashy 1990 season, Dykstra suffered a series of setbacks. The following year, Dykstra's gambling troubles caught the eye of Fay Vincent, the commissioner of Major League Baseball. Vincent, a former vice chairman of Coca-Cola, was familiar with Lenny because he was a Mets fan and had watched him from the Shea Stadium stands prior to becoming commissioner.

These gambling problems, which were well known among Dykstra's teammates and friends, were just now making their way up to the commissioner's office. "In Atlantic City I saw him lose $50,000 in twenty minutes on blackjack, chewing tobacco and spitting it on the floor," says Radomski, the Mets' clubhouse hand. "I've seen him lose $200,000 to $300,000 in AC in only a few hours and get markers for $150,000 and blow through them in no time."

He says that Dykstra would "get angry and start cursing and screaming and kicking the table and shit," but that the casino would "put up with it because he used to lose a lot of money. He was a bad gambler."

Specifically, Vincent had heard that Dykstra lost $78,000 in high-stakes poker games in Mississippi. He requested a meeting with Nails and went down to Clearwater, Florida, where the Phillies held their spring training.

"There was no office or place to meet privately, so we ended up meeting in the men's room at the Clearwater Phillies spring training complex," Vincent says. "A friend of mine stood outside and shooed people away while Lenny and I went inside." Dykstra had declined the baseball players union's offer to have a lawyer present. Instead, he was willing to talk to Vincent man to man.

"I thought it showed a certain self-confidence and willingness to confront reality," Vincent says. "He wasn't going to make obfuscating, or legally subtle, arguments. I was very impressed with that." As the two men stood there in the bathroom, Dykstra turned to Vincent and said, "'I'm frightened of you because you just threw Pete Rose out of baseball and with a flick of your tail you can throw me out,'" Vincent recalls. "'Baseball is my whole life, and I'm frightened to death of what you're going to do.'"

Rose, who was managing the Cincinnati Reds at the time of his controversy, lied to investigators and was banned from baseball for betting on games his team played in. Today, he still maintains he never bet against his team.

Bart Giamatti, the commissioner who had instituted the initial ban of Rose, died eight days after the ruling. Vincent, who was deputy commissioner at the time, then took over the role of commissioner.[2]

"If you bet on a game in which you have an interest, you are banned for life, and nobody's come back from that," Vincent says. "If you bet on a game in which you are not a participant, you are subject to being suspended from baseball for one year."

However, the Rose and Dykstra cases had several major differences, he reports. Most importantly, Rose bet on his team's games, whereas Dykstra wasn't being accused of betting on baseball, And there was no rule in baseball banning gambling in general. However, Vincent was concerned about Dykstra's activities.

Looking at Dykstra, he said, "I'm not going to throw you out of baseball, but I do want you to listen to me very carefully. You're putting yourself in a vulnerable position where, if you start owing any real money to professional gamblers, they will ask you to do things I don't want you to do."

Dykstra could be "vulnerable to being influenced or pressured by mobsters or bad people into betraying the game." Dykstra agreed to halt his gambling immediately and was put on probation.

Vincent threatened to have "detective types" track Dykstra to make sure he was staying out of trouble. "He said, 'I'm going to shape up. You won't have any more trouble with me,'" Vincent recalls. "Now, can I be absolutely certain that he didn't do something in the dark of the night or around the corner that I might not have seen? I can't be absolutely certain, but my impression was that he was being direct. He honored his commitment as far as I can tell."

Just a few short months later, Dykstra narrowly escaped death when he wrapped his brand-new red 1991 Mercedes-Benz around a pair of trees in a single-car, drunk-driving accident on his way home from a bachelor party for teammate John Kruk. He almost killed himself and teammate Darren "Dutch" Daulton. Dykstra bruised his heart, broke his collarbone and cheekbone, and fractured three ribs—one of which punctured a lung. His blood alcohol was .179, which for someone his size was equivalent to drinking eight beers in an hour.

"He didn't pay attention to man's law or God's law," Tommy Herr, his Phillies teammate, once told reporters.[3]

While the near-death car accident and gambling troubles were cause for concern, some of Dykstra's teammates grew even more alarmed by what they witnessed in private. Wally Backman, one of the hard-partying Mets of the '80s, joined Dykstra in Philadelphia in 1991 and was troubled by what he saw. "There was one night before a game, Lenny had blood coming out of both his ears," Backman later told reporter Bob Klapisch. "I don't know how he played, but he did. Obviously, you knew it wasn't going to end well."[4]

"He's the kind of guy who takes a lot of risks in life—womanizing and drinking and whatever. He was not afraid of anything," says Bill Giles, co-owner of the Phillies. "He was one of those athletes that—and Pete Rose was another one I knew—that believed they were above the law of the land, kind of like Tiger Woods."

Dykstra broke his collarbone again later that season while running into an outfield wall in Cincinnati, and on opening day in 1992, a Greg Maddux pitch broke Nails's left wrist.

Then, in 1993, Lenny brought the magic back, nearly willing the Phillies to a World Series victory. "He was really a red-light player that year," Giles says. "When the team was out of the hunt, Lenny didn't play too well. But when you put him in a crucial game, the best comes out of him."

One of those times was Game 5 of the 1993 National League Championship Series against the heavily favored Atlanta Braves. Dykstra belted a full-count fastball from right-handed reliever Mark Wohlers over the center field fence, leading the Phillies to a 4–3 victory, helping to knock off the Braves in six games and send the Phillies to the World Series.

He would be even better in the World Series, batting .348, smacking four homers, scoring nine times, and driving in eight runs. In the decisive Game 6, Dykstra stepped to the plate in the seventh inning, once again needing some fireworks—big ones. With runners on first and third bases, the Phillies were on the verge of defeat. They were trailing 5–1 with little time remaining. Thinking he'd "better do something before it's too late," Dykstra worked pitcher Dave Stewart into a "cripple count"—three balls and one strike. Zoning in, he launched the next pitch into the right field stands, quieting the Toronto crowd as the Phillies continued the rally to eventually take a 6–5 lead into the ninth inning.

"When Lenny hit that three-run home run in Game 6 of the World Series, I remember sitting in the box with Lee Thomas [the team's general manager] and all our executives and saying, 'We have just won the World Series' because the momentum had shifted," Giles recalls. "Then of course we end up blowing the game." Mitch "Wild Thing" Williams, who had received death threats after losing Game 4, struggled before serving up a meatball to Toronto's Joe Carter, who hit a walk-off, series-ending homer.

In the ensuing days, newspapers ran headlines such as "Bullpen Cost Phils a Title and Dykstra MVP Trophy" and "If Only Dykstra Could Pitch In Relief."[5]

Dykstra finished second in the MVP award voting and was rewarded with a hefty $25 million, multiyear contract after the season. "Lenny said, 'I'm not the best player in baseball, but I think I'm in the top 10 percent, and here's the range I think I deserve,'" Giles recalls. "We had pretty quick negotiations, and I gave him 25 million bucks."

At the time, the deal made Dykstra the highest-paid leadoff hitter in the history of baseball. It would also be his last big league contract.

After the World Series defeat, Major League Baseball unleashed Dykstra on Europe, selecting him as the game's goodwill ambassador on the Continent. While in Paris, Dykstra and his twelve-person entourage, including Terri and his business manager and longtime friend Lindsay Jones, dined at the La Tour d'Argent, a famous restaurant overlooking the Seine said to have been frequented by Henri IV.

After arriving late, Dykstra refused to follow the restaurant's protocol and remove his cap, according to a *Sports Illustrated* piece by reporter Ian Thomsen.[6] Instead, Dykstra had his interpreter lie and say that he had injured his head playing baseball and that he couldn't expose the wound to the open air. He could have followed the rules, but why bother if he didn't have to?

After settling in for dinner, Dykstra recounted how one time at Caesars Palace in Las Vegas he had enjoyed a bottle of delicious dessert wine. The name sounded something like Chateau d'Yquem. The good people at La Tour d'Argent had a bottle of 1937 Chateau d'Yquem and informed Dykstra it could be his for only 16,000 francs, or a little more than $2,700, according to Thomsen's account.

The wine is one of the most difficult in the world to make, and that particular bottle had survived World War II in the battle-ravaged country. The proprietor had hidden the bottles to protect them from the Nazis. There were only five bottles from 1937 and 1938 left when Dykstra arrived.

He ordered a bottle, and then, remembering he was supposed to be at the Chicago Pizza Pie Factory across town to sign autographs, he bolted from the restaurant, leaving his entourage to enjoy the restaurant's famous duck dishes in his absence. When he returned, the group enjoyed the "best wine in the world," and Dykstra dropped his Visa to pay the $13,000 dinner tab. Then he ordered another bottle of Chateau d'Yquem for the road.

CHAPTER 6

THE TAJ MAHAL OF CAR WASHES

By the time that magical 1993 season arrived, injuries were already plaguing Dykstra. He had played in just 145 out of a possible 324 games the previous two seasons and knew he wasn't going to be able to make a living terrorizing opposing pitchers for the rest of his life. He started thinking about life after baseball.

It had taken everything he had to claw his way out of a benign middle-class existence, and there was no way he was going to slip back into a mediocre life. NEVER! He needed to parlay his baseball earnings into an even-bigger war chest.

"Before I take a dirt nap, I'm going to build myself a financial empire," Dykstra told *Sports Illustrated* at the time.[1] Only he didn't know exactly how to go about it. A handful of ideas he pitched to Giles, the Phillies' owner, didn't take off.

"He would come to me maybe two or three times with business ideas," Giles says. "He wanted to do a debit card with his picture on it and things like that. I said, 'Lenny, I'm not going to get into that with you.' He was always thinking about how to make a buck."

Dykstra had a particular interest in real estate because "it's real" and there's a limited supply of it. He also wanted to go into what he considered a low-risk business that "couldn't be replaced by a microchip." After carefully weighing his options, Dykstra decided to take a whack at the Southern California car wash biz.

The car wash business was a natural fit for a guy like Dykstra. He had always been entranced by luxury cars, and his blue-collar persona meshed perfectly with the cash-heavy, workmanlike profile of the car wash business. On the field, Dykstra became known for his perpetually dirt-ridden uniform. Surprisingly, off the field, he was obsessive when it came to germs. A business centered on cleanliness made total sense.

Dykstra brought the start-up cash, and longtime buddy Lindsay Jones brought the business savvy. Jones was one of the kids who had packed the Dykstra family garage for high-intensity Ping-Pong tournaments and later became a part of Dykstra's European traveling party.

The men "had a lot of the same personality—they were exactly the same," recalls Brian Dykstra. They both lived life in the fast lane. They reveled at the chance to sneak off to Las Vegas or Atlantic City for late-night baccarat and high-stakes card games, which they did during the off-season and several of Dykstra's stints on the disabled list. They would drink, gamble, party, and do God knows what else.

The friends embarked on a mission together to create the greatest, most luxurious car washes known to man. But before they could make "some serious cheddar" from the new business, they needed a place to build it. According to Dykstra lore, his search led him to a slice of land in Corona, California, that an old lady had been living on and had purchased decades earlier for $43,000. As Lenny tells it, he drew up an oversized sweepstakes check for $1 million and knocked on the elderly woman's door.

"Hi, I'm Lenny Dykstra, and I want to buy your property for a million dollars," he said, noting that the woman's knees buckled and the expression on her face made him worried she might drop dead. "I said, 'Don't die on me; I really need that property.'" She didn't die, at least not then, and by December 1993, just a few months after the Phillies' unlikely World Series appearance, the first Lenny Dykstra Car Wash began soaping up cars in a section of North Corona, California, known as McKinley Hills.

"He played the game the way you're supposed to, and he carried that over into business," says Brian Dykstra, a sales manager at the car wash. "A lot of people saw him coming up to the plate grabbing his crotch and spitting out chewing tobacco, and they thought he was a dummy."

However, he had a plan.

Knowing the grueling, 162-game baseball season would prevent him from keeping a close eye on the business, Lenny turned to his kid brother, Kevin, to watch over the fledging car wash. Kevin, who had been working as a minor league baseball umpire, got the call to run the day-to-day operations of the McKinley site.

Across the country in Philadelphia, Lenny continued to face a familiar foe: injuries. Light years away from his magical 1993 postseason performance, Dykstra laced 'em up just 84 times in the strike-shortened 1994 season. The following year, the notoriously rock-hard, tobacco-juice-stained turf at urine-scented Veterans Stadium, where the Phillies played their home games, continued to take its toll. Although Dykstra was still being paid the big bucks, he missed 100 games in 1995, owing in part to an arthritic right knee.

With the Phillies dead in the water, wrapping up a sub-.500 season, 21 games behind the National League's East-leading Atlanta Braves, Lenny's car wash biz was very much alive and well in the fall of 1995. It was a time of paradox for Nails. His baseball career was on the decline, but the Lenny Dykstra Car Wash business was ready to become a kingdom.

Learning from their space limitations at McKinley Hills, the boys knew they had to go big or go home. Lenny, Lindsay, and Kevin scouted out a prime location in suburban, middle-class Simi Valley, forty miles northwest of Los Angeles, for the new castle. The two-and-a-half-acre lot was big and situated in a family-oriented part of California. The location offered a steady flow of commuters looking to keep their cars in tip-top shape. If you build it, they will come, the boys thought with dollar signs in their eyes.

"A lotta rooftops here, bro," Lenny later said in an interview with *Esquire* magazine. "And they're all families, commuters. So they've got two cars, and they put a lot of miles on them. And there wasn't much competition. What guys are here, we're gonna send them to their fucking room!"[2]

The expansion plans came at the right time for Dykstra as the bottom was about to fall out of his baseball career, bringing the reality of a life without baseball and its supersized paychecks clearly into focus. After playing in just 40 games, his 1996 season was over by May. He was in serious trouble. His back pain was debilitating, and he had numbness in his legs. Dykstra had played through stiffness. He had played through soreness. He had played through massive hangovers and self-imposed sleep deprivation. He had played through fatigue from all-night poker games and partying binges. But he couldn't play through this.

The official diagnosis was spinal stenosis, a congenital condition that causes narrowing of the openings in the spinal canal where the nerves pass through, creating painful pressure on the nerves. Even for a guy who was tough as nails, this was scary stuff. Hoping to relieve some of his eye-watering pain, Nails underwent the knife two months later, which sidelined him for the rest of the year. Sporting a gruesome, one-inch-wide purple scar running the length of his back,[3] Dykstra struggled just to get out of bed in the morning following his surgery.

His playing career was in jeopardy. With the Phillies crawling to a 67-win season, worst in the National League, manager Jim Fregosi's job was clearly on the chopping block. Nails knew it was time to make his move. On the last day of the season, Lenny reached out to Bill Giles with a proposition.

"He called me up one Sunday after the game and said, 'I've gotta come talk to you, I know you're going to fire Fregosi,'" Giles recalls. "He said, 'My back's hurting. I'm not sure how effective I can play, so the way to win again is to make me the manager.'"

Dykstra wanted to name Darren Daulton, the popular but oft-injured veteran Phillies catcher as his bench coach. He also wanted John Kruk, a Philly fan favorite who had retired the year before while playing for the Chicago White Sox, to be his hitting coach. "Lenny said, 'You'll have the most popular team and draw lots of fans.' I said, 'I don't think that's in the cards, Lenny.' He called me a couple of more times after and said the same thing—that I should hire him as manager, which of course I did not."

Instead, the Phillies went with Terry Francona, a onetime opponent of Dykstra's. Although the rest of the players pushed to get in game shape during the spring of 1997, Dykstra couldn't manage any hard exercise. One wrong move could put him out of commission for days, weeks, or even months. Players and members of the press turned away as the once great member of "Macho Row" hobbled past them in the team's clubhouse like a wounded animal. It was tough to watch Dykstra wincing in pain. In the end, the entire 1997 season was lost—he didn't play in a single game.

Literally on his last legs, a broken-down and battered Dykstra stared into the baseball abyss. To the surprise of many who thought he was surely done, Dykstra reported for duty in the spring of 1998, shuffling into the Phillies' spring training facility in Clearwater, Florida.

Setting the stage for the unlikeliest of comebacks and possibly the feel-good story of the year, Dykstra hardly resembled the man who just months earlier could barely walk. Despite living with the back of a seventy-year-old man, the thirty-five-year-old appeared in better shape than he had in years, running drills with his teammates and shagging fly balls in the warm Florida sun.

All he had to do was stay healthy, and he would be anointed the starting center fielder. It was only logical, he thought. He was a proven major league hitter, and fans adored him. And he was making the big bucks.

But unfortunately for Dykstra, it wasn't that simple. This was 1998, years removed from his or the Phillies' last productive season. Most of his teammates from the 1993 season were long gone—either retired or scattered elsewhere throughout the league.

Dykstra was a stranger in his own clubhouse, a fossil in a rebuilding club. And Dykstra wasn't doing himself any favors. A notoriously slow starter, he was having trouble getting back into the swing of things. He hadn't played in a major league game in a year and a half, and it showed. He was healthy for the first time in years, but he was about to find out that wasn't enough.

Francona, the manager, and Ed Wade, the team's general manager, summoned Dykstra for a chat. They said they needed to see more out of their former All-Star. His past accomplishments, although important to the organization, didn't guarantee him a starting job. Dykstra wasn't the Phillies' only option in center field—in fact, he likely wasn't their first option. During the off-season, the team had imported twenty-seven-year-old Doug Glanville, the team's center fielder of the future.

Dykstra walked away from the meeting with Francona and Wade dejected. "The feeling I get is they have no confidence in my ability, and if that's the case, I think they should release me," Nails told reporters afterward. "Maybe I scared [Francona] because of how good shape I'm in and I'm able to go to the post every day."[4]

The already slim odds of resuscitating his dead-as-a-doornail career grew bleaker by the day. Dykstra's struggles continued as Glanville flashed the leather in the field and impressed at the plate. It became increasingly clear that Dykstra was part of the Phillies' past, not their future.

With Dykstra openly criticizing Francona in the clubhouse, the press described the situation as a soap opera. It was disruptive to the club and was casting a "big, dark cloud" over the team, Francona later said.[5]

Then nature intervened. A little more than a week after the meeting with Wade and Francona, Dykstra put his comeback on hold owing to his barking back. One of the world's leading specialists delivered the sobering news: if Dykstra continued to play, he might suffer dire long-term consequences. It was time to step away, time to do something else.

"I knew I couldn't play the way I wanted to play; the way people remembered me," Dykstra later told the *Daily News*. "People looked at me different and I knew the party was over."[6] In June, the once heroic Nails said he would never play ball again; he officially submitted his retirement papers in November, twenty-nine months after his last appearance in a major league baseball game.

———

No more belly flops onto the cold, hard, cementlike turf at the Vet. No more dipshit general managers or jerkoff coaches to deal with. With baseball on the back burner, he could focus on the only team that mattered to him now: Team Dykstra. Now he had the time to spend on the car washes and his family—two things that often went hand in hand. As the car wash business expanded, more family members got involved.

Just one month after officially hanging up his spikes, Dykstra opened the Simi Valley palace with pomp and circumstance. The festivities included appearances by Ken Caminiti (an MVP third baseman), Hall of Famer Rod Carew, and former Phillies player and manager Larry Bowa.

Just a few years later—in 2003—Dykstra added the third jewel in his triple crown when he opened the final car wash in South Corona, California. Just off Interstate 15, that location included a gas station and 19,000-square-foot retail shopping center.

The car washes are not run-of-the-mill, boring wash-and-wax places. "They're like palaces; they're not like car washes," Brian Dykstra tells me. "There's nothing like them."

Lenny compares the car washes to the Taj Mahal, the revered 1600s structure built by Mughal emperor Shah Jahan as a tribute to his favorite wife, Mumtaz Mahal. Although such a grandiose comparison sounds a bit odd to many, consider that the car washes have green or pearly white marble countertops and Kohler fixtures in the bathrooms, as well as cherrywood cabinets and leather chairs in the skylighted waiting areas.

Inside are gigantic fish tanks filled with expensive creatures, televisions all over the place tuned to sports stations, sports memorabilia showcases (there was a Mickey Mantle jersey on display in one of them), and an entertaining story. As far as car washes go, these are pretty damn nice.

"I had Butterworth fixtures," Dykstra said in a later interview broadcast on HBO's *Real Sports* program on March 10, 2008. "I had granite, just like he did. I had the same shit he had. I don't even know what the Taj Mahal is. In fact, somebody said that . . . I just took it and ran with it."

CHAPTER 7

CRAMERICA

The dramatic transformation of Lenny Dykstra from stubby, blue-collar, dirt-under-your-fingernails baseball folk hero into successful businessman didn't begin and end with the car washes. The beating he took in the stock market during the dot-com crash of 2000–2002 is really what shaped the next phase of Dykstra's life and springboarded him from local California car wash kingpin to a mainstream, Main Street resurgence.

The lead-up to the market's dot-com crash was a modern-day gold rush, with investors speculating heavily on unproven stocks in hopes of finding hidden nuggets. A lottery-winning, get-rich-quick mentality took over, and many of the traditional methods for assessing a stock's value went right out the window.

In this environment, stock prices soared on hope and optimism—particularly among newer Internet-based companies. It looked as if the party were never going to end, and few wanted to jump off the gravy train prematurely. The price of a share of stock was being set, in many cases, by investors based on a company's cool new technology or perceived future moneymaking potential, not its current fundamentals.

Young CEOs who had started companies out of their dorm rooms were becoming multimillionaires seemingly overnight. Hordes of companies with whacky-sounding names launched on a nearly daily basis. Many of them incorporated dot-com into their corporate identity, proud their firms were on the cutting edge of this new frontier.

The new strategy for many of these companies was to get as big as possible as quickly as possible in order to dominate their respective playing fields. They would often give away their products and services for free, accepting huge quarterly and annual losses in order to grab a bigger slice of the market. They believed that if they built enough brand awareness and customer loyalty, they could make money later. And investors often turned a blind eye to current business problems and held irrational faith that they would hit it big down the road.

With little or no money coming in, these companies turned to venture capitalists or the investing public for funding, often via initial public offerings (IPOs). An IPO occurs when a privately held company first offers the investing public a chance to buy some shares of its stock. Instead of judging companies on their plans to achieve profitability, investors often examined companies' burn rate, which measures how quickly an unprofitable company without a clear path to profitability is blowing through its stockpile of cash.

Companies such as TheGlobe.com, a social networking Web site that was a sort of grandfather to MySpace and modern-day behemoth Facebook, were born into this environment in 1998. Started by two Cornell college students, the initial price of the stock was set at $9 a share. However, on the first day of trading investors clamored for the stock in the same way millions of teenage girls had gone bonkers for the Beatles decades earlier. They drove shares of TheGlobe.com as high as $97 its first day of trading. At the time, TheGlobe.com's IPO was considered the most successful in history.

However, the honeymoon didn't last long as the company continued to bleed money and the stock price plummeted. A little more than a year later—in late January 2000—the company's founders resigned. By 2001, investors could buy several shares of the company's stock with spare change they found under their couch cushions.

Online pet supplies retailer Pets.com was another popular dot-com bomb. Largely cited as one of the most spectacular failures of the dot-com craze, the company spent a boatload of cash on building its brand and infrastructure, while sacrificing profits to grow its customer base.

The company did a great job at raising its public profile through its mascot, an antagonistic, unnamed, doglike sock puppet with buttons for eyes and a microphone in its paw. The puppet gained a cult following, appearing on television shows such as *Good Morning America* and *Nightline*. The puppet even had its own giant balloon in the world-famous Macy's Thanksgiving Day Parade in 1999. A few months later, Pets.com paid $1.2 million to air a spot during Super Bowl XXXIV.

The problem was that the company's business model had gaping holes in it. Pets.com offered free shipping and big discounts on its merchandise to try and grow its customer base with the intention of upselling customers to bigger-ticket items. Not only didn't that work; the company also was losing money on most of its sales owing to the steep discounts and the cost of shipping.

The success of this branding initiative ended up contributing to the company's demise. As more people turned to Pets.com, its customer base grew, and more customers equaled more money-losing transactions.

Dot-coms weren't the only ones to suffer during the stock market crash of 2000–2002. Between the market's peak in March 2000 and its bottom in October 2002, companies collectively shed $5 trillion in market value. The Internet tornado engulfed many investors, wiping out huge chunks of their wealth. Dykstra was one of the many people caught in the twister's path, unable to find shelter from the massive storm. According to Dykstra, his broker mismanaged his retirement nest egg so badly that it lost 80 percent of its value—falling from $2 million to just $400,000.

Dykstra didn't understand what had happened to his money—he only knew that it had evaporated in an instant. "My financial adviser, who was robbing me blind, introduced me to his best friend the broker," Dykstra later told me. He privately referred to the broker as "Wally Wall Street."

"When I lost this money, I went to my broker . . . and I said, 'What the fuck happened to my money?'" Dykstra later told HBO *Real Sports* reporter Bernard Goldberg. "He started making up all these excuses. I didn't know what he was talking about. I was humiliated."

The problem, as Dykstra came to learn, was that he had too much exposure to tech companies that blew up when the bubble burst. His broker told him he was invested in safe blue-chip, top-tier mutual funds. Dykstra didn't understand what a stock was, let alone a mutual fund, which is essentially a basket of stocks.

And he didn't realize that many of the different mutual funds he owned had a lot of the same underlying stocks in their basket, making them more alike than most people realize. That can be a good thing when a stock is on the rise, but crushing to a portfolio when the stock tanks, like many did following the dot-com crash in 2000.

As Dykstra walked out of his devastating meeting with Wally Wall Street, he vowed to never allow himself to be in that situation again. He then set out on a mission to take control of his finances, yanking his remaining money out of the market and putting it into a bank account.

He ordered more than thirty newsletters, bought CDs and DVDs, and gave himself one year to learn everything he could about the stock market. He used his name to open doors in the world of finance, seeking coaches and mentors. In addition to having his ex-teammate Dave "Head" Hollins introduce him to his brother Paul, a stockbroker at Wachovia, Dykstra offered his baseball know-how to one of his neighbors in exchange for private stock market tutoring.

Dykstra even wrote to people he saw on television, such as legendary investor Warren Buffet, asking for help. Some replied. Others didn't. One of big-ger fishes to take the bait was Jim Cramer, who is often dubbed the "Mad Man of Wall Street." A self-described "banking-class hero," Cramer set out to make financial news entertaining and bring it to the masses. Following a successful hedge fund, radio show, and financial news Web site, Cramer carved out his most recent niche by making the stock market more accessible and easier to under-stand on *Mad Money*, his television show on CNBC, which began in 2005.

In stark contrast to the sleepy, often dry, and boring stock news programs, Cramer's show has been described by some as Pee Wee's Playhouse meets Wall Street. Known for his hyperkinetic mojo and his enthusiastic use of the term "Boo-Yah," Cramer has also been dubbed Wall Street's "Pied Piper of Capital-ism" by *USA Today* in a December 2, 1997, article.

With his sleeves rolled up and his tie hanging down, Cramer fields calls and e-mails from viewers and enthusiastically and decisively rattles off his take on a handful of stocks each day on his show in segments such as "The Lightning Round." Cramer, a gnarling, balding, middle-aged guy with a reddish-white goatee, uses props such as plastic bulls, stuffed bears, buzzers, whistles, and gongs to entertain his audience.

"Regular people really do love the show, and it is despised by every 'acade-mic' and graybeard out there," Cramer said in a September 2008 interview with the *Players Club* magazine. "They truly can't stand it. The antipathy and the love are both extreme; I mean, I can eat a dinner at La Dolce Vita in Belmar, New Jersey, and people crowd around me and 'boo-yah' me. But if I were in a room with investment 'pros,' they would only do the 'boo' of the boo-yah."

Cramer's path to the top, which eventually led to his crossing paths with Dykstra, took years. Growing up, Cramer loved sports. One of his earliest jobs was selling Coca-Cola, and later ice cream, to fans in the 600–700 level of Vet-erans Stadium in Philadelphia. Really, though, Cramer wanted to be a sports reporter or columnist.

When he went to Harvard, he became president (a fancy name for editor) of the *Harvard Crimson*, one of the most prestigious college newspapers in the world. There he rubbed elbows with future captains of industry, including Steve Balmer, the current CEO of Microsoft, who ran the business side of the *Harvard Crimson*.

After graduating magna cum laude from Harvard in 1977, Cramer spent a month covering the Philadelphia Eagles football team before moving to Florida and reporting on one of the most gruesome chapters in American history. Liv-ing down the block from Florida State University's Chi Omega sorority house, Cramer is said to have been one of the first reporters on the scene of the 1978 slaughter there by pretty-boy serial killer Ted Bundy.

Bundy, known for his boyish good looks, went on a multistate rampage over several years, attacking, abducting, and killing dozens of young women and girls. He bludgeoned, raped, and killed most of his victims, even engaging in necrophilia with some of the corpses. He admitted to killing thirty women in Washington, Utah, Colorado, and Florida but is suspected of having killed more—some estimates exceed one hundred women.

After escaping jail in Colorado for the second time, Bundy fled to Florida, where he bludgeoned and strangled Lisa Levy and Margaret Bowman while they were sleeping at the Chi Omega sorority house. He then attacked two other women there before beating a fifth female student a few blocks away. He left town and continued his rampage before being stopped by a police officer for driving a stolen car.

"I knew he was a killer," Cramer said of Bundy in the 2008 *Players Club* interview. "He wore a wool fisherman's sweater and it was never less than one hundred degrees with 100 percent humidity. He always winked at me. I was at Big Daddy's one night when he was there. It turned out to be my fave bar. I probably bought him a drink. I loved buying guys drinks." Bundy was eventually sentenced to death and was fried in the electric chair on January 24, 1989.

Cramer moved from Florida to California, continuing to cover the ugly underbelly of society as a crime reporter for the *Los Angeles Herald*. However, his career and life took a major turn for the worse when a burglar broke into his home and stole everything he owned—including the bed. He became homeless, living in his car, a rundown Ford Fairmont, for several months. He says he was harassed by the police and even slept with a .22-caliber pistol.

"I had a jaundiced liver, mononucleosis, loved the bottle and borrowed from everyone and stiffed every creditor—most of whom caught up with me in the ensuing years," Cramer told the *Players Club*. However, that experience transformed him. "The car thing created someone who was so insecure about money that he decided he had to be filthy rich. . . . It made me who I am. I could not take being poor."

Cramer returned to Harvard, where he reignited his long-lost love of stocks. He studied law but lived for stocks, often leaving stock tips for callers on his answering machine greetings. His machine messages caught the ear of Martin Peretz, a professor at Harvard and editor of the *New Republic*, who handed Cramer a $500,000 check and asked him to invest the money for him. Cramer reportedly earned $150,000 for Peretz over a two-year period.

From there Cramer further cut his teeth as a stockbroker for the ultra-wealthy at Goldman Sachs for three years before starting his own hedge fund. Peretz, and future New York governor Eliot Spitzer, who had been a Harvard classmate of Cramer's, were among the fund's early investors. Cramer claims his fund earned a hefty average of 24 percent per year over the fourteen years he managed the fund (he retired from the fund in 2001). It also made Cramer a lot of money—he says he earned tens of millions of dollars during that time.

In 1996, Cramer and Peretz launched a Web site and company called TheStreet.com, which has since expanded into a host of interrelated Web sites. TheStreet.com Web site focuses on financial news, trading, and the stock market, mixing traditional news with commentary. A chunk of the site's content is available for free, but it also maintains a subscription-only area.

TheStreet.com was born into that tech fervor of the late 1990s and was not immune to its many pitfalls. On May 11, 1999, the day its stock debuted on the Nasdaq, TheStreet.com traded as high as $70.12 per share. Within two weeks, the stock had plunged all the way to $30.44 a share, and by late 2001, it had fallen all the way to about a buck a share.

Initially, Cramer had some distance between himself and the site. "Cramer provided a lot of general ideas and direction, but he was restricted by his position as a hedge fund manager," says Dave Kansas, the original editor in chief of the site. "He couldn't be in the news room, he couldn't provide specific ideas, he couldn't hire/fire, and we worked to ensure that the separation was maintained, for his sake and for ours. He was able to educate us on how markets worked, and his own writing was prolific and absolutely crucial to the site." After leaving his hedge fund in 2001, Cramer became much more active with TheStreet.com.

Several years later, Cramer received an e-mail from someone claiming to be . . . Lenny Dykstra. At first, Cramer thought the letter must be a gag, but after a few exchanges, he realized it was Nails and asked for an autograph for his sister. Dykstra sent a signed poster saying, "Nan, I love you," and the relationship between Lenny and Cramer blossomed.

Cramer respected the way Dykstra applied the same skills he had used in baseball to the stock market and eventually asked him to write a column for TheStreet.com. Dykstra also appeared as a regular guest on Cramer's radio show.

"Cramer was a big fan of Lenny's on the East Coast," says Lenny's younger brother, Kevin, who was working at the car wash when the correspondence began. "Lenny's name was good. It was a win–win for both of 'em. They could use each other's names. They fed off each other."

Despite being a rookie in the world of stocks, Dykstra began writing the column for TheStreet.com in 2005. Although his column wasn't typical fare for the site, readers came in droves to see what Lenny Dykstra would say next. He told readers which stocks were in his lineup and which were "on the bench."

He noted that certain companies were "batting leadoff" or that a specific stock pick was a "single," "double," "triple," or "home run."

The tips would appear in columns with headlines such as "Dykstra: Around the Horn of Plenty" or "Dykstra: The Mentality of the Closer."

The columns weren't just about sports or about the stock market—everything and anything was fair game. For example, after quoting a line from Charles Dickens's *Great Expectations*, Dykstra wrote, "I know it will come as a shock to most, but I am not a literary buff." In another column Dykstra quoted lyrics from Billy Joel's song "Pressure."

Dykstra explained to readers how he had adopted one of Warren Buffet's famous quotes as his own personal motto. "Be fearful when others are greedy, and greedy when others are fearful" was written on a piece of paper taped to his computer screen so that he could see it each morning before trading.

Atop Dykstra's lighthearted columns was a picture of him donning a red baseball cap and showing a puzzled look on his face. Readers loved it. Whether they took the columns seriously or not, they were something different on a site that could be very thick at times. And Dykstra seemed to have a knack for picking stocks.

In one early column entitled "Dykstra: How to Keep This Rally Alive," he noted that the "first-game jitters are gone" and that he had made a profit from Symantec, his "leadoff hitter" from the week before. He had bought Symantec at $19.95 and sold it at $22.18, a profit of $2.27 a share. Dykstra gained a following, and as his popularity soared, he and Cramer became better friends.

The inclusion of such a column, however, represented a drastic shift in the direction of the serious financial Web site. In the beginning, the site's main goal was to provide scoops and analysis in "real time" so that it could affect the stock market during the day, Kansas says. "We also wanted to entertain and provoke in order to rise above the cluttered fray. Our best stories were real shoe-leather reporting pieces that broke news and changed the conversation."

Dykstra's column, however, was part of a larger initiative to feature columns by celebrities, such as famed chef Rocco DiSpirito, Chicago Bears linebacker Hunter Hillenmeyer, and Heisman Trophy winner and perennial NFL standout Tim Brown, to drive more traffic to the Web site.

Kansas, who had departed years before the celebrity push, says he was surprised to see his former publication feature Lenny Dykstra as a columnist. "It seemed almost bizarre," Kansas says. "I also knew Cramer as a deeply loyal Philadelphian, so it made some sense at that level."

Although the celebrity initiative was initially met with mixed reviews by the journalists at TheStreet.com, Dykstra's column was cause for particular concern to many in the newsroom because of the investment style and approach, which dealt with an infrequently written about vehicle known as deep-in-the-money calls, a type of option and an investing system that calls for throwing more money at losing positions.

CHAPTER 8

JOCKS AND STOCKS

It was a miserable and drizzly evening in December 2007, and I was sitting on a wooden stool in a crowded dive bar on the Upper East Side of Manhattan, waiting for my friend Dan Ryan. He had called earlier in the week to say he had an intriguing business proposal to discuss.

The watering hole was hosting a diabetes fund-raiser, a cause near and dear to my heart. I had been diagnosed with Type 1 diabetes in 2000 at the age of twenty-three, and I need to take several insulin injections each day in order to live. It was a classy move on Dan's part to pick that venue, I thought, as I scanned the faces in the packed room, anxiously awaiting his arrival.

Dan and I had worked together at a company called Money-Media the year before. I was the managing editor of *Ignites*, the company's flagship publication. He sold advertising. Despite its unusual name, *Ignites* is a wildly successful daily electronic newsletter that is delivered to more than 50,000 executives in the multitrillion-dollar mutual fund industry each morning.

I had been recruited to join *Ignites* in 2004 after covering the largest scandal in the mutual fund industry's history for a rival publication. Eliot Spitzer, future governor of New York, Cramer pal, and the attorney general of New York at the time, had been slugging it out with the industry's heavy hitters.

Back then I was a young reporter on the front lines digging for stories. Fund shops were frantic—Spitzer was embarrassing them in public, parading incriminating internal e-mails in front of the press, and twisting the arms of industry giants such as Bank of America, Alliance Capital, and AIM Investments until they capitulated to his demands: hundreds of millions of dollars in fines, penalties, and restitution each. It was a horrific time to be a mutual fund exec, but a great time to be a reporter.

Just six months after I joined Money-Media—at the age of twenty-seven—I was promoted to managing editor of *Ignites*. That was a big step in my career, and I felt my star was clearly on the rise—at least in my own little universe. During the ensuing years, I worked hard along with my team of reporters and editors to build on the publication's success, while the company's sales staff pushed for aggressive price increases, which they usually got.

However, by the time I got Dan's call, I had been running *Ignites* for almost three years and was a bit burned out. The work had become routine. I reported to the head of editorial for the entire company, so there seemed little room to grow professionally.

Plus, Money-Media was on the block. The founder and owner of the privately held company wanted to cash out. I began to think about how to take my career to the next level.

Dan, by all accounts, was thriving since his departure from Money-Media. He was now heading up Doubledown Media's capital markets advertising sales. The firm had launched a few years earlier and sported titles such as *Trader Monthly* and *Dealmaker.*

At that time, top executives at the firm claimed Doubledown was "recession-proof because of its rarified audience: men whose average net worth is between $3 and $5 million and who want to read about other men like themselves." Plus, Doubledown was hiring new staff and expanding at a time when much of the economy was struggling.[1]

When Dan showed up, he began telling me about this once-in-a-lifetime magazine project he was working on with Lenny "Nails" Dykstra. With a smirk on his face and a sort of disbelief that he was even speaking the words, Dan, a diehard Phillies fan, described the Players Club (TPC).

The Players Club was both the name of Dykstra's company and a magazine used to showcase the company's core message. Doubledown was partnering with Dykstra on the magazine portion of the venture. On a very basic level, the Players Club was designed to be an all-encompassing, one-stop resource for the unique lifestyle needs of professional athletes. If a pro athlete needed anything—from relocation services after being traded to a new team, to a last-minute birthday present for his wife—the Players Club was there to help.

The way it worked was simple. Rather than trying to build the enormous infrastructure to offer all of these services itself, the Players Club's intended to create strategic alliances with elite companies in various industries, such as financial services firms, jet charter services, custom home builders, or luxury car brokers.

For example, if Dallas Cowboys quarterback Tony Romo wanted to build a one-of-a-kind beachfront castle on some tropical island paradise and needed a referral from someone he could trust, the Players Club would put him in touch with its premier custom home builder, Windstar Homes.

Because the Players Club wasn't trying to sell anything to the athletes directly, its real value would come in the hand-holding it provided. And the Players Club would have a certain amount of credibility because it had been started by a former player who understood their needs and would be spread by current and former players. "Player reps," a loosely based network of retired players established and financially incentivized by TPC, would recruit new players into the club. Dykstra described it as "players helping players."

As I would later learn, Dykstra often drew a wheel—a small circle surrounded by a larger circle—when trying to illustrate TPC's business model. The smaller circle would be labeled "the Players Club." Along the perimeter of the larger circle would be the names of the various services. Dykstra would then draw a line from the smaller circle to one of the services on the perimeter, creating a spoke in the wheel. He called it "building bridges." The Players Club would walk each player seeking help across a bridge to a specific strategic partner that could help him or her.

However, for all the glitz and glamour of private jets and fancy cars, the core message of TPC entailed a much less sexy subject: annuities. Dykstra started the Players Club as a way to help professional athletes avoid going broke after their playing days were done. He had seen too many athletes pawning their world championship rings and trophies because they were in dire straits and needed cash.

"Players who've won championship rings have ended up living under bridges," Dykstra wrote in his column in the inaugural issue (April 2008) of the *Players Club* magazine, noting that "professional athletes have ended up working after their retirement for the same money they were giving away in tips."

Most professional athletes retire at a much younger age than the vast majority of the general population, giving them a limited number of years to earn big bucks. They also have to survive many more years in retirement than most people—many without a new source of income. Many live an expensive lifestyle, and without new paychecks coming in after retirement, the money simply runs out.

Dykstra hoped to encourage players to sock away as much as $500,000 a year or more into an annuity. It was a way for them to secure a regular payout once they retired. To Dykstra, the Players Club was about "changing fucking lives" while underscoring the importance of family.

"There are many reasons that 80 percent of athletes get divorced," Dykstra wrote in that first edition. "Money is certainly one of them. . . . Seventy-eight percent of NFL players will either be broke, divorced or jobless within three years after they're done playing."

Dykstra planned to convey this core message through a free monthly magazine, which would be placed inside the locker of every athlete in each of the ten major sports—NASCAR, soccer, baseball, football, basketball, hockey, and men's and women's tennis and golf. The concept was essentially to wrap the financial message in a luxurious lifestyle magazine that highlighted players and the things they were interested in.

Along with doing a little good, Dykstra wanted to make money. From a business standpoint, he saw the magazine as the key to unlocking the $60 billion of wealth in the professional athlete market and launching his own personal net worth into a new stratosphere. He could make money by charging the strategic partners a pretty penny for access to professional athletes in the club and for strategic partner designation. He could gain a commission on each sale as well. He also believed that high-end advertisers would pluck down large chunks of cash, providing a significant secondary revenue stream for the business.

The magazine had to be high gloss, printed on the heaviest stock paper, and it had to be overflowing with lush photographs and top-shelf articles. Just because it was free didn't mean it was going to be flimsy or cheap looking. However, Dykstra had no idea how to produce such a high-quality magazine, so he turned to Doubledown for help.

The magazine, Dan told me, would launch in just a few short months. "We'd like you to write a few articles for the magazine from time to time, but I have something different in mind for you," Dan said, switching gears.

Doubledown, which specialized in print publications, wanted to break into the world of e-newsletters, one of which would feature Dykstra's stock market advice. If Doubledown did, in fact, move ahead with this new initiative, Dan thought I was the right man for the job considering my work with *Ignites*. He asked me to meet with Doubledown president Randall Lane.

———

I waited for Dan to confirm the meeting. Days turned into weeks, and I began to think the odds of ever meeting with Lane were slim to none. In the interim, Money-Media was sold to the *Financial Times*, the London-based salmon-colored newspaper that rivals the *Wall Street Journal*. I was relieved and renewed.

Just as I, and the rest of the staff, began to settle in with our new employer, Dan resurfaced, asking me to drop by Doubledown's offices to meet with Lane. As Tony, Lane's assistant, escorted me down the cramped, dimly lit corridor, I could see the newsroom filled with worker drones glued to their computer screens, quietly going about their business.

We arrived at the last office on the right, and I stepped inside. Lane's office was spacious and illuminated by the daylight streaming through the windows. Lane surfaced from behind a large stack of papers, magazines, and boxes and invited me to have a seat.

He was a tall, middle-aged white guy with an unassuming build and a thin, reddish-brown Fu Manchu. His sideburns stretched all the way to the bottom of his ears, but he had very little hair on the top of his head. His attire was professional but laid back—suit pants and a button-down white-collared shirt, with the top two buttons undone. No tie.

He glanced at my résumé, and looking up, he set it down on the desk. Leaning back in his chair and pressing each fingertip to the corresponding finger on the other hand, making a teepee with his hands, he jokingly asked me how mad Andrew Sollinger would be if I resigned from *Ignites* to work with him. Sollinger was the top business guy at Money-Media and a friend of Lane's.

His question was an effective icebreaker and immediately put me at ease. His manner was informal, and his tone was slightly nasally, as if he were fighting off a cold, as he described how each newsletter in the "Jocks And Stocks" e-newsletter division would feature stock picks from a single well-known public figure.

"The Dykstra Report" would be the first launched and was the lynchpin of the group. The plan was for Dykstra and me to chat each day about the pick he wanted to feature and what he wanted to say in his column and I would ghostwrite it for him.

Dykstra's options-picking record had impressed Lane. As 2007 drew to a close, Dykstra had refined his system and established a loyal following. He posted a scorecard on TheStreet.com that allowed readers to follow his wins, losses, and picks still in play.

Between February, when he began keeping track of his picks, and the end of November, Dykstra had 107 winning picks and just 2 losers (with 13 picks still in play). The majority of the wins were for $1,000 or so, while one of the losses cost Dykstra more than $40,000. However, despite the one major disaster, Dykstra was still ahead by $149,050 for the year.

Wanting to fully focus on the *Players Club*, Dykstra then decided to take an open-ended hiatus from TheStreet.com. During that time, Lane suggested to Dykstra that they expand their business relationship beyond the magazine to also include a newsletter and offered him what he characterized as a sweetheart deal. "Lenny's special. We gave him a really good deal to get him on board," Lane said to me.

Plus, Dykstra had accumulated the e-mail addresses of 5,000 of his readers at TheStreet.com who, he said, would be willing to pluck down wads of cash to subscribe to his newsletter, Lane told me. He knew "The Dykstra Report" could be a big-time moneymaker.

During our second meeting the following week, Lane expanded on the other newsletters he expected to include in the "Jocks And Stocks Division." Eric Bolling, a well-known commodities trader and television personality, was already on board and raring to go, Lane said. Just a few months earlier, Bolling had joined Fox Business Network from CNBC, the network that airs Cramer's show *Mad Money*. On CNBC, Bolling appeared on a show called *Fast Money* and was known as the Admiral. While still working at FOX, he would be the focus of a new Doubledown newsletter entitled "Bolling for Dollars."

Even though Bolling was much more well known for his market commentary than his athletic ability, he had been drafted by the Pittsburgh Pirates organization when he was a much younger man. Slowed by injuries, he decided to take on the New York Mercantile Exchange instead. There, his trader's badge sports the letters RBI, a nod to his baseball past. Bolling's most recent show on Fox Business, *Follow the Money*, was canceled in early 2012.

The other big personality Lane said he had signed up was Pete Najarian, an options trader and TV talking head. Najarian, known as the Pit Boss on *Fast Money*, had played linebacker with the NFL's Minnesota Vikings and Tampa Bay Buccaneers. He and his brother Jon, who had played briefly for the Chicago Bears, also cofounded "OptionMONSTER," an options newsletter.

Although Dykstra was a hit with fans and day traders, professional traders wrote him off as a sideshow gimmick. Bolling and Najarian, however, both had well-established track records in the world of investing. They would provide some much-needed credibility.

Richard Suttmeier, an older, heavyset gentleman, rounded out the division's initial four newsletter characters. Suttmeier had been a bearish market commentator for years, appearing on various television shows and in many newsletters, including TheStreet.com's RealMoney site.

Dykstra first stumbled across Suttmeier while watching CNN's *Talking Stocks* program over the 2004–05 holiday season and decided to look up his phone number. "I get a phone call, and I thought it was one of my buddies playing a game with me," Suttmeier says. "I soon discovered that by chatting with him, it was him and he did get hurt in the market."

From there Suttmeier taught Dykstra how to read a stock chart, the basics of technical analysis, and how to tell the best time to enter and exit a stock position. At first, Dykstra would call Suttmeier every day and they would have a "long, drawn-out conversation" about what was going on in the market.

As time went on, Dykstra and Suttmeier became better friends. So when Dykstra was finally in a position to throw Suttmeier a bone, he did, bringing him into Doubledown. Suttmeier's newsletter was definitely the oddball of the group—he was not the athletic type and was much more senior than the other three. He also wasn't nearly as famous. Lane brought Suttmeier into the mix as a favor to Dykstra with the hopes the newsletter could generate at least a small revenue. Anything would be gravy.

During our third and final meeting, Lane put an official offer on the table— $100,000 a year plus an annual bonus equivalent to 5 percent of the division's profits. The offer was 20 percent above my base salary at *Ignites* and offered a potentially life-changing bonus. Lane said that on the upside, my bonus could approach $250,000 in the best-case scenario, although it was likely to be less— at least initially.

The beauty of the offer was that a lot of it depended on me. I would get to create something brand new from the ground up and benefit significantly if it succeeded. Aside from Lane setting up the relationships and contracts with the personalities, I would be given a blank canvas. Lane wasn't a micromanager and was willing to cut me in on a share of the profits. That was the break I had been waiting for.

CHAPTER 9

MOVIN' ON UP

In a flash the man known as Nails appeared from the elevator bank and then just as quickly disappeared. Through the partially transparent glass windows of the conference room, the dozen or so of us gathered for the editorial meeting watched as he whisked past us, his cameraman struggling to keep pace as they both faded out of sight down the hallway.

There was a collective sigh from the fidgeting group. Sure, Dykstra's offices were much nicer than ours, but the entire Doubledown Media team had to trek across Midtown Manhattan to get there and Dykstra was already very late. The *Players Club* magazine was just weeks away from its premiere, and every second counted. Although there were issues still to be discussed, the meeting was just as much for the cameras as anything else. Dykstra was being filmed for an episode of HBO's *Real Sports with Bryant Gumbel* set to air the following week, on March 10, 2008.

I had accepted Doubledown's offer but wasn't even on the payroll yet, and I didn't know anyone in the room other than Lane. I didn't really have a reason to even be at the meeting.

As we all waited for Dykstra to arrive, his fresh-faced, spiky-haired, twenty-five-year-old "assistant" Dan Della Sala leaned his upper body through the doorway of the conference room, scanning the room hurriedly with his finger. "Mr. Dykstra would like to see Chris Frankie," he said with the nervous energy of a young man with an impatient boss. The meeting was being moved to Dykstra's office, and only a few of us were invited.

As I scooped up my black leather work bag from under the table and slung it over my shoulder and followed Dan swiftly down the long winding hallway, my mind drifted back to early 1987 when I was nine years old and the Mets had just won the World Series. The Smithhaven Mall in Smithtown, Long Island, near my house was celebrating the grand opening of a new food court area, and Dykstra was going to be on hand to greet fans and sign autographs. I knew I had to be there, so I dragged my mom and older sister, Dee, to the mall for a chance to meet Nails face to face.

By the time my mom pulled our car into the overflowing parking lot, hordes of fans were already waiting for Nails to arrive. We thought we were early. We were wrong. The line stretched from inside the new annex and snaked all the way around the outside of the mall, wrapping around several corners. Barricades were set up to keep autograph seekers out of the street.

After we had stood in the line under drizzly and overcast skies for four hours, security personnel delivered some bad news: Nails had to leave! Anyone beyond a blue-and-white wooden barrier they placed in the line should head home—Nails didn't have time to see them. I was devastated—we were only fifteen people behind the barrier.

As the crowd started to disperse, my mom grabbed me by the hand. We were not about to be denied. When the security guards turned their backs, we slipped into the line—this time in front of the barrier. We were hardly able to contain our excitement that we had pulled it off.

As Dan and I approached Lenny's office at the end of the hall, I chuckled to myself, thinking back to how I had gotten to meet Nails all those years ago and how he had used a big black magic marker to sign his name over other autographs, which were all in blue pen, on my prized World Series Champion 1986 Mets baseball. After he signed the ball, we waited outside the mall to catch one last up close glimpse of Nails. As he hurried out the exit, I called out to him and he waved and said, "Hey, little dude," before hopping into a waiting car.

Snapping back to the here and now, I remembered I was being called before Lenny Dykstra the businessman and my new boss. I had to focus. First impressions are important.

As I entered the room, Dykstra half rose from his chair, extending his right hand. "Chris, good to meet you," he said in a slurring lisp. The man in front of me was outfitted in business attire and a tan-and-white Maybach baseball cap, with straight gray hair peeking out from the sides. That was his typical uniform those days.

Maybach, a superlux German car company that I and most everybody I knew had never heard of, was Dykstra's newest infatuation. When asked why he wore a Maybach hat as opposed to a Mets or Phillies cap, Dykstra would typically respond with some variation of "I already helped the Mets win a World Series and the Phillies the National League. Now I'm gonna take Maybach to the top." And for good measure he would note that the Mets and Phils no longer paid his salary.

He quickly plopped back into the leather desk chair and awkwardly hunched over one of his two open laptops, which were hastily propped on Dan's desk. Dykstra wasn't in this office much, but when he was, he used Dan's desk as his own, leaving Dan to stand on guard nearby in case Dykstra needed something. Dykstra was slowly surfing the Web, opening countless browser windows with his swollen fingers as he uninterestedly listened to Lane, occasionally glancing up and letting out an "uh-huh" or halfhearted "oh."

He had retreated to his office to escape the hot lights of the camera and to conduct the meeting the way he wanted to, in relative privacy. On that day, Lane was trying, to no avail, to hold Dykstra's attention just long enough to get the former big leaguer to make some key decisions about the soon-to-be-printed first edition of the *Players Club* magazine.

Dykstra looked disheveled, but seeing him with anything other than a #4 slapped on his back seemed unnatural anyway. Besides, I didn't really expect him to look as polished in his Park Avenue office as most of the slick Wall Street types I had encountered during the previous eight years as a financial journalist. That was part of his charm—he was still Lenny Dykstra. I respected the way he had reinvented himself after his playing days. And so what if he didn't fit the mold? There were already enough slimeballs in suits on Wall Street.

However, Dykstra's apparently fragile state was troubling. Most of his teeth were gone, and the remaining ones were hanging on for dear life. Dykstra's love affair with wads of tobacco, which lined the inside of his cheek for the better part of his playing career, had taken their toll, as he illustrated to us when he took out his false teeth and jokingly held them inches away from Lane's face. Lane was obviously grossed out but tried to laugh it off. It was funny in a twelve-year-old-boy kind of way.

I was stunned to see the impact that years of balls-to-the-walls, reckless abandon, hard-nosed play on the diamond had taken on him. I suspected that Dykstra wasn't just suffering from "Crashing into Too Many Walls Syndrome," although he acted like a boxer who had taken too many blows to the head. When he said, "I left pieces of myself all over the National League," I knew exactly what he meant. On the diamond, no one tried harder. And it was no secret that Dykstra was as reckless with his body off the field as he had been on it.

He had celebrated his forty-fifth birthday a month earlier, but if I didn't know better, I would have guessed he was pushing sixty—at least. Many of his teammates from that '86 World Series Champion Mets team looked healthy and together, including Mr. P., former pitcher Ron Darling, and first baseman Keith Hernandez, both of whom were helping their old teammate with the *Players Club*.

Hernandez, who was nine years Dykstra's senior, was a featured food critic. Darling, a Yale-educated ballplayer who was much more polished and well spoken, helped Dykstra with his presentations. He had been born three years before Dykstra.

Next to these guys, Dykstra looked like . . . a broken-down fossil.

This was not how I had envisioned the meeting in my head. Dykstra seemed to be struggling in his own skin and uninterested in a lot of what was going on around him in a slightly autistic kind of way. We talked about what Dykstra wanted to talk about, and no one else was going to steer the conversation. When in his presence, everyone operated on Lenny time. It's just the way it was. Lumpy or not, Dykstra was in charge.

Dykstra continued to play on his laptop, beating on his mouse, and telling stories, including one about Game 6 of the '86 World Series and that "arrogant motherfucker Roger Clemens," who had been a starting pitcher for the opposing Boston Red Sox. It didn't get much better than listening to Nails tell war stories about *the* Game 6.

However, I knew I needed to keep a professional face on. And I certainly wasn't about to let on that I had been a huge Mets fan growing up. I wanted Dykstra to look at me as a professional first and foremost, not as a fan (I was able to keep that secret throughout most of my employment).

Dykstra rarely made eye contact with anyone in the room, firmly entranced by his glowing computer screens. When Lane tried to discuss "The Dykstra Report" newsletter, Dykstra seemed surprised.

"Are we really doing this?" he said, his blank stare looking in Lane's direction. "Yeah, yeah, Lenny, don't you remember we talked about this?" Lane said. His tone was lighthearted, and he spoke to Dykstra in a very nonthreatening, jovial manner. It was obvious he was treading carefully. It reminded me of the way an adult son might speak to an elderly parent suffering from Alzheimer's disease.

It didn't matter; Dykstra didn't want to chat about the newsletter. The *Players Club* was his primary focus right now, and it was less than a month away from its red carpet kickoff.

I was worried about Dykstra's nonchalant attitude toward the newsletter. I had just quit my job to come to work with him. "Don't worry; that's just Lenny being Lenny," Lane said to me after the meeting. "We'll get everything going," noting that sometimes Dykstra lost focus.

Eventually, Dykstra began grilling me about my past experience. When I answered, he listened, but his attention drifted off if my answers ran too long. It was a delicate balance that I quickly learned I needed to master if this experiment were going to work. I told him that Money-Media, the company I had last worked for, was sold to the *Financial Times* for tens of millions of dollars.

"All right, bro, you cashed out. Good job." He misunderstood, but I had his attention—he respected money. I told him that, unfortunately, I wasn't the owner and hadn't lined my pockets with dough from the sale. However, I had left my job to come work for him, and I could help make HIS newsletter a big success. Even though Doubledown was my new employer, I knew whose name was on the top of "The Dykstra Report" and that ultimately Dykstra needed to know he was the boss if this project had any chance of success.

"Where do you live, bro?" he asked. I told him that I had a modest place on the Upper East Side of Manhattan. Before I could elaborate and tell him it was a small one-bedroom apartment in a prewar walk-up, Dykstra interrupted with the theme song to the '70s TV show *The Jeffersons*. "Movin' on up," he rattled off with a slight chuckle before again noting that I must be filthy rich. My attempts to correct him were going nowhere, so I went with the flow, saying lightheartedly, "I do okay for myself." As the meeting came to a close, I grabbed my coat and thanked Dykstra for the chance to work together.

"We'll talk, bro," he said enthusiastically, glancing up at me as I headed toward the door, leaving Lane and another Doubledown exec behind. I had to get back to *Ignites*, where I was finishing out my remaining days. Then Dykstra stopped me, looked me in the eye, and said something I will never forget: "I'm all about accountability, bro. It's key." Those words made me feel instantly better. Although unusual, Dykstra was a stand-up guy and wanted to do things the right way, I thought.

CHAPTER 10

NAILS NEVER FAILS

Following his retirement from baseball, Dykstra never fully stepped away from the limelight, but he wasn't quite at the forefront of the public's collective attention either. He signed autographs at random card shows, appeared at Mets reunion ceremonies, wrote columns for TheStreet.com, and was seen regularly at his California car washes.

Then WHAM! Out of nowhere in March 2008, a much older and seemingly more mature Lenny Dykstra with gray hair and a potbelly was making waves for conquering a new playing field: Wall Street. Within the month, Dykstra would attain Golden God status, being accepted as an accomplished businessman, media juggernaut, newly minted financial genius, and selfless hero for the brotherhood of professional athletes. His story was once again being told to the masses.

He built the financial empire he had set out to create a decade and a half earlier. In fact, he made more money off the field than he ever had on it. He was now living in an $18 million mansion, in an exclusive mountaintop country club, that he had bought from hockey legend Wayne Gretzky.

In typical Dykstra fashion, his reemergence was an all-out, in-your-face assault. It unofficially began on March 10, 2008, when HBO's *Real Sports with Bryant Gumbel*, a monthly sports newsmagazine television show, aired a wildly entertaining and popular segment entitled "Nails." The piece skyrocketed Dykstra to new heights of stardom. It showcased Dykstra's luxurious lifestyle, which included "the best house in the world," his "bird" (a private jet), the expensive German car that he had bought for "four-hundred large," and, of course, baseball.

It also chronicled his unlikely ascent to stock market guru and protégé of Wall Street titan Jim Cramer, the sale of his incredibly lucrative car wash empire for $55 million, and the *Players Club* magazine. The piece was shocking.

"If there was one guy we thought was going to be successful in the stock market, it would not have been Lenny," Mets legend Gary Carter later said to me. "Lenny was all about baseball, and he liked to party and enjoy life and everything else." Kirk Radomski, the Mets clubhouse hand, Dykstra's pal, and steroids dealer, puts it this way: "If you had an intelligent question to be answered, you didn't go to Lenny Dykstra. But if you wanted the guy who would play the hardest, you went to Lenny Dykstra."

Dykstra's former teammates weren't the only ones who were stunned. The *Real Sports* segment kicked off with a monologue from host Bryant Gumbel in which he said that during Dykstra's playing days he was a "monosyllabic, simplistic, tobacco-chewing, hard charger on the field and a party animal off of it." Dykstra seemed to be the embodiment of the dumb jock stereotype, he added, implying later in the segment that Dykstra's stock-picking skills might be akin to a monkey tossing a dart at a page full of stock symbols.

Nonetheless, the piece was a roaring success. "Of all the television pieces I've ever done—and I started at CBS in 1972—I have never received more reaction to a piece than the Lenny Dykstra piece," HBO *Real Sports* reporter Bernard Goldberg tells me. "It's not because it was magnificently written or anything like that. It was that Lenny Dykstra is the perfect character for television."

It's the walking contradiction that's so mesmerizing. "He sounds like Yogi Berra on a bad day, but he's saying things that sound pretty smart," Goldberg tells me. "He's got a stock strategy he's talking about. He's talking about business. He's talking about how to make millions. In an entertainment culture, you couldn't take your eyes off him."

Lots of people succeed on Wall Street, and many ex-athletes move into the business world after their playing days are done. That story isn't all that interesting. But because Lenny Dykstra did it, the story is downright astonishing. "If Bill Bradley had started a business, we would never do a story about him," Goldberg says of the NBA Hall of Famer who became a senator and then a presidential candidate. "Why? Bill Bradley's father was a banker. Bill Bradley went to Princeton. Why's that interesting that a guy that went to Princeton would start a business? Lenny is NOT Bill Bradley."

As the segment kicked off, Dykstra told Goldberg he didn't like to read. He said that during his playing days "those little words" hurt his batting eye and were "too confusing" and that reading made him "think too much." An almost incredulous Goldberg asked in response to Dykstra's distaste for reading, "And I'm supposed to follow your investing advice?" Nails's reply: "Yeah, only if you like money."

However, more shocking than the mansion, the car washes, the private jet, and the expensive car combined was Dykstra's bromance with Jim Cramer.

Sitting in a director's chair inside his *Mad Money* studio filled with all sorts of chaos and knickknacks, Cramer told Goldberg that Dykstra was a smart dude.

"People don't think of Lenny as sophisticated. But I'm telling you, Bernie, he is not only sophisticated; he is one of the great ones in this business," Cramer said, his arms waving, eyebrows rising, and eyes bulging. "Okay, so let me tell you the truth about Lenny Dykstra," Cramer continued, his voice growing louder, "If I didn't know any better, I would tell you everything you hear from Lenny is an act because there's just no way that you would ever feel like he's as smart as he really is. Now there are probably four or five people in the world who, if they sent me an e-mail telling me to learn a stock, I would actually take them seriously. He's one of them."

Goldberg says Cramer's endorsement was the clinching factor for the *Real Sports* team when deciding to do the story on Dykstra. "When Jim Cramer said that 'he's one of the top stock pickers I've ever known' and he said it publicly, he said it openly, he said it on camera, that was it. We were off to the races on that one," Goldberg explains to me.

"People in the media love a juicy story, and Lenny seemed to fit the bill. Now all of a sudden, Jim Cramer loves him—Cramer is a story-sparker," says John Korpics, creative director at *Fortune*, who worked on the first issue of Dykstra's *Players Club* magazine. "Cramer's the ringleader. He stands in the middle of the room and rings bells and whistles. A guy like Lenny is great for Cramer because it's fun to build up the image."

However, Cramer's faith in Dykstra extended beyond TheStreet.com. Cramer later told reporter Ben McGrath of the *New Yorker* that if the duo had met back when he was still running his hedge fund, he would have brought Dykstra on board. Cramer told McGrath that the problem with Dykstra was that he "is so weird and crazy in person that people miss his intelligence that comes across in his e-mails."

The wide-ranging *Real Sports* segment also touched on the Players Club and its mission of helping players make smarter financial decisions. "People think [you make] $10 million, but when you pay your agent, you pay taxes, you buy the nice house, help the family out," Dykstra told Goldberg, counting off each item on his fingers, "okay, now you got . . . your dick in your hands basically," noting that players also have very few skills outside of their sport, limiting their ability to continue to make money.

As the piece drew to a close, viewers saw a close-up of Dykstra saying that he knew people were laughing at him behind his back and his foray into the world of investing. "Yeah, fuck them," he retorted. "We'll see who's laughing when you want a loan, motherfucker."

Seemingly disconnected from the rest of the overly positive HBO *Real Sports* segment was a final, uncomfortable exchange about steroids. *The Mitchell Report*, baseball's investigation into steroids, had been released a few months earlier and had implicated Dykstra.

Goldberg asked about it. Dykstra, removing his sunglasses and looking Goldberg straight in the eye, said he never took steroids. Goldberg then relays how, off-camera just a few minutes later, Dykstra said he lied about not taking steroids, only to later recant that admission in a follow-up phone call, saying he was joking when he said he took steroids.

Despite the odd back-and-forth steroid talk, the HBO piece was an overwhelming success and the fan mail poured in. It wasn't just baseball fans in New York and Philly. Women in their sixties, people from Alaska and Singapore, and folks who had never heard of Nails but loved his story were sending e-mails wishing him well. They understood the way he felt when he found out his retirement nest egg had disappeared at the hands of his broker. They shared his frustrations about Wall Street. They could relate to his distaste for reading and to how people underestimated him because his intelligence was masked by his slovenly appearance.

Real Sports was just the beginning of the massive fanfare, and with each magazine feature or newspaper article, the drumbeat grew louder. "Doubledown and Lenny were both puffed-up marketing machines," says Dan Ryan, the Doubledown sales executive who recruited me. "When those two forces collided, it was atomic for two months. It was 'through the roof' exposure. Lenny Dykstra became mainstream America talk—not just sports world talk or New York or Philadelphia talk. It was meteoric."

As I prepared to launch the newsletter, Dykstra continued to dominate the headlines. Over the next month he appeared in the *New York Post*, *Daily News*, the Associated Press, and *Forbes*, *GQ*, *Bloomberg*, *Kiplinger's*, and *Inc.* magazines and on the television shows *Fox & Friends*, *Money for Breakfast*, *Night Talk*, CNN, and others. He even cracked the pages of the hoity-toity *New Yorker* magazine with its article "Nails Never Fails" on March 24, my official start date at Doubledown.

After the massive, five-thousand-word *New Yorker* article, "People started to say, 'Wow, Lenny Dykstra . . . the *New Yorker* is saying what a great businessman he is,'" according to *Fortune*'s Korpics. But despite the overly positive headline, the article was neither an endorsement nor critique of Dykstra's business acumen. Rather, it was a glimpse into the daily life of a reemerging folk hero from the childhood of author Ben McGrath, a self-proclaimed buttoned-up guy. It helped build the mystique surrounding this odd but engaging character.

After all, Dykstra was a good baseball player, but he really made a name for himself as a character, a "maverick self-brander," McGrath tells me. Very few ballplayers write an autobiography after their rookie season. Dykstra did. It's not often that little boys all over the tristate area plaster posters of platoon players on their bedroom walls. That real estate is typically reserved for the superstars—the Derek Jeters, Darryl Strawberrys, and Gary Carters of the world.

However, in the mid-1980s when Dykstra was splitting time with Mookie Wilson and even journeyman Tom Paciorek, Mets fans were buying Dykstra jerseys and hanging up the famous Nails poster in which a shirtless Dykstra, wearing eye black and holding a bat, is standing on a floor covered in nails.

McGrath wanted to capture the "spark" attached to Dykstra and not just show a "crazy, sleep-deprived idiot who's starting a magazine," he says. "I wanted to let people say, 'Wow, this guy is crazy, but he's kind of entertaining.'"

Although captivating like the HBO piece, the article had a markedly different feel. The *New Yorker*, for all its prestige, is often accused of looking down on its subjects in a very restrained way that seems arrogant. In this article, Dykstra was still living large, but he wasn't always the same happy-go-lucky guy we had seen weeks earlier on *Real Sports*.

Because Dykstra doesn't go to sleep for days at a time, he just starts behaving like a "lunatic," McGrath tells me. "He zones out of the conversation and then picks up halfway through and he's sort of trembling."

"The thing that struck me the most at first is physically he is not well. I remember going back to the office after the interview saying, 'This guy is going to be dead in ten years,'" McGrath recounts. "In retrospect, I think I might have hammered more on the odd juxtaposition of this guy who is positioning himself as someone teaching players how to lead successful lives while he's this physical shell of a person."

Typically, people trying to help others avoid the pitfalls of fame and fortune say, "Don't make the same mistakes I did." But Dykstra's "message wasn't 'look at me, you can do better'; it was 'look at me, you can be like me.' I think most people would look at him and be like, 'Whoa, what happened to you?'"

The article was a collection of bizarre, yet entertaining tales, painting Dykstra as an eccentric, misunderstood, harmless, but semilovable guy. In one anecdote, Dykstra talked about how many older businessmen looked at him like he "got hit with an idiot stick—took ten lashes on the way in."

However, the most vivid and bizarre image was of Dykstra and McGrath meeting at a cul-de-sac adjacent to a barren dirt field filled with crows near

Dykstra's mansion. He told McGrath he goes there to "get away from the humans," then popped his trunk open, leaned in, and began to pound away at the keys of one of his laptops, using the lid of the trunk as a shield from the sun.

Dykstra continued to do this for the next hour as he juggled calls with his lawyers, designers, and staffers, before switching to another laptop in the front seat. When that one stalled, Dykstra clicked the mouse wildly, inadvertently opening a plethora of windows, making matters worse and forcing him to switch to yet another laptop in the backseat. "I'm very frustrated with this spinning of the wheel," he told McGrath.

In the final scene of the article, at the Four Seasons near his home, Dykstra had the waitress weave an extension cord through the restaurant so that he could play on his laptop. After a pair of women tripped on the cord, Dykstra exclaimed, "Why is everyone walking through here? It's a fucking magnet."

However, the article ended on a light note, with Dykstra joking with the waitress about his need for a jolt of caffeine. "Uh-oh, we need some more juice. Firepower. Some ammunition, right here. I'm going under. We're going into withdrawing mode."

When the article finally came out, Dykstra wasn't thrilled with the way it made him look. In the weeks following, Dykstra was a presenter at the National Magazine Awards and made a bunch of jokes at the expense of the *New Yorker*, according to McGrath. "I think he got a sense during the fact-checking process that there were going to be some things in there that he wasn't going to be happy about. At one point he even told the fact-checker, 'Did you remember to put in there that I have a twelve-inch schlong?'" McGrath recalls. "He sort of went off the rails a little bit."

In the end, after the initial bite of the article wore off, the only thing that mattered to Lenny was its big proclamation, written by an editor and not McGrath, that "Nails never fails."

CHAPTER 11

PAINFUL DOROTHY

In the weeks leading up to the *Players Club* launch party, I continued during the day to finish up my final weeks at *Ignites* while at night and on the weekend laying the groundwork for the Jocks and Stocks Division and Dykstra's newsletter. I knew I had to hurry the hell up because I would have only a week between my official first day at Doubledown and the launch party.

All of us working behind the scenes could already sense that the newsletter was going to be something special. Customers were lining up to fork over buckets of cash to preorder. "The Dykstra Report," which was originally priced at about $500 a year, was quickly jacked up to $995 for an annual subscription at Dykstra's request. It didn't matter—fans were willing to pay it. We were raking in tens of thousands of dollars for a product that didn't even exist yet.

However, by my first day in the office, I had already learned that success with Dykstra came at a steep price: lots of stress and chaos. He was likely at any given moment to throw a wicked curveball in my direction, and there was nothing I could do but to take my best cut at it. And he wasted little time testing me.

I had just finished up a late night at *Ignites* and was about to head home when I got a call from Dykstra. I hadn't spoken to him one on one yet, so I was nervous. I listened as Dykstra launched right into a long and winding speech about the *Players Club* before abruptly cutting the conversation short. "I have to go, bro. I'll call you right back." I chuckled to myself realizing that I had barely gotten in a word edgewise.

Not wanting to miss the follow-up call or have to chat with the noisy city street in the background, I sat in my deserted office boxing up my belongings, waiting for my phone to ring. After more than an hour, I decided to head home. I stepped out into the dark Manhattan night, walking past an empty Bryant

Park. There, in the swirling, howling winds outside Grand Central Station, my cell phone rang.

"Yeah, hey, it's Lenny," said the muffled voice on the other end of the line. He sounded anxious and annoyed, as if the call were an unpleasant formality he did not enjoy making. I could barely hear him. I ducked in between the two sets of glass doors leading into the station so that I could decipher what he was saying.

"Look, bro, I don't think I wanna do this newsletter thing," he said. "I'm sorry, but it's not gonna happen." I was stunned and didn't know what to say. Lane had told me everything was all set.

There really wasn't much else to say. He could have hung up. Instead, breaking the ice or simply halting the awkward silence, Dykstra asked about my qualifications again and my commitment to the project. I told him I had quit a good job to come work with him. If he was on board with the newsletter, I explained, we could make a lot of money together, but I understood it was ultimately his call whether or not he wanted to do it. I assured him that if we decided to move forward on the project, I had the know-how to mold whatever vision he had for the newsletter into a whopping success.

He seemed a bit worried about losing control of the project, so I made it abundantly clear I knew he was the top dog. He asked me to keep him informed of all the newsletter's happenings and to carbon copy (cc) or blind carbon copy (bcc) him on all of my e-mails relating to "The Dykstra Report," even the ones that seemed inconsequential. I agreed.

I could sense a change, and his icy attitude started to thaw. "I like you, bro, and Diane says you're okay," he said somewhat reluctantly, referring to one of his lawyers who was also one of my sources at *Ignites*. "We'll figure something out, but it's important that you keep this conversation between the two of us."

Then, without much explanation, he bolted. "All right, bro, I gotta go. Keep it stiff." Although the phone call was troubling, I walked away feeling exhilarated—like I had just saved the day and my job. As I passed through the subway station's turnstile, I thought to myself, this must be one of those "Lenny being Lenny" moments Lane had told me about.

I would soon discover Dykstra wasn't the only one I had to worry about. On my first day in the office, I learned there was a written contract between Dykstra and Doubledown for the *Players Club* magazine, but not for "The Dykstra Report," as Lane had led me to believe. With the newsletter, it was a handshake deal, Lane now explained. I was quickly learning a lot about Lane I wasn't overly thrilled about.

"One of the main problems, in my opinion, was that Lenny and Randall were too much alike," says Todd Tarpley, Doubledown's CTO. "They both liked to think big and move fast, do deals on a handshake and a slap on the back, and react on testosterone." I began to resent Lane for withholding this important piece of information from me, and it was only my first day on the job. I felt manipulated.

Despite my reservations, I decided the best way to motivate Lenny to sign the contract was to make him happy with the product.

As I began meeting my new coworkers, I realized that nearly everyone in the company had experienced a Lenny being Lenny moment and that I should get used to it. Most of the moments were harmless or just plain weird. When I told other staffers that I was hired to work with Dykstra, there was a lot of eye rolling or good-natured but sarcastic remarks, such as "Good luck with that."

For Rachel Pine, who was global director of marketing and communications at Doubledown then and an investor in the company, Lenny moments included strange e-mails at all hours of the day and night and a series of bizarre meetings with Dykstra and his entourage. "He liked to send e-mails with every line of text in a different color and font from the next one," she says. Because Randall Lane "idol-worshipped" Dykstra, he insisted that a number of the company's staffers be available to Dykstra on a 24/7 basis.

Pine says Dykstra showed up at important business meetings with a "rotating cast of characters," including his personal pilots. "Usually private pilots don't sit in on meetings with their passengers." With Dykstra, I guess they did.

During meetings at Dykstra's luxurious hotel suites, he would let everyone know how much the hotel was charging him and then purposely order huge amounts of food from room service just so that he could "kind of fake complain about the bill," Pine says. He was not shy about flaunting his wealth either.

For Dan Ryan, his most awkward Lenny moment came during a meeting to discuss how "The Dykstra Report" should be structured. A subscription model was preferable to a pure advertising model, he said.

"Lenny had the impression that his page was the most popular page on TheStreet.com and it was earning hundreds of thousands of dollars a day just from advertising," Ryan says. "I tried to explain it to him—I told him that that wasn't the proper structure." Lane grasped the concept. Richard Suttmeier, who was also in the meeting, understood it. "And Lenny paid little or no attention to anything I said."

Suttmeier and Lane then stepped out of the Doubledown conference room to allow Ryan some one-on-one time with Dykstra. He continued to try and talk business with Dykstra, but Dykstra kept "reinforcing the point that his articles make hundreds of thousands of dollars a day for TheStreet.com solely on advertising—making an unreasonable amount of money that I knew from being in the business they couldn't make."

After about ten minutes, Dykstra looked up from behind his computer screen and asked Ryan, "You like pussy? Me and Suttmeier are gonna go get some pussy. We got a suite at the St. Regis." Ryan was stunned. "I didn't say anything, and then he went right back to the laptop and continued surfing around on different Web sites, and that was the end of it," Ryan says with a laugh.

As I began to hear more and more of these stories, I quickly realized Planet Dykstra was very different from any place I had ever traveled to, and I knew I needed a tour guide.

With Lane perpetually swamped or out of the office, I turned to Dorothy Van Kalsbeek, one of Dykstra's West Coast–based assistants. Dorothy, I found, was always very nice to me and more than willing to help. When I couldn't get Dykstra on the phone, I would call Dorothy. She was a true believer in Dykstra and his abilities. I felt I could trust her.

Dorothy had been with Dykstra since his car wash days, helping him nurture the *Players Club* from an abstract idea to a high-end glossy magazine. She had first met him when one of the car wash's employees called her up for help with the accounting software. Dykstra hired her on the spot.

She helped Dykstra prepare for the sale of the car washes. However, she quit owing to the stress of the job. "The next day Lenny hired me back, and then the day after that he fired me again," she says. "He hired me back, sometimes I think, just so he could be the one to fire me. Then two days after that, he had to call me and hire me back again." That cycle continued, and for the next few months their working relationship would be "on again, off again."

He could be a class-A jerk, but he could also be a really nice guy—Good Lenny, Bad Lenny. "He would come to the car wash and meet with people, and if somebody came in who was fragile and you knew he was fragile, Lenny would be the most decent guy on earth—very, very caring and very concerned about their well-being and bend over backwards to do whatever they need," she says. "And then if you got somebody who came in his office five minutes later who had a little bit of an attitude, he turned into an ass. It was like he matched his personality for the personality of the other person."

It was during one of the off again periods that Dorothy started sending Dykstra little notes about his columns on TheStreet.com. "I would see his column, and a few of them were cute, and I would comment on them and send him a little message," she says, noting he also started keeping a record of his picks' performance called the Stat Book.

He would post the Stat Book in his columns, but it was filled with errors, she says. "They didn't add numbers correctly. They weren't quoting the stock price right. They were really bad. So I was sending him corrections," Dorothy says. "He e-mailed me back and said that he was tired of the corrections and he wanted me to start working the Stat Book for him and he wanted me to do it right away."

Over the next several months, Dykstra taught Dorothy the ins and outs of his stock-picking strategy. "In return, I kept track of the portfolio for him," she says. "It was a good trade." However, somewhere along the way, their financial arrangement changed substantially.

Dorothy had submitted a number of invoices to Dykstra for the work she had done but would never get paid, she says. Finally, someone working for Dykstra paid her for all of the outstanding invoices.

"I thought I would be decent and kind, and I wrote Lenny an e-mail and I said, 'Thank you.' He sent me a nasty e-mail saying he had no intention of paying me. It was rather curt," Dorothy says. "He wanted me to do all this work and then didn't want to pay me. He was mad at me because I had gotten paid. I'm not quite sure why he has that problem with not wanting to pay people for the services that they do because most times he is very generous."

At the time, I didn't know the backstory between Dykstra and Dorothy, nor did I know that he didn't pay her—I only knew she was not a typical assistant. He already had one of those—her name was Joanie, and she worked out of his house handling his bills and daily schedules. Dorothy, on the other hand, lived and worked hours from Dykstra's home.

Dykstra kept Dorothy "hidden" and jokingly referred to her as his "night slave," often making her pull all-nighters to prepare presentations. "He ragged on her every chance he could, saying, 'She's busted, man. . . . She's NASTY. She wants to bang me,'" according to onetime Dykstra employee Samantha Kulchar. "He said she was his 'bitch,' . . . that he always wanted to get rid of her and he would fire her for sport and entertainment, then send her an assignment the next day to see her jump."

The words he used were cruel, but in a weird way. I thought he was horsing around and never meant to hurt Dorothy's feelings. Along with the insults, he would often say something like "She's a grinder, she works hard, and she's loyal. That's hard to find."

Despite calling her "painful," Dykstra relied heavily on her, and she enjoyed the work. Their relationship was odd but seemed to work for them.

I sought Dorothy's advice, and she offered up "Dorothy's 10 Simple Rules for Working with Lenny . . . and Being Effective," an off-the-cuff document she apparently created just for me. I was grateful.

Hi Chris,

I enjoyed our chat too, thank you.

In regards to your last question to me. . . . regarding tips for working with Lenny and enjoying it as much as I do. No one has ever asked that question before. I like it that you did, shows initiative. Nice!

Well, I gave it some thought and here are my rules. . . . They work. . . . Well, they work for me. You may have to develop your own rules because Lenny is a complicated guy and what works for me, might not work for you . . . but overall they are pretty simple . . . common sense really.

#1—Lenny is almost always right. . . . There are times when you may not think so, but you need to step back & look at it from his perspective and once you see his perspective you will be amazed just how right he always is. It's uncanny. So, seek his way of looking at things & see it for what it is . . . and you will learn in unexpected ways. And, if you don't think you can learn from Lenny and his unique perspective . . . leave right now & go back to your other job.

#2—Lenny hates excuses. So don't make any.

#3—Always be honest. 100 percent of the time, no matter what. He only respects honesty & he can see BS before you utter it. . . . It's like he can hear you thinking it.

#4—Things are only black or white, right or wrong . . . no gray area. What you see as gray . . . Lenny sees as excuses. . . . (See rule #2.)

#5—Lenny doesn't believe in circumstances beyond your control . . . and there are times when, well, shit happens. What do I do then? I take responsibility for everything, even when beyond my control. . . . Instead of saying, . . . Oh, poor me, it couldn't be helped, . . . I ask him for help. I say, I tried to do this . . . but it didn't work, do you have a solution for me? Or should I do this, this or this. This one works miracles . . . and again, it opens up unexpected doors.

#6—Lenny has to know what everyone is doing. So all your work has to be transparent with him. Include him in every little thing. I almost NEVER email anyone anything, without a cc to Lenny. He always knows what I am doing, or has the opportunity to know what I am doing, if he wants to. He has to know what I am doing & who I am talking to . . . and what I am saying, . . . etc. Don't try to work for him by working around him. If you keep him out of the loop, even inadvertently . . . it will be you that is left out, permanently. And, I have seen lots and lots of people come & go . . . quickly too, because they think they know their job & don't need Lenny's input any longer. WRONG! Lenny will learn from you & you from him, but only if you keep open the lines of communication . . . and allow him to direct you.

#7—Remember who you work for. It's the Dykstra Report not the Frankie Report. Look at that title every day. No matter what you put into it, the result will always be Lenny's vision, and ultimately his responsibility for all that you do. This one is hardest to follow, because it's difficult not to grow attached to your work. But you can't. Lenny gets bored with things looking the same so it will constantly be changing & evolving. Embrace the change . . . because with Lenny, the change will always be an improve-ment. . . . He always pushes it up to the next level . . . again & again & again . . . perpetual upward motion.

#8—Lenny is good at assigning the "impossible tasks," as I call them. . . . These are my favorite. . . . Get one of these done & you feel like you could do anything.

#9—Lenny is very difficult to please, he has the highest standards & exceptional taste . . . and can be downright picky when it comes to little details. So your A-game is a must, at all times. No half measures. Do it his way . . . all the way, or get out of the way. This isn't your garden variety 9 to 5 job. . . . If you want one of those, look elsewhere. Lenny works all the time & expects everyone else to put in as much as he does. You won't be able to keep up, trust me—that's next to impossible . . . but you have to be willing to put in as much as you can . . . and then give a little more.

#10—Lenny is all about the now. . . . With him, a great job yesterday . . . in the past. Over. Done. He personifies the concept of . . . "what have you done for me lately?"

Follow the rules & Lenny will push you in a direction you never dreamed possible & he will open up abilities, you don't know you have. He is very good at directing & motivating . . . and he will quickly learn how to get the good stuff out of you . . . but you have to let him.

Well, those are my rules . . . for the most challenging & clearly the most rewarding work experience you will likely ever find.

But, like I said above . . . you will have to tailor the rules to fit your personality & what you want to derive out of the experience.

Good luck, I am looking forward to the Dykstra Report & will be expecting great things from you too.

Dorothy

I was thankful for the insight but leery of some of the details—mostly the ones that seemed to excuse Lenny's detachment from reality. Demanding, I could handle. Impossible, I was nervous about. However, by that point I was fully committed. Quitting and going back to *Ignites* weren't an option. Plus, Dykstra's empire was growing and I was going to be a major part of it.

CHAPTER 12

LIVING THE DREAM

The red carpet and velvet ropes stretched all the way to the sidewalk in front of the chi-chi Mandarin Oriental as a crowd gathered around the glitzy hotel's lobby. The slowly setting sun was casting a blinding burnt-sienna glow down Sixtieth Street on Manhattan's wealthy Upper West Side as guests, such as tennis legend John McEnroe, Don Trump Jr., and his wife, model Vanessa Haydon, began to arrive for the highly anticipated $600,000 *Players Club* launch party, sponsored by Mercedes-Benz and Maybach. There was a noticeable buzz throughout the crowd and a nervous excitement in the air.

Once on the thirty-sixth floor, I could see the party was beginning to bustle in the spacious ballroom. The room was surrounded by three walls of windows, providing a dynamic, panoramic view of the lush, rolling trees of New York's treasured Central Park as night fell over Manhattan. There were ice sculptures and finely dressed waitstaff throughout the room holding trays of hors d'oeuvres or champagne. The party had a very lavish, go-go, 1990s-era magazine launch feel to it—it was "big league."

Next to the main stage were tables featuring delicious dishes from famed chef Marco Canora. Later, Grammy Award–winning hip-hop violinist Miri Ben Ari serenaded the crowd with everything from covers of Jay-Z to the national anthem during a miniconcert.

The crowd was an odd mix of people in suits and jackets, women in cocktail dresses, and young people in jeans and T-shirts. I ordered a beer at the bar and scanned the crowd for someone I knew.

Finally, there parked in front of the buffet, which was lined with an assortment of salads and seafood, was someone I recognized—Jim Cramer, the Pied Piper of Wall Street. Unlike his very outgoing, loud, on-screen personality,

Cramer was quiet, almost squirrely. Standing by himself with his shoulders slumped and his head down, looking toward the floor, he was rapidly shoveling shrimp into his mouth.

Maybe people were too shy to approach him, I thought. But I had met Jim years before when I was fresh out of college and worked as a markets reporter at TheStreet.com in 2000–2001 (I was let go from TheStreet.com a few weeks after 9/11). Jim and I worked in the same nearly empty newsroom most early mornings. When I arrived at 7:15 a.m., Jim was already at his desk across the newsroom, plugging away on the keyboard, excitedly shouting into his phone or causing some sort of commotion. He was intense.

Cramer and I didn't have any real interaction aside from sharing a few laughs at the company Christmas party or the occasional head nod in the hallway. However, my history with TheStreet.com was an icebreaker, so I walked up and reintroduced myself.

"Hi, Jim, I'm sure you don't remember me, but I used to work at TheStreet a while back, and I just started with Doubledown to run Lenny's newsletter," I said. Looking up, still munching on the shrimp, he just sort of nodded.

"I thought you did a nice job on the interview you gave to *Real Sports*," I said, thinking maybe that would get the ball rolling. "Thank you," he said in a monotone as he wiped the side of his mouth with a napkin. He then turned away and looked around the room. I took the hint. The conversation was clearly over.

As I walked away, I thought maybe he was unhappy that Dykstra was partnering with Doubledown on the newsletter and not TheStreet.com. Or maybe he just wanted to enjoy the party and not make small talk with someone he barely knew. Either way, I really couldn't tell and didn't think much more about it.

I looked around the room and noticed Don Trump Jr. and his wife attracting stares on one side of the party, while Henrik Lundqvist and Scott Gomez of the New York Rangers huddled together in a small group toward the back of the room. However, the *Players Club* party was missing a few key players.

First, Dykstra was nowhere to be found, which was strange because it was his shindig. Second, to the disappointment of many partygoers, the guest of honor and the cover boy for the premier issue was on TV and not mingling with the crowd. Derek Jeter and the rest of his Yankees teammates were playing against the Blue Jays in the final home opener at Yankee Stadium, which was closing at the end of the year. Originally scheduled for the afternoon before, the game was postponed owing to rain and rescheduled for the night of the party. What rotten luck for Dykstra, I thought to myself.

I found out later that it was a blessing in disguise. Dykstra "claimed countless times that his dear friend would attend the launch," says Richard Rubenstein. His firm, Rubenstein Public Relations, which represents a number of high-profile clients, such as Yankees third baseman Alex Rodriguez and the Trump Organization, was hired by Dykstra for the launch party and for securing media coverage for the magazine. "As a precautionary measure, we decided to confirm Jeter's attendance with his agent and found out that Derek was, in fact, not going to be there. We had to abruptly modify our media invitations accordingly."

At the party, guests thumbed through the photographically lush 168-page magazine, which contained a wide variety of finance and lifestyle pieces, including the "Better Half" column, a spread showcasing actress Eva Longoria, then the wife of NBA player Tony Parker. Dykstra characterized the spread and Longoria as "high octane." The cross-pollination of sports and entertainment didn't stop there. The magazine's "In the Front Row" feature was entitled "The Coolest Dork in Hollywood" and focused on Will Farrell's movie *Semi Pro* and his love for local LA sports teams.

The magazine also housed a fashion piece about "stylin'" with Pat Burrell, who was with the Phillies at the time, and a guide to the best restaurants in New York written by Dykstra's old Mets teammate Keith Hernandez. Dykstra's buddy former football All-Star Tim Brown of the Raiders penned a piece for the column "Off the Field, On the Money" about the need for a paycheck after retirement and about his two businesses: Tim Brown Racing and Locker 81 Fundraising Solutions. There were pieces about golf's "Fairways to Heaven," tennis-bad-boy-turned-lovable-television-commentator John McEnroe, a guide to Manhattan's finest shops, and castles, an ode to the house that Gretzky had built and Dykstra bought.

When the man of the hour surfaced on stage, he shuffled to the microphone. "For the first time ever, a player will have the ability to have guaranteed, recurring cash flow. . . . This is about growing up," he said in a slow, deliberate, easy-to-understand tone. "You either grow up or you die," he said, noting that "we're going to be part of something big."

To many at Doubledown, they already were. As Dykstra continued, Randall Lane watched from the back of the room. It was a proud moment. Dykstra told the crowd he wanted to thank someone he admired, someone he looked up to. Could he be talking about Lane? He seemed to be laying it on a little thick, but he and Lane had been through a lot in the weeks leading up to the party. Dykstra wanted to thank . . . Jim Cramer! "He's everything I want to be—a winner."

As Cramer, who was not involved in the magazine in any way, shape, or form, approached the stage, Lane and Doubledown's top brass watched in disbelief, the disappointment and anger obvious in their faces. Dykstra hadn't even mentioned Doubledown, the publisher of the magazine, or its staff at all during his speech—not even once! It was the ultimate sign of disrespect. The magazine's battle-weary staff stood deflated, stunned that their hard work wasn't even acknowledged. It may have been an oversight, they thought, but probably wasn't.

"I gave him the benefit of the doubt that he didn't understand the social protocol," says Doubledown CTO Todd Tarpley. "But I talked briefly with Randall a few minutes later, and [Jim] Dunning as well, and they were clearly not happy about it. That's when it became more clear to me that it was probably an intentional omission." Dunning was Doubledown's primary investor.

Not far from Lane stood Nicole Blades, who was immediately "blown away" by the snub and thought to herself, "This isn't going to end well." Blades had served as the *Players Club* senior editor from January through March but quit when she got an offer from a "legitimate" magazine. She was at the launch party purely as a spectator. "About a month in, I was like, 'This is ridiculous; this man is acting like a crazy person, and it doesn't seem like anyone can tell him no,'" Blades says of Dykstra.

As Dykstra posed for pictures on stage, accidentally backing into a heavy sign and sending it crashing to the ground, startling the crowd, Lane made a beeline toward the magazine's managing editor, Clifford Blodgett, and senior editor Jonathan Lesser. The duo, who were mentally and physically wiped from the marathon sessions it had taken to pull this masterpiece together, as well as the soon-to-be-completed second issue, were chatting about what they had just witnessed.

"Lenny knew exactly what he was saying, and when he got off the stage, he bragged about it," Blodgett says. "He knew that he had hurt our feelings. I was upset." When Lane got there, he gave Lesser and Blodgett the pat on the back that Dykstra had refused to. "Randall said, 'At the end of the day, you know what you guys did. You put out a good product, and you should be proud of it. Enjoy this party; it's yours too.'"

Blodgett and the gang had already been on quite the roller-coaster ride just to pull this magazine together. At first they were amused by Dykstra's stories, his one-of-a-kind dialect, and the outlandish things he would say. "Whenever I would bring up measurements, like that's a 42-inch TV or a 26-inch computer monitor, Lenny would be like, 'That's the size of two of Darryl Strawberry's cocks,'" says Blodgett, who had been a big Strawberry fan as a kid. The editorial team also got a sort of high from pulling off Dykstra's impossible tasks.

But there also had been a ton of carnage for a magazine only on its first official issue, and the moving targets Dykstra kept creating appeared harder and harder to hit. Aside from the humorous, yet frustrating time-sucking conference calls and "wink wink" jokes about taking steroids, a number of logistical issues kept popping up. First, at Dykstra's insistence, the magazine was ramped up from one issue every three months, to a bimonthly, and then to a monthly. That created a massive time crunch.

Then came the near-impossible mandates. "The things he wanted were so oversize and so pie in the sky, and we started to question 'Is this really well thought out?'" Blades says, while noting that Dykstra was always nice to her. On deadline, he would instruct the editorial staff to call Jack Nicholson or some other big star and just "get the interview." When trying to plan ahead for the second cover, Dykstra sent the staff a list of his top five choices. It looked like this:

#1—Lebron James
#2—Lebron James
#3—Lebron James
#4—Tim Duncan
#5—Lebron James

Then about a week before deadline, he changed his mind and wanted Chris Paul. The caveat: he wanted only original photographs and an exclusive interview. "He'd say things like he wants to get Tiger Woods on the cover. Those of us who have worked in sports journalism know there is a machine surrounding Tiger Woods," Blades says. "He would just be like, 'I'm Lenny and I'm an athlete, so these guys are going to do it for me.' And it was like, 'Some of these guys don't even know who you are.'"

In the months leading up to the launch, the *Players Club* editorial team had also been uprooted from Doubledown's headquarters and sequestered to Dykstra's 245 Park Avenue offices, away from their colleagues, fact-checkers, photo researchers, and editorial assistants. Technically, they were Doubledown employees, but they were on their own to work with Dykstra. "Randall wouldn't stand up to Lenny because then he knew Lenny wouldn't trust him," Blodgett says. "We thought we had someone going to bat for us, and then at the last minute Randall would say, 'Oh, do what Lenny said.'"

The team was also promised resources that never materialized. Dykstra said he would fly the *Players Club*'s editorial team to Florida and Arizona on his private jet so that they could spend a week or two there interviewing a ton of baseball players during spring training. They could then use the interviews for features throughout the year. Spring training came and went, and the Florida sunshine remained a pipe dream for the team.

However, most troubling was the staff turnover. I knew Dykstra was high maintenance, but sitting in my nook at Doubledown's headquarters, I was shielded from the extent of it. Over in the skyscraper across town, Dykstra has "gassed," or made Lane fire, several employees, while others, such as Nicole Blades, walked away unwilling to work through the bedlam. "Someone would come in, sit in for two meetings, and then you would ask about them, and they would be gone," she says.

When Dykstra met the *Players Club* staff for the first time, each of them had to basically reinterview for the jobs even though they were Doubledown employees. Blodgett recalls how one employee, a talented veteran journalist on the team, got the boot after an awkward conversation with Dykstra.

The editorial team, including Dykstra, headed over to Doubledown's offices together. Dykstra noticed a sign atop a taxi promoting eyebrow threading. "What the fuck is that?" Dykstra asked in a semiaggressive tone. The journalist spoke up in a matter-of-fact manner, explaining the procedure. The next day Lane called the employee into his office and told him he was fired because Dykstra didn't like him. "The guy didn't even get a chance," Blodgett says.

Others left of their own volition. Back in December 2007, while Dan Ryan and I were still discussing the possibility of working together again, changes were already afoot at the *Players Club*. Arthur Hochstein, who was the head art director at *Time* magazine, was fast becoming friends with Dykstra. Dykstra wasn't happy with the Doubledown designers and asked Hochstein for help.

Hochstein liked Dykstra and wanted to be involved with the *Players Club* but didn't have the time to fully commit, so he turned to another designer, John Korpics, to help with the inside of the magazine. "I enjoyed talking to Lenny, and I am a big baseball fan," Korpics says. "If it's a shell game, Lenny is the thing you are chasing. He has a certain cachet to him if you grew up around sports or grew up in the New York area."

Although Dykstra was a bit unusual, Korpics found him fun to talk to. "He's like the Tasmanian devil. You stand back and listen to him say these outrageous things and watch him do this crazy shit. It's kind of funny." However, the long rambling phone calls that lasted for hours and the e-mails at 4 o'clock in the morning had only a certain amount of charm.

Things began to sour between Korpics and Dykstra over money. Korpics says he needed upfront cash because he was going to make commitments to photographers and other people he had to pay to get the job done. "Lenny kept missing the deadline in advancing me the money. He missed an agreed-upon date twice for money," Korpics says. "The third time the money didn't show up, I just said, 'We're done.'"

In response to Korpics's resignation e-mail, Dykstra insulted him. "Thank God! Your whining is/was fucking killing me!" Dykstra wrote. "And just to let you know, you are not that good! . . . and on top of that: YOUR SO FUCKING SELFISH, YOU DON'T EVEN SEE THE BIG PICTURE."

With Korpics out in late January, Dykstra cut Hochstein a sizable, five-figure check, and he went to work on the first issue of the magazine. "There's a real ugly side to Lenny. This is not a friendly, overly intelligent baseball player athlete. This is a guy who bangs his head against a wall to get things done," Korpics says. "He'll pull out a knife in a fight—he's that kind of a guy. I felt bad for him when our relationship ended. I knew this bile he was spewing was going to infect everything around him."

Unaware of the social politics going on at the party and not knowing Clifford Blodgett or any of the magazine's staff or its turnover problem, I got ready to head home. For me, it was a good night.

CHAPTER 13

BAD MACHINES

It was 7:45 a.m., and I was dressed in a black suit and tie, standing in the hall-way outside of Dykstra's luxurious suite at the Carlyle Hotel on New York's Upper East Side—it's an "old-money" boutique hotel on Madison Avenue. I had been banging on the door to no avail for what felt like an eternity.

A little after midnight the night before, Dykstra called me and asked me to join him for breakfast at his suite. He really liked my ghostwriting style and wanted to discuss the newsletter in more detail, he said. I was excited—more face time with the big boss. Dykstra was much more pleased with the prospects of "The Dykstra Report" than he had been during our earlier conversations. The makeshift Web site we had slapped together for the newsletter had included everything Dykstra asked for, and the presales were rolling in.

Still standing in the hallway, I dialed Dykstra on my cell phone but got no answer. Great, what was I supposed to do? Just wait? I knew how easily he soured on people, and I didn't want to let that happen with me. Remembering Dorothy's ten rules, I decided to wait. My phone rang about fifteen minutes later. "Hey, Chris, what's up, bro? I saw that you called," Dykstra said in a hushed but friendly tone.

"I'm here for our meeting, Lenny—I'm outside your door," I said, trying to sound upbeat despite my anxiety. "No, no, no bro, that was supposed to be hours ago," he said. I had arrived at the right time but knew Dykstra was more than a little disorganized. It wasn't a huge deal. "I'm at the studio filming *Fox & Friends* now," he said. "I'll tell you what, come by the hotel tonight at 11:30 p.m. Bring your girl. We'll get some work done and hang." Click—he hung up.

I walked out of the Carlyle and caught my connecting subways over to Doubledown's offices. Following the launch party, talk of Dykstra's snub and its potential repercussions were circulating like wildfire among the rank and file.

Word on the street was that Lane's bosses—the money guys—were pissed at the disrespectful gesture and wanted to pull the plug immediately.

Could the relationship be salvaged? And did Doubledown really want to salvage it? I was getting the feeling that the answer to both of those questions was a resounding no.

I was growing increasingly concerned about my suddenly murky job security. It was highly unlikely that Doubledown and Dykstra would continue to work together on the newsletter if bad blood caused their partnership on the *Players Club*, which was a much bigger venture, to fail.

Plus, I had a number of unfortunate surprises my first week at the company that gave me even greater pause. I learned from my colleagues about Doubledown's reputation for taking its time to pay freelancers and vendors and about its growing financial problems. Additionally, when I started, Lane and Ryan seemed to be the only two people at Doubledown who even knew about the Jocks and Stocks Division. I couldn't get a budget from Lane, and I had to fight for internal resources, which some of the managers didn't want to make available to me because of the budget situation.

I was uneasy about the handshake deal between Dykstra and Lane when I first heard about it. When the relationship soured, I was flat out worried. And it made me wonder whether Bolling and Najarian, the other two key members of the newsletter division who were not signed to contracts either, would bolt if Dykstra walked away. I began to get a sinking feeling in the pit of my stomach.

Our meeting time—11:30 at night—had come and gone, and Dykstra was nowhere to be found. My girlfriend, Rhea, and I had been sitting on the sofa in front of the elevator bank at the Carlyle Hotel for about an hour, quietly chatting. We were starting to grow uncomfortable as the hotel staffers glanced at us just a little bit longer each time they passed by, as if to question whether the two of us actually belonged there or had just wandered in off the street and parked ourselves down on the couch.

Finally, and without warning, Dykstra blew in like a hurricane, bringing the hustle and bustle of a busy midday Midtown Manhattan sidewalk with him even though it was after midnight. He was wearing a suit, had a bag strapped over his shoulder, and was holding another one as his loud voice echoed throughout the lobby. His arrival stirred the hotel staffers.

As he headed straight toward the elevators, he spotted us and pulled the cell phone away from his cheek for a split second. "Hey, Chris, give me a few minutes to change and then come on up," he said, as he handed his bag to the elevator operator, never missing a beat.

When we arrived at the room, Dykstra was much more laid back. He was wearing a faded orange T-shirt and washed-out royal-blue sweat shorts (Mets colors). He was hobbling with a noticeable limp and appeared to be in significant pain. Rhea followed me into the room and then made herself comfortable on the couch while I joined Dykstra at a small, messy table on the side of the room where his computer was set up.

Sitting just two feet from Dykstra, I could tell something was really off. He was not the same guy I had seen just a few minutes earlier rumbling through the lobby, operating at a million miles a minute. He had a glazed-over, distant look in his eyes. I knew he had had some serious back problems during his baseball career and subsequent surgeries. I wondered if his new limp and sedate condition were somehow related to that or to some sort of pain medication or muscle relaxer.

"I pulled my hammy at that TV show this morning," he said as he asked me to grab a magazine off the table for him because he was in too much pain to get it himself.

Overall, the *Fox & Friends* interview earlier that morning was a positive one for Dykstra. In it, he was loose, carefully deflecting questions about womanizing and the wedding-dress stalker who had showed up to Mets games all those years ago. He joked with the hosts about how he was now known as Thumbtacks instead of Nails because of his lumpier, softer physique.

However, he also got injured. Host Brian Kilmeade had seen the HBO *Real Sports* segment "Nails" and wanted badly to reenact a portion of it in which Dykstra got into a fistfight with Dodgers catcher Rick Dempsey at home plate at Dodger Stadium. Dykstra moved out in front of the set's coffee table as Kilmeade squatted down pretending to be Dempsey. Kilmeade directed one of the female hosts to get behind him and act like the umpire.

"I took out Dempsey," Dykstra said while standing over Kilmeade, who was excitedly bantering with the other hosts. "It was June and I was hitting .400. He was brownnosing the ump." Reenacting what happened that day, Dykstra turned to the "ump," pointed off in the distance, and said, "You see that scoreboard out there. What's it say? .400. You know why it says .400? Because I know what a strike is, and that's not a strike."

Kilmeade, wearing a dark suit and a light blue tie, stood up just like Dempsey had more than a decade earlier. "I'm so sick of you fucking brownnosing the umpire. Then we just went," Dykstra said, showing a flash of his past quickness as he playfully grabbed Kilmeade by the shoulders and started to pretend wrestle. With the other hosts laughing and cheering and Dykstra and Kilmeade tussling, the wrestling match quickly turned more serious.

Kilmeade, gaining the lower position for leverage, grabbed the back of Dykstra's leg and pulled it out from under him, causing him to fall backward onto the hard floor and Kilmeade to fall on top of him. There was a loud clanking noise, and Dykstra shouted, "Good takedown" as the duo continued to roll around on the floor. Dykstra pinned him, and they both got up laughing.

Excitedly and almost proudly, Dykstra exclaimed, "I pulled a hammy." One of the other hosts revealed that Dykstra had fallen directly onto the microphone's battery back, which was positioned on his lower back. After Dykstra joked around that the match had been staged and he had been trying to make Kilmeade look good, the show's hosts called for a doctor. Dykstra declined.

"I'll be all right; I'm not playing tonight," he said. "He actually took me down pretty good. It felt good. . . . I don't need anything. Tape it up and go. If you can't play, tape 'em up and roll 'em off the field and put another guy in." In the HBO *Real Sports* clip, Dempsey looked bruised and battered. In the reenactment, Dykstra was the one on the losing end.

Back at the Carlyle, Dykstra couldn't block out the throbbing pain coming from his injured hamstring. "Dude, you won't believe how bad it is," he said with a wince and a groan. Rolling up the leg of his shorts to reveal the tightened muscle, he said, "Look at it, bro," as if trying to convince me. I didn't need any; I could see the obvious pain in his face and hear it in his voice.

"Bro, feel it; it's bad," he said. It was an awkward moment. I knew Dykstra was sort of showing off his injury as a badge of honor the way one player might to a teammate. But it was still weird. I took my index finger and reluctantly poked at his leg. It was almost as if his hamstring were made out of cement. "Lenny, you should see a doctor. I think you did some real damage," I said to him. "Naw, I'm fine," he said, showing he was still tough as nails.

As we turned back to work, Dykstra took me on a detour. Before long, I was being shown pictures of Dykstra's new airplane and given a tour of all of his favorite Web sites. That continued for the better part of the following two hours before Dykstra turned his attention to Rhea, who was still on the couch flipping through the channels on the flat screen television mounted to the opposite wall.

She knew Dykstra used to play for the Mets, but hanging out with him wasn't the thrill for her it was for me. She liked Dykstra well enough, and the hotel was nice, but it was approaching 3:00 a.m. Trying to be a good host, he asked, "You like ice cream? I live on the stuff." Before we could answer, he picked up the phone and ordered a few bottles of Coca-Cola, as well as three ice cream sundaes—his with the hot fudge and an entire extra bowl of whipped cream on the side.

While we waited for room service to arrive, Dykstra began gimping about the room in search of *Players Club* magazines as he sang the chorus to Bruce Springsteen's "I'm Going Down" over and over again. "I'm going down, down, down. I'm going down, down, down," he rattled off in a slow, mumbling voice. Trying to make conversation, I asked if he was a big fan of the Boss. "Naw, rock 'n' roll makes me think of drinkin' too much," he said, cupping his hand and shaking it next to his head as if to motion that booze scrambled his brain.

Before long, Rhea and I joined the search, looking through stacks of papers scattered throughout the room. "Hey, bro, can you do me a favor? I have a couple of suitcases in the bedroom. Will you guys go see if the magazines are in there?" Dykstra asked.

One thing was immediately clear: Dykstra did not travel light. Clothes—suits, ties, shoes—were just mixed together and jammed into his overflowing suitcases. Inside one bag was a gigantic jumble of hundreds of DVDs. Still another large bag was packed with an odd mix of baseball cards and photos of Dykstra from many different brands and spanning several years.

As a kid, I had collected baseball cards and so had learned the importance of protecting them to preserve their value. Bent corners were a bad thing. Some of these cards in Dykstra's bag, however, looked as if they had been put in the spokes of a bicycle speeding through the streets of Flushing on a rainy June day. Not only weren't they in any protective casing; some also were bent in three or four places, while others were ripped in half.

I couldn't imagine what he was doing with the cards. I later found out that many of them had been sent to Dykstra by fans seeking an autograph. He kept them instead and was now lugging them all over the country.

We couldn't find the magazines and retreated to the main room, where the ice cream had arrived. As Dykstra made fast work of his ice cream, I pulled out a syringe to give myself an insulin injection. The needle caught Dykstra's attention. "Bro," he said with a smile and an exaggerated tone. I explained that I was diabetic and had to take a shot whenever I ate, especially when eating sweets. "My boy Dave Hollins is diabetic. You two should talk," he said.

We finished our ice cream at about 4:30 a.m. The meeting had run way longer than I expected, but it went well and was fun. We didn't get a whole lot of work done, but Dykstra was becoming more comfortable with me. Maybe that would help smooth things over between him and Doubledown, I hoped.

With the night winding down, I stood and thanked Lenny for his hospitality. "You guys can stay over," he said. "I have extra beds. I've got this whole place, and it's just me here." It was a nice gesture and one he had made several times earlier in the night as well. But I declined, and Rhea and I headed out into the chilly predawn air on Seventy-Sixth Street for the short walk home and some much-needed rest.

―――――――――

As April rolled on, the relationship between Dykstra and Doubledown deteriorated at a rapid pace, placing me squarely in the middle of an escalating cold war. Dykstra had stopped replying to Lane's e-mails and wouldn't return phone calls from nearly anyone at the company—except me!

He and I had to communicate because I was ghostwriting his stock market columns. "The Dykstra Report" was not yet quite ready to launch as a subscription product,[1] yet Dykstra had asked me to pen free columns he was again publishing on TheStreet.com to alert his loyal readership he was back. The plan was to scale back the freebies on TheStreet.com once "The Dykstra Report" went live, he said. That way he could still collect a paycheck from TheStreet and use its broad reach to promote his newsletter with Doubledown.

During the daytime, I would call Dykstra's office and try each of his four cell phones several times in hopes of getting his stock pick for the next day. I wanted to get a jump on the column, which had to be edited and posted to the Web site by no later than 9:30 a.m. the next morning. However, as his relationship with Doubledown got worse, Dykstra became less likely to take my calls during the daytime because I was at the Doubledown offices. If he answered, he would immediately say that he had to go, promising to call me right back. He never did.

Then the midnight calls from Dykstra began. Those were followed by the increasingly common 2:00 a.m. conversations. In the beginning, the calls would slowly trickle in, but before I knew it, I was fully sucked into Dykstra's 24/7 world.

That's when I made my first big blunder. When chatting with Dykstra one night at about 2:00 a.m., we were discussing potential picks for the morning's column. As was typical with his dizzying calls, he changed his pick a few times. I must have gotten confused and put the wrong call letters in the column. I still didn't fully understand options, so the error wasn't an obvious one to me. However, after receiving an e-mail the next morning from one reader alerting me to the mistake, I sent Dykstra a note acknowledging the error and telling him we had to correct it.

"THIS IS A FUCKING NIGHTMARE," he wrote back.

A LOT OF PEOPLE BOUGHT WHAT YOU TOLD THEM—THIS IS BAD! . . . WE ARE NOT PLAYING A GAME—THESE PEOPLE ARE INVESTING MIL-LIONS OF DOLLARS ON WHAT I SAY. . . . YOU ARE SUPPOSED TO BE MY EDITOR.

He said that the pick would still turn out to be a winner, but that he was suddenly unhappy with my ghostwriting ability and wanted to go over the way I was writing the columns. Up until this point, he said he had really liked my writing and style. Now, not so much.

I wrote him a long note back taking responsibility for the mistake, but also outlining a process for ensuring accuracy in the columns going forward. We needed some ground rules, and I had to set some boundaries. Part of it was his responsibility, I said, and I asked him to send me an e-mail each night with the final pick so that there would be no confusion. "I like that—a process. You're a smart dude," he said to me on the phone the next night with his patented slow-motion laugh. I felt good, like I had earned some respect from him. And we had a workable process.

———————

Dykstra and I were fast becoming pals. In between asking about my family and about Rhea, Dykstra would give me the pick and we would chat about the newsletter, which was on its way to bringing in $65,000 in its first few weeks prior to the launch. But he also wanted to know what was going on at Doubledown. What had Lane said to me? Had I heard anything about the magazine?

Dykstra wasn't the only one probing me for information. Lane also wanted to know what was going on in Lennyland, placing me in the awkward position of being caught between Lane, who was technically my boss, and Dykstra, who was really now becoming my boss. I tried to tow a very fine line, hoping that the newsletter's success and the credibility I was building with Dykstra would be enough to keep him at the table.

With Dykstra, I never really had any info on the magazine to share because I wasn't involved with it. I mostly listened to Dykstra vent, and when I had something to share, I would be 100 percent honest—as per Dorothy's advice. I would keep him up to speed on the newsletter and about what Lane was telling me—which wasn't hard because Lane was trying to stay positive.

With Lane, I had to strike a more diplomatic tone because Dykstra was talking awfully tough. I tried to convey the urgency of the situation to Lane without needlessly relaying the insults. When Lane would say things like "Oh, that's just Lenny being Lenny," I would respond by saying something like "I think it may be more serious than that" or "I definitely think you should sit down with him because that's not the impression that I get from Lenny." I wanted the two sides to work things out, but I didn't want to be a negotiator.

That time period became a very confusing one for me. Dykstra would tell me the relationship was dead in the water one night, and the next day I would go into work at Doubledown, and Lane would say, "Lenny is just being Lenny; it will all work out." I wanted to believe Lane because he had more experience dealing with Dykstra than I had, but in the back of my mind I knew he wasn't totally upfront with me from the get-go.

My hunch about Lane was further cemented during a mid-April meeting with Eric Bolling in Lane's office. The three of us sat down to discuss the "Bolling for Dollars" newsletter. Bolling was really keen on working with Dykstra—it seemed to be a prerequisite for working with Doubledown. He asked Lane if Dykstra was on board, and Lane assured him that Dykstra was indeed.

Sitting next to Bolling, I couldn't look him in the eye. I knew that things could not have been worse between Dykstra and Doubledown, and I wasn't about to embarrass my boss in front of a potential business partner, but I was angry. Lane's remarks made me trust him even less.

At first I felt that perhaps Lane had put the horse before the cart when he hired me without having Dykstra inked to a deal. I reluctantly gave him the benefit of the doubt even when I first learned about the supposed handshake deal for the newsletter. That night I told Dykstra that Bolling had come to our office and wanted to work with him. "Bolling's not doing it with Doubledown, dude. I talked to him. I told him the truth," Dykstra said to me. "Watch out for Randall. That guy's a bad machine."

CHAPTER 14

GOING, GOING, GONE

The night had slipped away, and before I knew it, it was dawn. My attempts to cut out of the late-night/early-morning marathon meeting at the Carlyle were unsuccessful at 4:00 a.m. and again at 6:00 a.m. With the new morning sunlight slowly illuminating every inch of the massive suite, I realized I was going to have to adjust my expectations if I had any prayer of keeping pace with Dykstra.

When I first arrived at the hotel, Dykstra had commandeered several of the hotel's staffers to run errands for him, using them like they were his own personal assistants. It was chaotic, but tasks were getting done. By half past seven, we hadn't accomplished any work in hours, derailed by Dykstra's meandering stream of consciousness.

Nonetheless, he wanted me to stay. Working through the night would become a regular occurrence when Dykstra came to town, which was about one week per month. His days were jam-packed with meetings, so the predawn hours were the only time he had left to meet with me. I simply had to tough it out.

"Bro, you hungry? Why don't you order us some breakfast?" Dykstra said, motioning to the phone atop a desk in the corner of his suite. Glancing up from typing on the laptop perched on the coffee table in front of him, he said to order him a thick stack of pancakes and three espressos. I got a bowl of freshly cut fruit.

As the food arrived, Dykstra picked up his laptop and moved over to the table, dragging a long trail of jumbled wires behind him. His laptop was plugged into a power strip, which was also supplying juice to a number of his other electronic devices, including cell phones, chargers, BlueTooth, and another laptop. As the power strip dragged across the hardwood floor, it pulled the devices crashing to the floor and into a massive heap of wires, metal, and blinking lights next to him. I scurried to catch his MacBook from being yanked to the ground, and then I joined him at the table.

"You know, I fired my whole fucking family—my brother, my mom, all of 'em," he said to me out of the blue, shaking his head in disbelief. "They were stealing from me." I was not surprised to hear these accusations—I had heard some rumblings. Underneath a number of online articles about Dykstra in the days following the launch party were some ugly comments. They appeared to be from someone who knew him well. I had asked Dorothy about them, and she told me she'd seen them too and suspected they were from Kevin Dykstra, Lenny's kid brother.

She said he was jealous of his superstar brother. Lenny gave Kevin every chance in the world, but he was simply too greedy, Dorothy said, as she told me how Lenny accused Kevin and another employee of running a scam at the car wash. In her mind, Lenny had no choice but to cut him loose. I took Dorothy at her word—I had no reason to doubt her.

Back at the hotel, I didn't know what to say in response to Dykstra's comment. I thought that he must lead a pretty lonely existence, never knowing whether the people around him were truly his friends or just "starfuckers," as he called them, hanging around because of the money and the lifestyle. After all, whom could he trust if he couldn't trust his own flesh and blood? I could tell this weighed heavily on him, but he didn't linger long on the topic.

Remembering he had an important meeting with Citigroup's execs in Midtown in a little more than an hour, Dykstra woofed down half his plate of pancakes and then hurried to his bedroom. Shouting from the other room, he asked, "Bro, can you tie a tie?" He said he could never master it himself. I felt sorry for the guy—he was a complete mess.

As he went to go get cleaned up, I looped four of his ties and put them on the bed so that he could choose one when he got out of the shower. I left some slack so that he could pull the winning tie over his head and tighten it himself. I was starting to feel more like a personal assistant than an editor, but as I learned, when you work for Lenny Dykstra, you leave your job title at the door.

As Dykstra got ready, I packed my bag and his. I knew he was running really late. He emerged from his room with his hair still wet, dressed in his suit and tie, and wearing his Patek Philippe watch, which he showed to me while shouting, "$65,000—I paid sixty-five grand for this. Can you believe that?"

We rushed through the lobby and out the side entrance of the Carlyle to a double-parked black SUV. I tossed Dykstra's bags in the back and reached out to shake his hand. All I could think about was my waiting bed.

"Good work, bro, but I need you to do me one more favor," Dykstra said to me, pulling a business card from his pocket. "I need you to run over to Kinkos for me." He wanted a stack of twenty-page color presentations printed up on the double for the meeting in forty-five minutes. "Do they have the electronic files on hand already?" I asked him. "Um, don't worry about that; we don't have time" he said, handing me a booklet he had mocked up for American Express bigwigs earlier.

"Dorothy really fucked this up," Dykstra said. "She's so painful." Then, pointing to the logo on the business card he had placed in my hand, he said to replace the AMEX logo with the Citi logo, and he pointed out the pages where I needed to swap out the brands. "I'll pay you back later; just keep the receipts." He gave me the address of the meeting and hopped in the SUV. He rolled down the window, and as the SUV pulled away, he shouted, "Have it there in thirty minutes, okay."

Great! One of those impossible tasks Dorothy had warned me about. I raced over to Kinkos. If Dykstra showed up to the meeting empty-handed, it would be my head on a platter as a result. After nervously waiting in the long line, I explained to the clerk that my boss was Lenny Dykstra and I needed some packets printed immediately. They knew Dykstra—he had pulled this stunt before.

However, the young man behind the counter informed me that such printing jobs usually took twenty-four hours and would be particularly difficult without the original electronic files. Furthermore, pulling the Citi logo from the business card might be a problem as well, owing to its small size and low quality.

Nonetheless, I didn't have the luxury of time to fuss over details. The clerk pulled me to the side and said he could help, but it was going to cost me. He handed me an envelope and said I should go wait next to a counter by the door. When the presentations were done, he would deliver them to me there. At that time, I should leave the envelope filled with cash on the counter, and he would stuff it in his pocket when no one was watching.

"How much?" I asked. "Whatever you think is fair," he replied and then went to work on the order.

After I had been pacing back and forth near the door for about forty-five minutes, Dykstra called me and he was pissed. "Where the hell are you, Chris?" he yelled into the phone. "You're embarrassing me." I explained the situation. "I don't care. Just bring me what you have right now. The meeting's about to start." He hung up.

The problem was that I didn't have anything to give him, and I couldn't show up empty-handed. I went back to the counter for a status report and learned they were making just one "presentation." I reminded them I needed five and needed them "yesterday."

About thirty minutes later, we made the exchange by the door. I placed $140 in the envelope. I really had no idea what to give, but that was most of the cash I had on me.

I jumped in a taxicab and waited nervously as we sat in midday bumper-to-bumper Manhattan traffic. Citi's offices were at least twenty minutes away. I was sure this would be my last day working on Team Dykstra.

As the taxi slowed in front of my destination, I had the door open and was ready to jump out before the car even stopped. I slapped a $20 bill in the driver's hand and hurried up the steps. After clearing security and taking a long elevator ride up, I was greeted by a young woman, an assistant to one of the Citi execs.

I expected to simply drop off the presentations, but instead she ushered me down the hall and into the meeting. She opened the door to reveal five or so executives, plus Dykstra, sitting around a long wooden table and making casual conversation.

I took a deep breath and walked in—the conversation came to a halt. Everyone turned toward me. "Hey, Chris, my man, come on in," Dykstra said, looking up. Turning to the other execs, he said, "Chris works for me."

I apologized to the group for being late, taking the bullet for Dykstra. I introduced myself, shaking each executive's hand as I passed out the presentations. After some brief chitchat, I excused myself. "Lenny, if you need anything else, give me a ring," I said. "I have a couple of items to take care of this afternoon."

I had pulled it off! I had just saved the day yet again—what a high. That night at the Carlyle, Dykstra praised me for coming through in the clutch and asked me what he owed me. "You walked in there with confidence . . . like you belonged," he said. "I like that."

I told him I didn't have a receipt for the presentations because I had to grease some palms off the books. Worried he might think I was overspending his money, I told him I had paid $120. It was silly, I know, but I didn't want to appear wasteful with his money. I was willing to eat the extra $20. He pulled out his checkbook and said, "You did a good job, bro," noting he was giving me a few extra bucks for my troubles.

I looked at the check, and he had written it out for $150,000. I handed it back to him, and he playfully snickered as he crossed out a few zeroes.

———

My efforts had made Dykstra like me more but hadn't changed his opinion of Doubledown one iota. The sobering reality was that Dykstra and Doubledown were still at odds.

At first the two sides agreed to part ways over the *Players Club* magazine but still work together on "The Dykstra Report." That arrangement fell apart quickly too, and all signs pointed to a nasty and bitter divorce.

It quickly become obvious I had to back one horse or the other or just walk away altogether. On one side there were Doubledown and Lane, whom I didn't trust. If Dykstra left, I would likely be relegated to writing articles for publications I had little interest in, such as *Private Air* or the *Cigar Report*. My bonus incentive would be gone too, and I doubted the company would keep my bloated salary on the books.

On the other side, I had Dykstra. I had no illusions about whether he was the kind of guy I would want to date my sister, but at least I respected the way he reinvented himself, and I began to appreciate his veiled intelligence. Dykstra, in my view, was high risk, high reward. Doubledown was the exact opposite: high risk, no reward.

Then the situation came to a head. "I need you to meet me over at the Carlyle right away, bro," Lenny said hurriedly into the phone. He was speaking so fast his words were blending together. "Randall Lane is trying to sabotage my magazine. I need you here right away."

When I got there, the room was a mess and Dykstra was clearly rattled. "They're holding my magazine hostage," he said, explaining that Doubledown refused to print the second edition of the *Players Club* unless he paid them hundreds of thousands of dollars.

Doubledown claimed Dykstra had not yet paid for the printing of the first issue, and it would not extend him further credit. Dykstra was livid. He asked Lane for an itemized list of expenses and said he was given an Excel spreadsheet with random numbers plugged in. Dykstra felt Doubledown was padding its invoices and claimed he wasn't seeing see any actual receipts.

Either way, the *Players Club* was only a month old and already in jeopardy. Missing the print date could be devastating. It would be embarrassing and halt all momentum Dykstra had bought from the positive press and the $600,000 launch party. It could scare away advertisers and luxury partners, including companies like Citi.

Dykstra's magazine had to be printed in stages because of its laminated cover. It took a certain amount of time for the laminate to dry, and he had a specific window to print the magazine and collate it with the cover so that it would come out perfect. If he missed the scheduled date, it would become a logistical nightmare to reschedule dual time on the presses, which were usually booked solid weeks in advance.

Dykstra, however, had a plan. He flew cross-country in the middle of the night on a private jet and touched down in New York, where he found a sympathetic helper. The design shop that worked on the magazine agreed to turn the files needed to print the magazine over if Dykstra agreed to protect them from any potential lawsuits from Doubledown.

"Publishing businesses have very few real assets. Things like lists and content are all they have," says Rachel Pine. Allowing Dykstra to steal the files is "like Tiffany leaving the door unlocked overnight." With his end around still unnoticed by Doubledown, Dykstra sought out a new printer.[1]

"You have to quit Doubledown right away," Dykstra told me. "Don't even go back." He said he wanted me to work directly for him and build his newsletter. "You've done a good job—I like the way you work. It'll be fun." Plus, he said he was reuniting with Cramer—he had a deal lined up with TheStreet.com, and there would be plenty of money to go around.

Besides, I had no other option as Lane would likely fire me once he pulled the plug on "The Dykstra Report," Dykstra said. The thought had crossed my mind too. However, I told Dykstra that he was wrong and that even if I was fired, I had options. He wasn't the only game in town.

I was flattered he wanted me to work directly for him, but I was leery too. I would no longer have the protection of working for an established company with benefits and a potential buffer between me and Dykstra. I knew working for Dykstra would be the toughest challenge of my life.

He asked what Doubledown was paying me, and I told him $100,000 a year plus a bonus. It wasn't the first time he had asked me, but he scoffed, saying "They're not paying you that, no way." I offered to show him my pay stub. We went through a cat-and-mouse game a few more times before he said he would pay me $5,000 every two weeks, offer the best health benefits in the world, and include a year-end bonus equivalent to 20 percent of the newsletter's sales.

In return, I would ghostwrite his columns and manage all aspects of the newsletter, run his New York office, manage his other employees, and pretty much handle any task he sent my way. "Take the weekend. Discuss it with your parents, your girl. I want you to feel good about it," he said.

I sent Lane my resignation letter, putting what I considered the worst chapter of my professional career to rest. "The job is turning out to be very different than what I was offered," I wrote. I didn't mention Dykstra's proposal or my likely acceptance of it. I could have been more forthcoming with Lane, but after what he had pulled, I didn't feel I owed him anything.

CHAPTER 15

FAMILY FEUD

Beneath my desk at Doubledown was a basketball-sized hole in the stained carpet that my chair would get caught on every time I tried to move. The Internet would often shut down for hours at a time without warning for maintenance, and the office was dark and cramped.

Dykstra, on the other hand, gave me my own spacious office on the thirty-ninth floor of 245 Park Avenue. The lobby was palatial, security was tight, and the ceiling was sky high—like a giant cathedral. I could recline in my office chair, put my feet up on the windowsill, and look out upon the iconic Chrysler Building, with its famous crown illuminating the New York City sky.

Feeling we had both been screwed by Lane and Doubledown, Dykstra and I bonded, my faith in him and his good intentions growing stronger the more we worked side by side. I believed in Dykstra. I did not believe Lane. Dykstra had credentials—in my mind he was legit. Plus, he had expressed confidence in my abilities, telling everyone I was his "main man" in New York.

I felt as if I had been rescued from a sinking ship slowly capsizing in rough waters. In reality, the storm clouds stretched well into Dykstra's past and cast a long shadow on his future.

Unbeknown to me, the legal disputes, handshake deals, and business ventures gone awry were piling up—the most devastating stemming from the car washes. A series of interrelated disputes between Lenny and Lindsay Jones and between Lenny and Kevin wreaked havoc on everyone involved and split the Dykstra clan in two, with Lenny on one side and almost everyone else on the other.

September 5, 2003, should have been a joyous occasion. Lenny was opening his third car wash. Instead, it marked the beginning of the end of the Dykstra family dynasty. Although he didn't know it when he woke up that morning, this would also be Jones's last day.

The relationship between Jones and Dykstra spanned decades, beginning in Garden Grove as kids. As adults, Jones was Dykstra's business manager and playmate—during Dykstra's playing days, he and Jones would head to Atlantic City or Las Vegas to party, drink, and do God knows what else.

However, Dykstra and his longtime friend had been on a violent collision course for years, ever since Dykstra had stopped drinking, according to his brother Brian. "Lenny used to show up in Simi Valley for meetings with a vodka bottle in his suitcase." Then he quit—cold turkey. "My mom was really happy."

It was a battle Dykstra was familiar with—he struggled with addiction for a long time, says Jimmy Stewart, a friend and former business associate. The two men met years earlier in rehab.

At that time, Dykstra was like "a little kid, just worn out, just desperate," Stewart says. "He absolutely brutalized himself." In addition to snorting recreational drugs such as cocaine and drinking heavily, Dykstra was abusing prescription drugs. He was taking up to fifty pills of the heavy-duty painkiller Vicodin per day, according to Stewart and Brian.

Stewart and the others in their recovery group "would have to watch over Lenny constantly because he was afraid. It was just his demons he was constantly fighting. The way he dealt with them was the drugs and the alcohol. He would medicate himself because he didn't want to feel."

When he was sober, he was "humble and he was down to earth," Stewart says. "Lenny has got a really good side to him." He is also very sharp. "He understands people," Stewart says. "He has really good insight into human behavior."

Sober, Dykstra started paying closer attention to how his car washes were being run—and he wasn't too happy with what he discovered. "Kevin and Lindsay were around during the time when the money and the stardom and the fame were just at an all-time high," says Terri Dykstra, who wed Lenny in 1985 and filed for divorce in 2009. "They just took what they wanted. A lot of the stuff Lenny condoned. When Lenny stopped playing and things weren't flowing like they were before, I think Lenny started telling them, 'Wait a minute—you can't spend my money, and you can't just take what you want.'"

When he found out what was going on behind his back, he was devastated, according to Terri. "Lenny funded all of the car washes. Lindsay didn't put a dime into it, but Lindsay reaped all the benefits," Terri says. "Lenny would give him a piece of everything he was doing." When she confronted Lenny about Lindsay, he would go to bat for his old friend, saying he deserved a cut of the profits. "From day one I complained about Lindsay. He's a scumbag beyond scumbags—just the worst."

Dykstra eventually agreed with his wife. He believed Jones was stealing from the business and confronted him the day of the grand opening. He accused him of demanding kickbacks from contractors and raiding cash registers at the car washes to buy drugs and pay off gambling debts, allegations Jones denied.

What happened next is not entirely clear. Dykstra contends that Jones quit. Jones and several other witnesses say he was fired and permanently banned from the properties.

That's when the family ties started to unravel, says Brian Dykstra. Jones sued his former partner, filling the lawsuit with Dykstra's dirty laundry. He offered "proof" of Dykstra's alleged steroid abuse and claimed Dykstra had helped him bet on Phillies games in 1993, a cardinal sin in baseball.

Jones said Dykstra turned to a Florida bodybuilder named Jeff Scott for his steroids over an eight-year period. A report from the *Los Angeles Times* alleged that Dykstra paid Scott, a convicted drug dealer, $20,000 plus "special perks" and that Scott claimed to have injected Dykstra with the juice more times than he could count.[1]

The report also said that in an effort to bulk up because he was playing for a new contract, Dykstra took five different kinds of steroids during the Phillies magical 1993 season. After that year, Dykstra signed a $25 million pact with the Phillies, making him the highest-paid leadoff hitter in Major League Baseball at the time.

However, the more troubling allegation was that Dykstra had helped Jones bet thousands of dollars on baseball games in 1993, just two years after promising baseball commissioner Fay Vincent that he would steer clear of gambling-related trouble. The winnings would be used as a form of payment to Jones, he claimed, but if the bets didn't work out, Dykstra vowed to cover any losses.

The messy allegations looked more like an attempt by Jones to twist Dykstra's arm enough to force a favorable settlement. It didn't work. Never one to back down, Dykstra came out with guns blazing, submitting an arbitration claim against Jones, accusing him of embezzlement and fraud.

Armed with the best lawyers money could buy, Dykstra was ready to go to the mat. "I had to hire Daniel Petrocelli, who is probably one of the top five attorneys in the world," Dykstra later told WFAN's Mike Francesa. "It cost me $6 million bucks to get my business back."[2]

Petrocelli had first made a splash in the headlines as the lawyer representing the family of Ronald Goldman in its civil lawsuit against former NFL star and actor O. J. Simpson. Goldman, a twenty-six-year-old model and waiter, had been stabbed to death along with O. J. Simpson's ex-wife, Nicole Brown Simpson, on a pathway outside her home.

A young Petrocelli persuaded a jury that O. J. Simpson was responsible for the wrongful death of Ronald Goldman, and Simpson was ordered to pay $33.5 million to the Goldmans.

When the arbitration ruling came down in the case between Dykstra and Jones, it wasn't even close—Dykstra won by a landslide. The arbiter ruled that Jones was not entitled to any compensation for his alleged stake in the businesses. He found that Jones had taken more than $2 million from the business without permission and owed $328,000 in unpaid loans. When all was said and done, Jones was ordered to pay $2.9 million in damages—$500,000 of that in punitive damages.

"Once Lenny got awarded that arbitration, he thought he was invincible," says Kevin Dykstra. "He knew he could lie and beat the system. It's all about having people on your side and teaming up on people." What Kevin didn't realize at the time was that his head would be next on the chopping block.

Following the fallout with Jones, Lenny grew increasingly paranoid. "Whatever he was taking, it really affected his brain and the way that he thought to where he started believing everybody's out to screw him," Terri says.

With the arbitration behind them, Lenny and Kevin prepped the McKinley Hills car wash site for sale. By February 2006, it was a done deal—Lenny had cashed out to the tune of $11 million. Kevin asked for the 10 percent cut he says Lenny had promised him years earlier. Instead, he got a pink slip.

After Jones was fired, Kevin says Lenny went on the warpath to stack the deck in his own favor. In addition to asking Kevin to get his friends in the police department to harass Jones, Lenny instructed him to destroy the only complete accounting records of the businesses, which could be used to help determine the true value of the partnerships and Lindsay's 25 percent stake.

Kevin also says that Lenny used his position of power to strong-arm his employees into lying during arbitration. Kevin, his uncle Wayne Neilsen, and two other former employees of the car wash later signed official documents declaring they had perjured themselves during the arbitration case. Kevin claimed he had lied under oath because Lenny pressured him to do so and he didn't want to lose his lucrative $250,000 a year job—a job used to support his wife, a stay-at-home mom, and three kids.

He testified that he and Jones stole money from the businesses and that Jones destroyed cash register receipts to hide the missing money. "Lenny set him up and screwed him out of his money and made me pretend I stole all this money with Lindsay to get him out of the partnership so he wouldn't have to pay Lindsay all this money," Kevin says.

However, the biggest kicker, Kevin claims, is that against his own best interests, he testified that Lenny had never promised him a 10 percent interest in the car washes. He says Lenny's lawyers felt testimony about the oral agreement would be detrimental to the arbitration case against Jones. He never imagined that the lies he told on Lenny's behalf would be used against him, he says.

After all, they had a handshake deal, and, according to Kevin, there were plenty of witnesses, including Lindsay Jones, Brian Dykstra, Michael Croswell (Lenny's business manager), Wayne Neilsen, Marilyn Dykstra, and their stepfather, Richard DeCento.[3]

"For a long time, I think Lenny verbally told Kevin, 'If I ever sell the car washes, I will give you a percentage of what I sell them for,'" Terri says. "When he did sell 'em, he didn't give him anything and he fired him. He told him, 'You've been stealing from me the whole time.'"

Lenny later described the whole incident as "ugly" to WFAN's Mike Francesa. "It was one of those situations where you forgave and you forgave and you forgave, but eventually you have to have tough love," he said. "You tell 'em, 'That's it. You keep taking, I'm going to fire you.' So, I had to fire 'em."[4]

The boys' stepsister Brenda Dykstra believes Lenny's version of events. "I can't believe how the family all turned their backs on [Lenny]. He had done so many good things for everybody."

Kevin probably did take advantage of his job at times by playing too much golf when he should have been at work, going to the casino too often, and giving out too many free car washes, Brian Dykstra says. However, Kevin's sins were a far cry from the theft Lenny was claiming, he says.

"Here's how the bottom line played out for our family. Lenny decided he's got to eliminate Kevin," Brian explains, noting that Lenny sent someone else to fire Kevin. "At the time, my mom was at Lenny's house. Kevin calls my mom, crying, 'Lenny just eighty-sixed me from the company.' My mom just lost it and freaked out on Lenny at his house."

Lenny tried to explain to her that Kevin was stealing, but she didn't want to hear it. "Then shit got ugly, and Lenny calls my stepdad, Richard, and says, 'You need to come and get *your* wife,'" Brian says.

Luckily, the situation didn't escalate, but that wasn't the end of the bloodbath. Wayne Neilsen, Lenny's uncle (his mom's brother) and a nine-year employee of the car washes, was given his walking papers two weeks later. He reportedly refused to take sides in the Lenny versus Kevin dispute.

"I was there during the gambling. I was there during the steroids. I ran his businesses. I know Lenny better than anybody," Kevin Dykstra says. "He's got all the fans that loved Lenny. They just see him as a baseball player, and he was a great baseball player. I was his biggest fan. But I saw the dark side—all the lies like he still does and the claims that everyone steals from him. It's bullshit."

Then one day, without even telling Brian until after the deal was finalized, Lenny sold the two remaining locations for a whopping $40 million. Brian says Lenny refused to pay him the $12,000 in vacation pay he was owed or the sweat equity Lenny had promised.

However, with pockets full of cash and the nightmare of the car washes behind him, Lenny sought to fly even higher with the *Players Club*, away from his brothers, whom he nicknamed the Criminals.

"Let's put it this way," Brian says. "I'm not going to say who is right and wrong here. I just basically keep my job and basically love my mother and my brother Kevin. How's that? Most beautiful family you could ever imagine."

CHAPTER 16

LOCK AND LOAD

Randall Lane "thinks I'm going to buckle," Lenny told the *New York Post* for a May 2, 2008, article. "I don't buckle—I go to war."[1] Dykstra struck first, and within days of my resignation, he and Doubledown were embroiled in a nasty and bitter legal slugfest, hurling lawsuits at each other like 100-mph beanballs.

The partnership between Dykstra and Doubledown had begun with much optimism. In a July, 30, 2007, e-mail from Dykstra to Lane included in the lawsuit, Dykstra tells the Doubledown president, "You are the kind of person that I WANT to partner up with; by the way, *we are partnering up. . . . And I never lose money for my partners, as it is unacceptable!*" However, the relationship "rapidly soured" in 2008, and the fallout sapped some badly needed momentum from the company.

The dispute boiled down to this: Dykstra claimed Doubledown unfairly jacked up the costs associated with the *Players Club* magazine and used his name without his permission by launching "The Dykstra Report" newsletter. Dykstra told friends and business associates that Randall Lane was "messing with my livelihood" by sabotaging the *Players Club* and the newsletter and "breaking the law by trying to blackmail me." Lane adamantly denied the accusation. Dykstra told others that Doubledown was the "the lowest scum of the earth!" and demanded his lawyers "throw the book" at Lane.

Dykstra wrote to one longtime friend that Lane "has no idea what pain is. . . . He stole my $650,000. Now he will pay! As you know, when it comes to lawsuits—I GO THE DISTANCE—AND I WILL PUT THEM OUT OF BUSINESS!"

The fallout resulted in the ugliest divorce—personal or professional—that Dykstra assistant Dan Della Sala had ever seen. Lane and Dykstra were both intent on making "life miserable for the other person . . . trying to get at each other and screw each other over any way possible," he says. "It was two egos trying to destroy each other."

For her part, Dorothy says she always thought Lane was "a snake in the grass. From the very first time I spoke with him on the phone, I had an uncomfortable feeling that he was not a trustworthy person." Dan felt the same way.

Doubledown, on the other hand, said Dykstra was a disaster. "Dealing with Lenny Dykstra was like herding cats. Everything had to be big league, but big league to him did not have the financial accountability it needed to have," says one former Doubledown senior exec. "There was too much shooting from the hip from a guy who was really accurate with his guns in one industry, but really inaccurate with his guns in publishing."

The company claims Dykstra repeatedly shirked his financial obligations beginning in 2007, when he began to exhibit signs of cash flow problems. Reading that in the lawsuit really irked me because Lane had known there was trouble months before he hired me.

"Over a relatively short period of time, Dykstra proved himself to be a mercurial, difficult client whose many idiosyncrasies and demanding personality imposed substantial costs on the planned publication and created excessive burdens for Doubledown," the company states in the lawsuit.

One of those costs was hiring Arthur Hochstein, design director at *Time* magazine, as a consultant, as well as *Time*'s photography director, despite the fact that Doubledown already had designers working on the magazine. "Together, the *Time* magazine duo spent hundreds of hours working with Dykstra and generated tens of thousands of dollars in unnecessary costs, such as a single assignment that alone cost almost $60,000," the lawsuit states.

Doubledown claimed Dykstra owed more than $587,000, including $59,000 lent to Lenny to pay vendors unrelated to the magazine. Part of that total was $200,000 Doubledown billed to Dykstra for work on the planned third edition of the *Players Club*, which was in the very early stages when the relationship collapsed.

Doubledown also sought $100,000 for expenses it says it incurred in connection with the development of "The Dykstra Report" newsletter, an absolutely ridiculous claim. Aside from my salary (about $8,333 per month for less than a month) and some development work done by the company's tech team, the expenses related to "The Dykstra Report" were minimal.

Plus, Doubledown and Dykstra didn't even have a formal agreement. Lane claimed it was a handshake deal, but it's clear from the documentation Randall provided in the lawsuit and from what I observed firsthand that certain details needed to be worked out.

However, Dykstra was aware of the newsletter's progress and benefited from the vagaries surrounding the status of "The Dykstra Report." He did not protest when the newsletter was bringing in tens of thousands of dollars or when I, an employee of Doubledown, ghostwrote his columns appearing on TheStreet.com, for which he was collecting a paycheck.

For its part, Doubledown had collected more than $75,000 dollars from more than 150 customers preordering the much-anticipated newsletter.[2] Lenny felt that since "The Dykstra Report" would never be launched in partnership with Doubledown, Lane should surrender the money to him.

Instead, Lane sat on the money, enraging Dykstra and underscoring the notion in Dykstra's mind and mine that Lane was a bad machine. Some of the folks at Doubledown weren't so thrilled either.

"I was absolutely shocked when I heard that Randall and Paul Fish [Doubledown CFO] were trying to keep the newsletter subscribers' money and not issue refunds," says Rachel Pine. "Randall told me that they were holding the money to try to pressure Lenny into actually doing the newsletter with them."

Despite my best efforts to avoid getting involved in this huge legal mess, before long I found myself walking through Midtown Manhattan toward the Upper West Side with Dykstra's "big gun" attorney, Dan Petrocelli—the lawyer who had successfully represented him against Lindsay Jones. I told Petrocelli everything I knew about the situation.

Petrocelli wasn't the only attorney Dykstra asked me to speak with. One afternoon when I received a phone call from Dykstra, he put me on speakerphone and told me two of his high-powered attorneys from K&L Gates were in the room. After Dykstra introduced the men, he turned to the real reason for the call.

"Chris, I have a very important question for you," he said in a serious, very businesslike tone, noting that my answer would be critical to his lawsuit. "I need you to think very carefully before you answer. Ready?" Dykstra asked me and launched right into his question. "How much pussy do you get?" Taken aback, and not sure if I had heard him correctly, I acted as if I hadn't heard the question at all.

In a slow, deliberate tone, Dykstra repeated himself. "Chris. . . . I want to know how much PUSSY you get?" Not quite sure what to say, I tried to lighten the situation with a joke that was largely ignored by the group. "All right, bro," Dykstra said, chuckling at how uncomfortable he had just made me. "I'll call you later. Keep it stiff."

—————

While the lawsuits played out in public, behind the scenes our small mishmash of Lenny loyalists tried to keep the gigantic wave of momentum generated by the *Players Club* launch party and HBO *Real Sports* episode from coming to a crashing halt. When we finally regrouped, we quickly realized that we were facing a monumental challenge. Lenny had lined up American Express Publishing to handle the content and design of the next two editions of the magazine, and *Time*'s Arthur Hochstein was still helping in a design consulting role, but the rest of the company had no infrastructure and no battle plan, with the ultradisorganized Dykstra leading the charge forward.

We had no office equipment or supplies, no payroll system or benefits, no magazine software or servers. Most importantly, I found out, we had no money and none of the potentially income-generating pieces of the *Players Club* were in place yet, such as the advertising sales staff or the preferred financial partner. So we had no way of offsetting the massive costs required to actually print and ship the magazine.

That was not the life I had envisioned while watching Lenny Dykstra, successful entrepreneur and multimillionaire, on HBO *Real Sports* just a month and a half earlier.

On the staffing front, we had just a handful of employees randomly scattered across the country, and several of them had little or no experience handling the tasks assigned by Dykstra. In California, Lenny had Gavin Dykstra (his adopted son) and Keith Peel (his brother-in-law) handle the magazine's distribution.

They were helped by Tim Murray, Dykstra's former flight attendant, and his wife, who lived in Nevada. Dykstra also had a personal assistant working out of his house—first Joanie and then Annie, neither of whom lasted very long. His flight attendant Amanda served as a personal assistant when Dykstra was on the road, and Dorothy, of course, was on board for whatever work was needed.

Our New York contingent was just two people—me and Dan Della Sala, whom Dykstra called "Junior." We worked out of "the best office in the world," the 245 Park Avenue *Players Club* headquarters, which consisted of three offices—one large corner office that used to house several of Doubledown's *Players Club* editorial staffers, and two smaller, but still sizable offices on each side. Dan sat in one of the smaller offices, while I was in the other. The large space in between us was empty. The three offices were connected via unusual sliding-glass windows, similar to McDonalds' drive-thru windows, which Dykstra had installed so that he could keep a watchful eye on his workers when he was in New York.

The offices were filled with cheap cookie-cutter-like office furniture, but the space had lots of potential and a world-class view. Despite the steep climb ahead,

Dan and I were optimistic. The *Players Club* concept was a good one, and even though working for Dykstra was challenging, it was also extremely exciting.

In my short time working for Dykstra, he had already pushed me to accomplish tasks I thought were impossible, an incredibly satisfying feeling that I hadn't quite experienced before. We just needed to weather the violent storm, I thought. After all, we had both been given a great opportunity in our fairly young careers: to get in on the ground floor and help mold the future of potentially multimillion-dollar businesses.

Dan, however, was a bit more battle weary. He had joined the *Players Club* at the start of the year but had witnessed the carnage and chaos up close. He had survived the Doubledown fiasco and fallout because he worked directly for Dykstra on the business side of the Players Club, not the magazine.

In the days leading to my arrival, Dan was a forgotten man. He often unlocked the doors each morning only to shut down the office each night without having encountered a single person the entire day. Dan was being ignored by Dykstra, and I got the sense he was relieved to have me on board because I had Dykstra's ear.

As I began settling into my new surroundings, I learned Dan wasn't Dykstra's "assistant" but actually worked on one of the most important pieces of the Players Club puzzle. "I was Lenny's annuity specialist," Dan says. "It was my job to be the liaison for Lenny and the insurance companies." Dykstra knew that he wanted players to be able to purchase guaranteed income for the rest of their lives, but he also knew nothing about how annuities or their living benefits worked.

Dan fielded calls from players interested in the Players Club, but his most important role was supporting and advising Dykstra on annuities. Although he was not empowered to make any real decisions, he would set up meetings with the big bosses at the insurance companies and seek out new opportunities.

"Initially, I was working with representatives from AIG on their annuities, insurance packages, and everything they proposed to Lenny," Dan explains. In the days leading to the *Players Club* launch party, Dykstra sang the praises of AIG to anyone who would listen. In the first edition of the magazine, Dykstra even told readers that AIG was "rock solid" and that the way to secure a paycheck for the rest of their lives was to buy an annuity from the insurance titan.

In fact, that inaugural, 168-page issue of the *Players Club* featured a 9-page spread promoting AIG and instructing players to call Dan at 212-672-1986. Dan would then direct players to an AIG annuity specialist, fulfilling the Players Club's mission of walking those players across the "bridge."

Getting a well-known company in the slow-moving, conservative insurance industry to undertake such a partnership was tricky business. Dykstra was a wild card that could really help or hurt a company's public image, and during earlier meetings with AIG officials, his attitude was cause for concern. "We were at a board meeting with our financial partner, AIG, and Lenny promised to bring several key people that were involved in the Players Club, one being Ron Darling," Dan says. Instead, Dykstra brought his pilot and one of his writers. Neither man said a word.

When it came time to discuss the products AIG wanted to offer on the Players Club's platform, Dykstra dismissively said, "I don't care what products you put together as long as I get paid," according to Dan.

Looking around the room, Dan saw executives with their eyebrows raised and jaws hanging open in astonishment. That was not the attitude they were expecting. "I literally wanted to crawl under the table and hide," he says. "From that point on, Lenny did not hold the attention of anyone in the room."

That meeting did not kill the relationship, but a dispute over "getting paid" put serious stress on the venture. Dykstra felt AIG should pay a hefty, upfront premium to become the club's financial partner. "AIG wanted to pay commission first, because the Players Club was an untested product, and then possibly work towards paying money up front going forward," Dan says. "I could see the validity of both sides."

As the relationship with AIG soured, Dykstra began shopping his idea around to the insurance giant's competitors, telling Dan that "the insurance companies need us more than we need them." Clearly lacking perspective, Dykstra lost sight of the fact that he "was someone with a great idea and a start-up company" but with no clients and little capital, Dan says.

Keeping AIG on the back burner, Dykstra refused to return the calls of AIG's top brass or provide Dan with any substantial message to relay to the company's execs. "I kind of thought AIG was out the door but thought maybe we could salvage the relationship," Dan says. "At the same time, I would speak to Lenny and know he didn't want to do it and it was on me to find the new insurance company to deal with. From that point on, it was downhill."

CHAPTER 17

PINCH HITTER

It was a little after midnight at the Carlyle Hotel as Dykstra continued to stare down at his computer screen, oblivious to the ringing doorbell. Standing outside his suite were the two Ricks. Richard O'Connor was a tall, middle-aged, clean-cut white man with light hair, glasses, and casual business attire. Next to him was a shorter, rounder white man in a dark suit named Rick Probst.

I had met the men earlier in the day and learned that late the night before they had hopped on the red eye from LA to New York on short notice at Dykstra's behest to help with some Players Club business. Once in New York, the Ricks were supposed to dine with Dykstra. However, when evening rolled around, Dykstra was nowhere to be found.

"At about 8:30 at night, we hear from Lenny—he's at a steakhouse," O'Connor recalls. "We get there, and Lenny is sitting in a booth with some people from *Time* magazine." Since the rest of the group was almost done eating, one Rick ordered a glass of wine and the other simply got an appetizer.

No sooner did they finish telling the waiter what they wanted when Dykstra got up from the table, told the Ricks they should pick up the tab, and made a beeline for the door. "Rick wanted to knock him out right there," O'Connor says. "We get stuck picking up an $800 dinner."

Once back at the hotel, they exchanged terse e-mails with Dykstra before stopping by his suite to try and prevent the situation from spiraling out of control.

Moments before the Ricks appeared on our doorstep, Dykstra told me how he "sent them to their room," one of his favorite expressions for describing showing somebody up. He was very proud of the insulting e-mail he fired off to them, which read in part "You have brought nothing to the table. . . . Enjoy your trip back to the middle." Dykstra repeated the lines over and over, laughing and looking at me with a smirk.

At the time I knew none of the drama that was unfolding other than that Dykstra was tired of the men. "It's brutal, man; you have no idea," he said, casting a blank stare in my direction for emphasis.

Dykstra instructed me not to take calls from either man from now on, telling me they didn't know what the hell they were doing and that one of them was a "cokehead." I didn't know if that were true or whether Dykstra was just running his mouth, but I knew enough to follow my boss's direction.

Once in the suite, O'Connor tried to act as a peacemaker, keeping the conversation lighthearted. Probst, on the other hand, planted himself in a chair with his arms folded, boiling under the surface. Neither attitude mattered as Dykstra spent the majority of the time in his bedroom, avoiding the men and leaving me to make awkward chitchat with them.

Finally, the men decided to call it a night. "Are they gone yet?" Dykstra shouted with a chuckle as he emerged from the bedroom holding his laptop. "Did you see the look on Doughnut Boy's face?" he asked, referring to Rick. "Did you see it? Hilarious! I sent them to their roooooooms!"

Dykstra was in a much better mood after the Ricks had gone, and we began talking about "The Dykstra Report," which would later be rebranded as "Nails on the Numbers." Even though he had started his 2008 stock-picking campaign in late March, Dykstra's record was already 5–0, with $5,000 in profits.

Dykstra's stock-picking system worked like this: he would write a column telling readers to purchase ten specific options contracts for a company such as Sigma Designs. Each contract essentially allowed him to "control" 100 shares of the common stock at a fraction of the price, he said. So ten contracts meant he was controlling 1,000 shares. He needed the option price to increase by $1.00, and he would make a quick $1,000 profit (1,000 shares x $1.00 = $1,000 profit).

Six days after he picked it, Sigma moved up a buck and he was $1,000 richer. His next pick—GPS-maker Garmin—netted him a $1,000 victory on the very same day he picked it. He was on a roll.

In private, Dykstra attributed much of his success to his process. "I LITERALLY FOUND A LOOPHOLE IN THE SYSTEM. IT'S NOT ME THAT IS CHALKING UP THESE WINS—IT'S THE MODEL I BUILT, THAT IS THE KEY!" he told one of the magazine's writers in an e-mail.

He told me he was taking his system and his newsletter back to TheStreet.com. However, he said, the company moved kind of slowly, so in the interim he wanted to launch the newsletter and Web site on our own, and he wanted it done immediately.

Over the next few nights, I scurried to finalize the design. At Dykstra's insistence, we worked literally around the clock, and after we had put in several grueling all-nighters, the Web site looked sharp. It worked really well, but the business side of things, such as our ability to collect money and keep proper books, was not ready. We also couldn't provide subscribers with log-in information, making it difficult for us to shield the exclusive content from people who hadn't signed up for the newsletter.

Dykstra didn't care and insisted we launch the Web site immediately. He offered the following solution: have people who want to subscribe send their credit card information to us via e-mail. Instead, I synced the site with Paypal so that we could at least collect money through a reputable vendor. It was a temporary solution until we transitioned to The Street.com.

As the site went live, Dykstra told me that in addition to sending the newsletter to new subscribers, we should also send it to the customers who had signed up for "The Dykstra Report" with Doubledown as an act of goodwill while the lawyers for two sides worked things out. Remember, Dykstra and I both already had all their e-mail addresses.

Before long Dykstra became dissatisfied with the slow pace of negotiations with Doubledown and Lane's refusal to turn over the more than $75,000 he had collected for the newsletter. First, he repeatedly pushed me and Dan to call the cops on Lane and Clifford Blodgett, the previous managing editor, because they had removed an expensive, big-screen Mac computer from the Players Club's offices. Dan and Blodgett were friends, and before the police were called, Doubledown agreed to return the computer.

Unhappy that the police did not haul Lane away in handcuffs, Dykstra turned up the heat. On May 15, almost a month after he had split from Doubledown, Dykstra dictated a note to me that he wanted sent to all the subscribers who had signed up for "The Dykstra Report" with Doubledown. The note was sent to alert them to "a very serious matter" they should be aware of.

I pleaded with Dykstra not to send the note. Putting readers squarely in the crossfire was bad for business. He didn't care. It didn't matter that he was about to piss away potentially thousands of dollars, enrage customers, and possibly bankrupt his only successful, albeit young, line of business. This was personal, and he wanted to beat Lane at all costs.

He told the subscribers that "The Dykstra Report"—a newsletter they had paid for—had been started without his permission. "Doubledown Media has collected your money, but provided you with no services and will NEVER have the ability to publish the newsletter," the note reads. He told readers that he, the real publisher, had been sending them legitimate stock picks via e-mail as an act of goodwill, but that he could no longer continue to do so unless they were properly signed up. That would surely enrage readers, he told me, and cause them to put the pressure on Doubledown and Lane.

The note urged subscribers to call Randall Lane, the president of Double-down Media, and provided his e-mail address, work phone number, and personal cell phone number. He told them to demand a refund. If he couldn't get at the money, he sure as hell wasn't going to allow Lane to keep it. "This is a regrettable turn of events and your frustration is understandable," the note continues, before offering readers a 50 percent discount on a subscription to "Nails on the Numbers."

Readers were upset, enraged, and confused. The backlash was swift. Some thought the note was a scam because Dykstra refused to sign his name at the bottom of it. They wanted *us* to provide them with a refund immediately, duke it out with Doubledown ourselves, and leave them out of the dispute. Others thanked us and sought our help in getting their money back from the "crooks" at Doubledown. Much to Dykstra's delight, one really mad subscriber even told us he planned to contact the Attorney General's Office and report Doubledown.

However, many subscribers simply did not understand how we were sending them the picks each day if they had signed up with Doubledown, a separate, unrelated company. They were skeptical of our note. How did we get their information or e-mail addresses?

The whole thing was a huge mess and a real eye-opener for me. I had never really had my credibility questioned before, but I was suddenly fielding a steady stream of angry phone calls from customers calling me a "con man" and a "piece of shit." I understood why those people didn't know whom to trust.

Unlike Dykstra, I had a history with most of those customers and felt sorry for them. When they signed up at Doubledown, I sent them their welcome letters or chatted with them on the phone. I had been their point of contact since day one. By mid-May, I was on the other side of the table, telling them Doubledown, the company I had been working for when they signed up, was the bad guy. It was a tough sell for some.

Nonetheless, we started converting the subscribers to "Nails on the Numbers" and signing up new subscribers at a record pace. Before long, we had just shy of $50,000 in new money flowing in by the end of May. At first glance, Dykstra's note appeared to be a minor detour. However, just as we started to build momentum, we got sucker punched in the gut.

Forbes magazine ran an article entitled "Piggyback" questioning whether Dykstra was "relying on a seasoned stand-in" for his newsletter stock picks.[1] Only it wasn't really a question. The article suggested Dykstra was copying his picks from pal Richard Suttmeier.

Dykstra called such allegations a "smear job" and privately fumed, thinking the article had been planted by Randall Lane, once Washington bureau chief for *Forbes*. In September 2011, Lane returned to the publication as editor. I found it hard to disagree with Dykstra's logic. After all, both Suttmeier and Dykstra denied the allegations to *Forbes*, and the article did not have a single person on the record—not one!—suggesting Dykstra wasn't making his own picks. It didn't even have a single source hiding behind anonymous quotes suggesting Dykstra was a fake. It did, however, cite the Doubledown lawsuit.

Although the bulk of the text, headline, subheadings, and a bold chart was dedicated to showing the similarities between the two men's picks during April, the article used all of sixty-five words to tell readers that another analysis of Dykstra's picks from October 2007 showed that only four of the twenty-two recommendations were similar to Suttmeier's that month.

The article ended with the following question: "Why would anyone pay $995 a year for Dykstra's market insights when Suttmeier's *Sector Report* carries many of the same ideas days earlier and charges only $300?"

People say facts don't lie—but they do when they tell only half the story. The article neglected to tell readers how Dykstra's stock selection process really works. Instead of choosing from every stock in the world, Dykstra follows only stocks in his universe—a group of about 100 or so stocks that he accumulated over time and tracks on a regular basis. Since Dykstra follows a short-term trading strategy, not a long-term buy-and-hold approach, he often picks the same stocks multiple times in the same year, seeking to make small profits each time.

Several of Dykstra's picks from April that were similar to Suttmeier's were past winners, a fact the article never mentioned. The very first company listed on the article's chart was United Technologies, a stock that had won for Dykstra at least three separate times the year before. General Electric, Pfizer, and Texas Instruments were also previous winners that Dykstra had returned to that were mislabeled as copycats.

However, probably the article's biggest sin of omission was that Dykstra and Suttmeier used many of the same data points when determining what picks to make. That fact wasn't all that unusual considering Suttmeier taught Dykstra the basics of technical analysis.

In another example of the article's bent, it implied there was something crooked about the relationship between Dykstra and Suttmeier. The article cited

Doubledown's lawsuit, which stated the company entered into negotiations to pay Suttmeier to provide Dykstra with "research assistance" and "lists of recommended stocks daily."

Much like bigwig Wall Street traders have research assistants do their legwork, Dykstra hired Suttmeier's son Jason to provide a spreadsheet every morning containing all sorts of data on all the stocks in his universe. There was nothing unusual or underhanded about this arrangement, despite the article's implication otherwise.

The article also failed to explain to readers the difference between picking stocks and picking options (the latter are much riskier), and the article also didn't even mention the most distinguishing element of Dykstra's system: the "secret sauce." That part of the strategy mirrors a well-known gambling strategy called the Martingale System. It works like this: if you lose, you double your bet the next time and repeat this over and over until you win a hand, erasing your losses. You then return to the smaller, original bet and start the cycle over.

The stock world calls this strategy "averaging down." As a pick goes south, you increase your commitment to it, confident that you made the right decision at the outset and that when the stock or option eventually moves back up, your victory will be even bigger because you have more money invested in the pick. The reason for doing that is to lower the average price paid for contracts. The benefit of lowering the average in Dykstra's system is that it also lowers the price he seeks to sell the options contracts at. In other words, as the option price falls, he never finds himself too far below the surface. The secret sauce in Dykstra's system is knowing when to average down, and he provided updated prices in the Stat Book portion of his newsletter regularly—another key omission by the article.

The bloggers were having a field day with the article. It didn't matter that the piece had serious flaws; it had caught on like wildfire.

Headlines such as "Lenny Dykstra May Have Been Busted by Forbes" and "Lenny Dykstra a Stock Fraud?" were typical. Others stung a bit more. A *Deadspin* post entitled "Lenny Dykstra Remains a Fraud: Lenny Dykstra Still Pretending to Understand Stocks" pulled no punches, ending with the following sentences: "We're not sure why the Lenny Dykstra Is An Unlikely Financial Genius ridiculousness started in the first place, but can we all admit the jig is up now? Please? You've all seen him talk, right?"

In the media, perception is reality, and we were losing the ground war. There was a real feeling among the staff that things could spiral out of control. The mainstream press had largely shied away from following *Forbes*'s lead, but the blogs were running rampant. Below the blogs was a steady stream of negative reader comments, many referencing Dykstra's steroid use.

Following that was a wave of e-mails from existing newsletter subscribers asking me what the hell was going on. Many were the same subscribers who had received Dykstra's earlier letter about Doubledown keeping their money. Just because we had the truth on our side didn't mean we were going to come out on top. And Lenny was becoming impatient.

"YOU NEED TO WRITE BACK TO THIS COCK-SUCKER AND TELL THEM THE TRUTH, AND CLEAR THIS BULLSHIT UP ONCE AND FOR ALL!!" Dykstra wrote in an angry, shouting e-mail to Richard Suttmeier, the man he was accused of copying.

THESE FUCKING PEOPLE ARE SICK AND YOU NEED TO WRITE BACK TO THIS IDIOT AND MAKE IT CLEAR THAT YOU DO NOT PICK MY STOCKS, PERIOD! . . . THIS IS BULLSHIT BY RANDALL LANE. . . . YOU NEED TO TELL THEM THE TRUTH—THEY ARE TRYING TO HURT ME.

Dykstra demanded I coordinate our response and find out why Richard was taking so damn long to respond to his e-mails. It was a Saturday, and I was preparing to go to dinner for my birthday with my family when I stepped outside for a quick conversation.

I quickly learned Suttmeier was celebrating his wedding anniversary and did not appreciate being interrupted. With his wife yelling in the background about Dykstra and with a few drinks under his belt, Suttmeier barked into the phone, taking his frustrations with Dykstra out on me.

He was annoyed that the article referred to him as a little-known stock strategist, and Richard felt Dykstra was trying to screw his son Jason out of $6,000. He said that Dykstra had been paying Jason $2,000 a month to provide him with the stock spreadsheets, but that he had fallen behind.

I mostly listened—the man was clearly upset, and I decided I could absorb some of the verbal jabs because the situation would blow up if he said those things directly to Dykstra.

Following our call, Suttmeier sent a letter to *Forbes* and several other bloggers entitled "Lenny Dykstra's Stock Picks Are His Own." He noted that he and Dykstra were friends and retold the history of how he had taught Dykstra to read a stock chart. He also explained that his son Jason provided a "Table of Technical Levels" to Dykstra for his "universe of about 100 stocks. That's Lenny's Roster. It's Lenny who decides which stocks to put on the field of play."

Following the brouhaha, Suttmeier also appeared on *Tech Ticker*, a Web-based finance show on Yahoo! Hosts Henry Blodget and Aaron Task, who had previously edited Dykstra's columns at TheStreet.com, peppered Suttmeier with questions about the *Forbes* article in an attempt to set the record straight.

"My model portfolio and *Sector Report* is based upon finding stocks near fifty-two-weeks lows that have a 'buy' rating that should trade up," Suttmeier said. "Lenny's deep-in-the-money call options is finding stocks near fifty-two-week lows and then buying a deep-in-the-money call to ride that up. They're parallel there based upon the lessons he learned from reading charts."

Suttmeier reiterated that he was not providing Dykstra with picks. Blodget chimed in that even Cramer read other people's perspectives on stocks and didn't "divine" his ideas out "of the air." Suttmeier's newsletter was one of the items on Dykstra's "smorgasbord" of research and opinions each morning, they noted. Task added that many stock pickers, including himself, took input from several different sources and tended to lean on some sources they liked better than others.

After noting that he didn't get involved with options and he'd "rather not learn how to do it," Suttmeier provided viewers with this insight into Dykstra's approach: "He learned to read the stock charts, the research reports, just like he steps up to the plate as a ballplayer, reads the pitcher, reads the situations, and applies a power swing when he needs to or bunts or steals a base. That's the way he looks at the market."

CHAPTER 18

STRIKING OUT

As the spring of 2008 drew to a close, the Doubledown lawsuit was having its own repercussions. Around the same time that the *Forbes* article debuted, *New York Post* columnist Keith Kelly wrote an article entitled "Freelancers Strike Out: Doubledown-Dykstra Fight Is Costly to Writers."

Although the article was a fair account of the dispute between the two sides, it didn't shine the best light on Dykstra. Doubledown had contracted freelancers, writers, and photographers to work on the *Players Club*, but because Dykstra had printed the second edition of the magazine without the company's permission, Doubledown wasn't sending out any checks. Doubledown said it would "work diligently" with Dykstra to make sure the writers were "paid in full." However, shit rolls downhill, and the freelancers were clearly at the bottom.

Dykstra's lawyer told Kelly that all the freelancers should be paid "once we figure out where all the money went that Lenny gave [Doubledown]." However, at the urging of his confidants, including Arthur Hochstein, and realizing that reporters were the last people he should be making into enemies, Dykstra opened his checkbook to a number of the freelancers caught in the crossfire rather than wait for the court case to play out. It would garner some goodwill, he thought.

It wasn't all bad news in Camp Dykstra, though. By mid-June, just before "Nails on the Numbers" was due to be relaunched with TheStreet.com, Dykstra's stock-picking record had jumped to 22–0, with $26,900 in profits on closed-out trades. The *Post* article also noted that Lane was "reluctantly" offering refunds to customers of "The Dykstra Report."

The Dykstra clan was also basking in the excitement surrounding Cutter Dykstra, Lenny and Terri's eighteen-year-old son. Cutter was making headlines as the next generation of Nails to hit the ball field. "Young Dykstra Has More Than a Name: Son of Former Major Leaguer Has Talent of His Own," read one headline from MLB.com. The *New York Times* proclaimed a few months before the June draft that "Dykstra, Like His Father, Is Reckless in Good Way."

The kid, who was more polite and well spoken like his mom, but crashed into walls like his dad, played ball for Westlake High School in Westlake Village, California, when he began attracting the attention of major league scouts. Terri told the *Times* that Cutter was more "refined" than his dad and not "a pigpen away from baseball, like Lenny." At just shy of six feet tall and 180 pounds, Cutter was bigger than his dad at that age too.

"I want people saying that's Lenny's son," Cutter told *Sports Illustrated*. "I want people saying, 'He looks just like his dad. He plays just like his dad. He approaches the game just like his dad.' . . . When I get on the field, I want to put on a show for people."[1]

Cutter, however, wasn't always slated to follow in his dad's footsteps. Lenny didn't want Cutter to play baseball just because of the family legacy. "I would be there for him if he were, say, playing in the chess championships," Lenny told the *Ventura County Star*. "I never pushed him to play baseball. Heck, he was a great golfer. He is a great golfer. But he chose baseball. He's got a lot of talent. He's bigger and stronger than I was."[2]

In the days leading up to the draft, there was speculation that Cutter might be drafted as high as the first round, and he rapidly moved up several scouts' draft board. "He can fly and he's an offensive weapon," Lenny told MLB.com. "Cutter's got thunder to all fields and he's a run-scoring machine. His ceiling is very high. He is very raw. . . . He's going to play in the big leagues and . . . he's going to put people in the seats."[3]

With a scholarship to UCLA waiting in the wings, Cutter decided to enter the draft, just like his dad, and was scooped up by the Milwaukee Brewers organization in the second round, with the fifty-fourth overall pick. It wasn't as high as the Dykstra family had hoped, but it was nothing to be ashamed of either. Plus, the pick came with a sizable signing bonus and was the first step in the path to the big leagues. "He's going to go out and play pro ball; he's not going to screw around," Lenny told MLB.com. "It is my belief if you want to play and you get drafted in a high spot, you go after it and chase your dreams."

With Lenny back in California and Cutter preparing for life away from Thousand Oaks and the Gretzky mansion, I called my boss to offer my congratulations. "You must be very proud," I said to Lenny, who offered a quick "yeah" before changing the topic. Instead, he had a proposition for me. "Chris, do you have wheels?" he asked. I told him that I did, but that my car was more than a decade old. That was great news, Dykstra said, because he had a deal for me.

He was selling Cutter's souped-up black Charger SRT8, which had a number of aftermarket enhancements done to it. "It's a $60,000 car, but you can have it for $40,000 in cash. It'll be sweet," he said, noting that even if I didn't want the car, I could turn around and sell it for a hefty profit. Either way, he wanted to dump it. I told him there was no way I could afford to pay that much money, especially since he was way behind in paying me my salary. That ended the conversation real quick.

Instead, he sold it to Shannon Illingworth, the founder of Corona, California–based AVT, a publicly traded microcap company that made high-tech vending machines that Dykstra thought were awesome. Illingworth was introduced to Dykstra by the taller, slimmer of the two Ricks—Rich O'Connor. Illingworth, in turn, brought two of his pals, ex-NFLers, to a meeting with Dykstra. One of the men expressed interest in the Charger.

"Lenny kept calling me, saying, 'Hey, your friend's gonna buy the car? Your friend's gonna buy the car?' He was driving me crazy," Illingworth recalls. Instead, Illingworth reluctantly took the car, paying Dykstra $30,000 for it. "It's a beautiful car. I still have it. I love it."

However, Illingworth and Dykstra had serious business to discuss as well. Illingworth says he wanted Dykstra's help in getting the vending machines placed inside the locker rooms of Major League Baseball stadiums. AVT was a small company and could really use a boost.

The exact details surrounding the professional relationship between Dykstra and Illingworth would later become the source of heated debate and much confusion. In Randall Lane's book *The Zeroes: My Misadventures in the Decade Wall Street Went Insane,* which was released in June 2010, he claimed his reporting revealed that Illingworth paid Dykstra approximately $250,000 in a secret stock deal in return for promoting AVT via TheStreet.com and getting him access to Jim Cramer.

Lane said the stock was issued to Dykstra's brother-in-law, Keith Peel, without Peel's knowledge, in order to hide the impropriety from regulators. Lane's source? Rich O'Connor. In a column on *The Daily Beast*, Lane wrote that O'Connor showed him copies of the stock certificates he had snatched from Lenny's mansion.[4]

When researching *Nailed!*, I also spoke with O'Connor. He made the same claims to me repeatedly, but failed to produce the stock certificates. O'Connor had always been very nice to me, but I knew to be cautious about what he told me.

O'Connor had also told me a story involving Dykstra and the files for the second edition of the *Players Club* magazine that turned out to be wrong. I didn't suspect that he was lying on purpose, but rather that he made assumptions that turned out to be wrong.

When Lane interviewed Illingworth, he said that he denied giving Dykstra the stock, but that the idea for Dykstra to promote AVT stock on TheStreet.com was mutual. Illingworth filed a $100 million lawsuit against Lane and his publisher, the Penguin Group, for false statements and libel. "We are simply not going to allow anyone to publicly defame AVT in this matter without taking action against them," Illingworth announced in a press release. He later dropped the lawsuit, saying that he wasn't going to "beat a dead horse" and that he wanted to focus on the positives and run his company.

Illingworth tells me that Lane's allegations were "slander," designed as a "smear campaign" to sell more books. His business dealings with Dykstra were centered on gaining wider distribution for his vending machines, he reports.

"It wasn't stock promotion," he says. "There's a big difference between stock promotion and consulting." Illingworth was willing to pay Dykstra to facilitate such a deal with Major League Baseball. He told reporter Teri Buhl of HedgeTracker.com the stock in question was issued as a private placement with restricted shares, but that neither Dykstra nor Peel was ever actually given the stock and that the issue was canceled in early April because Dykstra and Peel didn't have the kind of influence they claimed to have.[5]

"We were negotiating an agreement, and it was contemplated and we were going to do something, but it was never consummated," Illingworth tells me. "We never gave it to Lenny. Never gave it to Keith. It was never given to them, period," he says. "You can't cancel stock if you [physically] give shares to somebody."

O'Connor says Illingworth was peeved he didn't get "more plugs" from Dykstra or a promised meeting with Cramer, and that's why the deal fell apart, according to Randall Lane's account.

To add insult to injury, Illingworth tells me his interaction with Dykstra left him $15,000 poorer. When the two first met, Illingworth became a quick believer in Dykstra and the magic wand he wielded. He showed Illingworth his stock-picking system and told him for a minimum investment of $12,000 to $15,000, he could make Illingworth serious cash.

"I was fascinated with it, but I didn't really get it or understand all of it," Illingworth says. "I told him I would get more people to put in if it works."

Illingworth says he put $15,000 into one of Dykstra's Trade King brokerage accounts and periodically logged in to see how his money was performing. One day, he was unable to log in—the password had been changed. "The money was gone, and I was pretty much done with him."

Unaware of the craziness among Illingworth, Dykstra, and O'Connor going on behind the scenes in California, I was simply told to treat Illingworth as a VIP and to hire another editor right away for a new newsletter called "Making Money with Microcaps." Dykstra said it would highlight different penny stocks—including AVT.

I told Dykstra he had to be careful when promoting a publicly traded business partner via any news service because of regulatory guidelines. "Don't worry. I'll have my lawyers check it out," Dykstra replied.

Back in New York, I knew the perfect person for the job. At Money-Media, I had worked with a reporter named Chris Witkowsky. He was a blue-collar kind of guy who could write about complicated, and often, dry material in an interesting way for directors of companies like Starbucks and Microsoft. I offered him a nice bump in salary and a year-end bonus tied to revenue. Chris was up for the challenge, turning away another job offer in order to join Team Lenny.

The following week I received an e-mail before I was to send "Nails on the Numbers" out to our 100 or so subscribers. Dykstra wanted me to include a "bonus" pick (AVT) in the column and sent me a chunk of text that I should plop into the column. It was supposedly written by Dykstra, but didn't sound like him at all. It featured Dykstra telling readers that as he was strolling though McCarron Airport in Las Vegas, he saw a man from Australia buying a prepaid phone from a large 011 Mobile Kiosk. He was blown away by the technology, which was made by AVT, and he went home and looked up the company on the Internet.

I knew the story was pure BS because Dykstra never flew with "the herd," his name for commercial airline passengers. He didn't ever waste his time at baggage claim, as he indicated in the story. Rather, he always flew on private jets and had his baggage hand-delivered to his waiting town car, SUV, or limousine. The writing was awful, and the message was nonsense, but it's what Dykstra wanted.

Illingworth, for his part, says he does not know where the text came from, noting that it was sent only to subscribers of Dykstra's newsletter and placed on Dykstra's own site, which weren't "that strong," and not posted on TheStreet.com. The column, which came out approximately two months after Illingworth claims he canceled the stock that was to be issued to Dykstra, wasn't part of a stock promotion deal, he says. Rather, "it was simply throwing a name out there in his newsletter, saying, 'Hey, this is a fascinating company; take a look at it.' That was it. . . . He was trying to get my attention."

Dykstra later asked me to pull the column off the site, saying it was "embarrassing."

CHAPTER 19

KEEP MOVING THE CHAINS

My job was consuming me. I couldn't go to dinner, a movie, or even the wedding of a close friend without being distracted by Dykstra. Part of it was my fault because even when Dykstra wasn't calling me, work was almost always on my mind—it was infectious.

However, I held out hope that over time my work-life balance would return to normal as we built a solid corporate infrastructure. That's what appeared to be happening. My main goal was to surround Dykstra with smart, loyal, intelligent, hardworking people. We were making progress.

In addition to Dan, Chris, and myself, Dykstra hired James Kouledianos from MLB.com and Sirius Satellite Radio to handle his publicity, help secure interviews, and lure potential player reps to the Players Club. Also in New York, Dykstra hired Joanne Katsch, a top executive at American Express Publishing, to help build the staff. She had connections we needed to publish the *Players Club* in-house. Dykstra believed that in addition to her qualifications, Katsch would help secure a partnership with American Express on a cobranded credit card and possibly the financial slice of the Players Club.

On the West Coast, we finally had a strong assistant in Samantha Kulchar, a Brooklyn-bred go-getter who also served as Dykstra's business manager. She was smart and organized, and she established a level of structure that provided all of us in New York with a certain amount of comfort.

The hard work also seemed to be paying off for me personally. I was building myself a nice second income stream. Dykstra was in discussions to lure Eric Bolling, and his "Bolling for Dollars" newsletter idea, to our company. Bolling and I began working on designs for the site, and I began editing his columns, which were now appearing on TheStreet.com. Dykstra had helped him secure the deal.

Dykstra's own deal with TheStreet.com called for him to receive a hefty payout—between 60 and 70 percent of sales of "Nails on the Numbers." Ultimately, Dykstra wanted Bolling to join his own stable of newsletters, and we would negotiate a similar deal, taking a slice of Bolling's cut.

Dykstra told me I could make extra cash editing Bolling. However, until their deal was hashed out, which was supposed to happen any day, Bolling and I decided to wait to discuss specific dollar amounts.

Unlike the vagaries surrounding my arrangement with Bolling, Dykstra set up a much more clear-cut deal between me and Tim Brown, the former Oakland and Los Angeles Raiders perennial Pro Bowl wideout. TheStreet.com wanted to feature Brown in a regular column, and Brown needed a ghostwriter, meaning I could make "a little extra glue on the side," Dykstra said. TheStreet.com would pay Brown $4,000 a month, and Brown, in turn, would pay me half, Dykstra explained.

Known as Mr. Raider because of his strong association with the team during his seventeen-year pro career, Brown also had won the Heisman Trophy in 1987 as college football's best player while suiting up for Notre Dame. I didn't know how far back their relationship stretched, but Dykstra said they were friends, and I had seen Brown preach the Players Club core message in a five-page article in the first edition of the magazine entitled "How I Built an Empire."

"Listen, my wife has a nice car, but she has her eye on a nicer car. That's real, brother," he wrote. "You also have to keep in mind that a dollar is not necessarily a dollar, not with taxes and paying your agent and living in California for sixteen years."

Brown also talked up his various business ventures: Tim Brown Racing and Locker 81 Fundraising Solutions. Tim Brown Racing's goal was to help diversify NASCAR and to become the first NASCAR team in which minorities owned the majority of the team. Locker 81's goal was to supplant cookies and candy with prepaid Visa cards as top fund-raising items for youth organizations. Brown's company made money from the sale of such cards, while helping to cut obesity in the U.S., particularly among kids.

In the article, Brown said he considered himself a "front office type guy" and that he took pride when people said he was "intelligent" or that he handled "the game the way it should be handled." To Dykstra, he was a "spear-chucker," a term he threw around pretty regularly. Dykstra thought he didn't "know shit about stocks, but I can help him with the picks, and you can write for him," Dykstra told me.

Brown's column for TheStreet.com was a watered-down clone of Dykstra's. It was much less complicated, and his system much more informal. Unlike

Dykstra's system, Brown's column focused on stocks and provided no guidance on when investors should exit a pick.

It did, however, feature analogies between sports (mostly football) and the financial markets, insights from a well-known athlete, and a catchy sign-off. Dykstra ended each article with the phrase "Always remember: Life is a journey, enjoy the ride" while Brown told readers to "Keep Moving the Chains!," a football term synonymous with keeping a drive alive.

Unlike Dykstra, my direct interaction with Brown was limited. I had one quick initial phone conversation with him about the column and our financial agreement and then mostly corresponded via e-mail.

Because Dykstra thought Brown wasn't very market savvy, he was going to help Brown select the stocks to feature in the columns and then would send me the picks along with his picks for "Nails on the Numbers." When writing the columns, I relied on the only piece of advice Dykstra gave to me: "Make Tim sound real humble . . . respectful."

With the near-instant success of "Nails on the Numbers," Bolling on the verge of joining the team, Tim Brown's column, "Making Money with Microcaps," and all the recent additions to Team Dykstra, the future suddenly looked bright again.

CHAPTER 20

MISERABLE MILLIONAIRE

When we arrived at his hotel, Dykstra was sitting alone in a small dark room. "I'm a miserable millionaire," he professed to James, Chris, and me as he groaned about the shitty accommodations and how one of the hotel's staffers had stolen $500 from him.

The Trump Tower was his new home because staffers at the Carlyle had been offended when he loudly used the word "nigger" in the lobby and had booted him out, he said. The three of us had been summoned to Dykstra's digs under the guise of a late-night meeting, but I knew it was an excuse for an extended hangout session with his new entourage.

Dykstra immediately perked up upon our arrival, and before long his primary focus became getting a new phone even though he had three other working cell phones. It was almost 1:00 a.m., and virtually all of the Verizon stores were closed, but Dykstra couldn't wait. James said he might be able to help and excused himself to make a phone call. That's when Dykstra dropped a bombshell on Chris.

"We're not doing the penny stock newsletter anymore," he said nonchalantly, before changing the topic back to his broken cell phone. I was mortified—this was Chris's first meeting with Dykstra, and I had just hired him to run "Making Money with Microcaps." As Chris and I sat there worrying about his future with the company, James came back in the room, delivering a sliver of good news: a friend of his owned a Verizon store in Manhattan and was rushing down from his home in the Bronx to open it up especially for Dykstra.

"All right, bro, good job," Dykstra said as he excitedly sprang up from the couch and marched toward the door. We followed. As we walked down the golden hallway with Dykstra in the lead, he slowed down and began to reenact some mischief from his glory days, lightening the mood significantly.

He told us how he, as a young party animal, would try and rouse veteran catcher Gary Carter from his bed late at night to join the boys down in the bar. Carter would typically stay in his room reading his Bible and had no interest in partaking in the night-after-night shenanigans typical of the 1986 New York Mets.

"I was all about staying in my room and getting my rest and being ready each day," Carter told me. "I was not one to go out."

Turning his back to some other guest's hotel room, Dykstra lifted up his knee and violently swung the sole of his shoe backward into the door, flashing a devilish grin in our direction. "I used to stand outside Carter's room horse-kicking the door until he came out," Dykstra proudly told us, his eyes widening as he peeked out from underneath his Maybach cap. He then repeatedly mock-kicked the door half a dozen more times, chuckling the whole time and looking at us to make sure we were watching.

"Oh, man, he hated it," Dykstra said, adding that he had pushed Carter too far one night and the Hall of Fame catcher opened the door and lifted him up by the collar. James, Chris, and I laughed. "No, bro, I'm dead serious," Dykstra said in a no-nonsense tone of voice. "He's a strong dude."

Carter recalled the event as well. "Oh, yeah, that was Lenny until I picked him up and pinned him against the door and told him never to do that again," Carter said. "I think he knew where I was coming from when I said that."

In the weeks leading up to our Trump Towers gathering, I had settled into a groove with Dykstra. I had been steadily transitioning the Doubledown subscribers over to "Nails on the Numbers," a massive undertaking, and Dykstra and I would chat on the phone starting around midnight each night about the newsletter, magazine, or whatever was on his mind.

In reality, we needed just five minutes to talk shop, but the calls often turned into marathon sessions, lasting hours. I suspected Dykstra called because he wanted company or needed to vent. He didn't have close friends by his side, and he loved Terri and their boys, but they weren't even living in the same house (Dykstra was in the Gretzky mansion, while Terri and their youngest son stayed at their other home).

So, for hours, I was Dykstra's sounding board. We did a little bit of work, he got things off his chest, and in the end he felt better. Determined not to let the hours slip away needlessly, I reserved this time to ghostwrite Dykstra's "Nails on the Numbers" column. While he talked in circles, I typed away, creating a more coherent version of Dykstra for his readers.

The hours sucked, but the chats gave me a chance to understand him better. Sure, Dykstra could be an abrasive jerk at times, but that was just one side of him. I empathized with the guy when he felt people weren't taking him seriously.

The initial thrill of working for Lenny Dykstra, Mets folk hero, wore off after just the first few weeks. What was left was what I considered at the time to be a deeply flawed, but decent, human being with overambitious dreams and a lot of physical and mental scars. I really wanted to help him (and myself) succeed.

One of the major reasons people didn't last in Lennyland was because they failed to take the time, or exhibit the patience, to figure out how to interact with the unorthodox and peculiar Dykstra. I, on the other hand, was equipped with Dorothy's rules and was learning a few things on my own.

The quick success of "Nails on the Numbers" also provided some much-needed relief to Dykstra's troubled empire. The company was created with no start-up capital, but as the president of Nails Investments, the publisher of "Nails on the Numbers," I was able to issue checks within six weeks of our launch date to all the vendors who had helped the newsletter get off the ground.

We also bailed out portions of Dykstra's capsizing Players Club. Although the Players Club and Nails Investments shared an office, they were completely different companies. However, in addition to paying freelancers who worked for the magazine from the Nails Investments account, I issued $34,000 worth of checks to pay off Dykstra's past-due May rent and on-time June rent for the Player's Club.

The revenue from "Nails on the Numbers" also allowed me to pay Chris regularly and to pay Dan, an employee of the Players Club, some of his unpaid back salary. From what was left I was even able to pay myself a small chunk of salary ($5,000 of $19,000 owed). Up to that point, nearly two months into my tenure, I had not collected a single paycheck.

I could have paid myself most of the salary I was owed, but then there wouldn't have been enough to pay Dan, Chris, or the vendors keeping the businesses running. As president, I felt I had an obligation to do what was best for the company and the staffers. I would eat last, a decision that was made easier because of the apparent success of the newsletter. I was confident I would be paid shortly, and as long as I had enough cash to keep a roof over my head and food in my belly, I was fine.

We were on track to make a lot of money and were doing things the right way. However, Dykstra quickly poisoned the well with his unreasonable expectations and huge unpaid bills that had nothing to do with Nails Investments. This was infuriating.

I was reduced to putting out Dykstra's latest financial fires seemingly on a daily basis. I would wake up in the morning to see an e-mail from Dykstra to some person I had never heard of before, telling him or her to contact me for their cash.

Dykstra's personal lawyer wanted his $15,000 monthly fee. "No problem," Dykstra told the lawyer; "Chris Frankie will pay you immediately." Tim Murray, his former flight attendant who was now head of distribution for the Players Club, hadn't been paid in quite a while. Again, not an issue he told Tim; just see Chris. These kinds of requests became commonplace, and pretty soon Nails Investments was broke.

Some bills were relatively small, such as Dykstra's phone bill, and others were huge, such as a $250,000 invoice from technology vendor Space 150. He was bankrupting the business and leaving me in the unenviable position of having to tell many people that I could not pay them the money Dykstra had promised because we simply didn't have it. Furthermore, I had to buy time with the vendors who worked with Nails Investments. We also couldn't buy office equipment, leaving me to work on my personal laptop and Chris to borrow one from his girlfriend. The whole thing was embarrassing.

Making matters worse was the fact that Dykstra was trying to weasel out of the deal between the two of us. Seeing his debt to me growing quickly, he wanted me to collect half my monthly salary from Eric Bolling. The request was absurd not only because the work I did for Bolling didn't warrant $5,000 a month, but also because editing Bolling's column was extra work for which I was promised extra pay.

"Did Bolling pay you yet?" Dykstra would ask me on a seemingly daily basis. "No? Man, these people think they don't have to pay. It's unreal." Bolling, in fact, had not paid me as he and Dykstra still hadn't worked out the parameters of their deal. In the meantime, I had begun editing his columns as a courtesy with the anticipation of a deal that never came.

Each time Dykstra complained about Bolling, I reminded him I was not going to ask Bolling for $5,000 a month. Dykstra, however, was insistent. "Eric owes you funds that you and Dan need to collect in order to replenish the Nails account so that you and Dan can pay yourselves," Samantha Kulchar wrote to me in one e-mail, echoing Dykstra's instructions. She also said Dykstra told her we should pay the business's other bills with the money from Bolling.

The charade was getting out of hand, and I knew I had to act. While I was at Dykstra's hotel one morning, he again started in on the Bolling rap. I was nervous because confronting Dykstra required a carefully orchestrated balancing act. "Lenny, Eric hasn't paid me yet, but my deal with him is independent of the money you owe me," I said in a respectful but firm manner. "I am holding you to our original deal."

He had been testing my boundaries. I stood my ground, and, to my surprise, he did not argue. Rather, he backed away sheepishly like he knew he had been caught trying to put one over on me. He told me he appreciated that I was putting the business first and not hounding him for money and that my day to get paid would soon come. "You get it," he said. "You see the big picture. I like that."

He told me he had money, but that it was tied up in nonliquid assets, such as his mansion and private jet. "I'm having some liquidity issues, but it's short term," he said. Dykstra told me that a multimillion-dollar loan would fund in just eight days and that he was working on securing a bridge loan in the meantime to help with our day-to-day expenses.

"I'm not used to this situation," Dykstra said to me, sounding deflated. "Usually, I'm the one with money and others come to me." This was not the bravado-filled Dykstra I was used to—he sounded defeated. "Hang in there just a little longer, bro. The money will come," he said to me, sounding as if he might have also been talking to himself.

The Gretzky mansion, which Dykstra had purchased for $17.5 million, was also on the verge of being sold for a hefty profit, Dykstra told me. "The house is recession-proof," he said. "There's no bad market for someone buying a $25 million house." Bloggers ran headlines such as "Lenny Dykstra Discovers Tennis Court, Wants to Sell Mansion," or "Lenny Dykstra's $29 Million House for Sale" and "Lenny Dykstra Has Lost His Kids."

He told reporters that the mansion is "a compound, it's not a house" and that he could "go for a couple of days and not see any other family members." Dykstra privately told me that singing legend Barbara Streisand was the buyer. She didn't end up purchasing the place, but Dykstra told me over the course of the next month that several other prominent celebrities were going to buy the mansion. Next it was actor Mark Wahlberg, followed by Paul Pierce of the NBA champion Boston Celtics.

Finally, he said the King of Pop was planning to join the other celebs in the Sherwood Country Club. "Tito and Jermaine Jackson came by today," he said with a laugh. "They're looking for a house for Michael." I asked Lenny if he really wanted to be responsible for bringing the circus surrounding Jacko to the quiet community. "You're right. Fuck him. Good call, bro."

Lenny's mounting money problems were cause for concern, but I believed the troubles were short term, like he said. I chalked up the chaos surrounding the invoices and unpaid bills to the typical craziness and disorganization that followed Dykstra everywhere. And it was hard not to notice that the big boss didn't appear too worried, as he continued to dart across the country in private jets and live large at expensive hotels.

Plus, random acts of generosity went a long way, even if they sometimes smelled fishy. Stuck at the office one night, I received a call from Dykstra with an unusual request. He wanted me to call thirty-six-year-old interior designer Bridget Nisivoccia, an advertiser in the *Players Club*, and get money from her for a paid advertisement in the magazine.

Nisivoccia, whom the *New York Daily News* described as a "pretty blond," would make headlines of her own just a month later as "yet another beauty" linked to Peter Cook. At the time, Cook was embroiled in a very nasty, bitter, and public divorce from former supermodel Christie Brinkley. That showdown included allegations that Cook had an affair with his then-eighteen-year-old office assistant, spent $3,000 a month on Internet porn, and was caught by his children masturbating to the sexually explicit material.[1] Brinkley also said Cook was caught by law enforcement buying drugs at a "gay" truck stop. Cook denied his ex-wife's allegations.[2]

"Tell Bridget I dropped the check she gave me into a puddle by accident," Dykstra instructed me. "It's unreadable." Instead of a replacement, he wanted her to bring $15,000 in cash to his hotel room immediately. "If she brings it, I will give you two bones, bro—2,000 bucks. It's easy money."

I knew the task wasn't worth a $2,000 payout, but I wasn't about to turn it down either since Dykstra was way behind in paying my salary. I jumped off the call and dialed up Nisivoccia, who said she couldn't make it that night but would come first thing in the morning.

Once at Dykstra's suite, I worked feverishly on my laptop. Dykstra, on the other hand, was out of it. He told me he had been awake for five days straight. I didn't know if this was another one of his exaggerations, but if his assertion were true, I didn't want to know how he pulled it off.

However, one thing was clear: Dykstra was a drooling mess. As he sat on the couch across from me with a pile of crumpled preproduction *Players Club* print-outs on the table in front of him, Dykstra fell in and out of coherency. One minute he was repeatedly mumbling "Bonesaw knows," a line from the movie *Spiderman*, at a barely audible level, and the next he was sleeping sitting up with his head slumped forward and his baseball cap covering his eyes.

At one point around 3:00 a.m., I looked over and Dykstra had whipped cream from his ice cream sundae smeared on his cheeks and a half-chewed Twizzler dangling from his mouth like a cigarette as he lay there asleep. This, I thought to myself, cannot be happening. But I knew he needed the sleep, so I went about my ghostwriting and editing.

By the time Nisivoccia showed up with her boyfriend, photographer Rob Tringali, a few hours later, Dykstra was awake, refreshed, and lucid, moving around the room like a man on a mission. She handed Dykstra a check. "What's this?" he said, looking up at her and holding the check in his open palm as if to indicate it felt light. "Chris told you to bring cash."

Dykstra insisted she run to the bank and get cold, hard cash. When she returned, she handed Dykstra an envelope stuffed with $100 bills. He counted out twenty and handed them to me. I was not used to carrying that much cash, but I folded it in half, slid the money into my pants pocket, and went on my way.

CHAPTER 21

CHRIS THE CONTROLLER

The "sure thing" loan Dykstra was banking on didn't pan out, leaving Chris and James to share the lone computer in the office. We no longer had much money from "Nails on the Numbers" coming directly to us either. Following the relaunch in late June, TheStreet.com began handling the publication's accounting. The plan was to send us a check once every three months.

The first payday was set for July 15. That meant that until we received the money, we couldn't reimburse any of the staff for company-related expenses or pay salaries. We also couldn't pay the office rent or institute health benefits or any of the other items Dykstra had promised. Plus, that money had to last us until the following payment three month later in October.

Back in the office, I tried my best to keep the staff on an even keel. Having killed "Making Money with Microcaps," Dykstra regularly sought a reason to sack Chris. I tried to find work—any work, including hooking up printers and running errands—for Chris to do until the *Players Club* finished its run with American Express Publishing. We could surely find a writing position for him on the magazine's staff once we brought it in-house, I thought.

However, for all the crazy mistakes Dykstra made, he also took extra steps to try and make me feel important to his team. In a beautifully designed media kit folder, he prominently listed the Players Club's executive team. It read:

Lenny Dykstra, Chairman and CEO
Willie Mays, Director of Player Development
Harold Reynolds, Director of Player Development
Wayne Gretzky, Director of Player Development
Richard Suttmeier, Principal and Investment Advisor

Paul Hollins, Certified Financial Planning Expert
Dan Della Sala, Sr. Certified Financial Planning Expert
Daniel Petrocelli, Corporate Litigator
James Kouledianos, Director of Media
Chris Frankie, Controller

I was stunned to see my name included alongside legends such as the Great One and the Say Hey Kid. I was even more surprised to see my title listed as controller. It's a financial designation that I had not previously discussed with Dykstra and that I was not qualified to hold. He later told me that he gave me the title because "you control things."

Dykstra's quest for information to include in a separate glossy booklet for the Players Club also led to one of the most embarrassing business meetings I've ever been a part of. Melissa, the managing director for a firm that helps companies with accurate financial projections so that they can secure funding, came to our office on short notice because we needed such projections right away. She was giving up her Friday night as a favor to her friend Joanne Katsch, one of the Players Club's top executives.

Once at the meeting, Dykstra told Melissa that he needed the projections at 11:00 p.m. that night. The work involved in pulling together a five-year income statement and complex financial calculation would take a few weeks at minimum, she told him. They needed to get down to business right away, and she began to ask him questions about the Players Club.

Dykstra, for his part, had little interest in letting Melissa run the meeting the way she wanted. When she inquired about the Players Club's revenue, Dykstra responded with a story about how during his playing days he used to bang chicks in his hotel room and let the "batboys hide in the closet and watch." When she asked about the company's preferred partners, Dykstra told how he had "impregnated three women in the same night and made them all get abortions."

When the meeting was over, Dykstra headed out, leaving Chris, Melissa, and me standing in the office. I noticed one of Dykstra's bags on the floor and darted down the hallway to return it to him. When I caught up with him, he directed me to walk with him.

We descended the thirty-nine stories in the elevator, passed through security, and walked out to the street to Dykstra's waiting car. He told me to get in. I declined because I didn't have my wallet, cell phone, or insulin. He insisted, saying that as soon as the car dropped him off at his hotel, he would have the driver bring me back.

The meeting ended up being yet another marathon chat, and by the time I returned hours later and convinced security to let me back in because I had no identification, Chris and Melissa were long gone.

Dykstra wanted Melissa's projections to be displayed in a high-end glossy booklet he needed for an upcoming event in California. Dykstra was planning a West Coast launch party for the *Players Club* that was going to be bigger and better than the one in New York and would make everyone forget about the Doubledown debacle, he said.

The new bash was slated for Monday, July 15, the same week Major League Baseball was playing its All-Star Game at Yankee Stadium and that ESPN was holding its annual awards show, the ESPYs, in Los Angeles. Dykstra engaged event planner Event Eleven to arrange a no-holds-barred blowout for 350 athletes, celebrities, friends, and potential business partners at the iconic Mr. Chow's restaurant, a celebrity hangout in Beverly Hills. The cost? An estimated $650,000 for a five-hour party.

The centerpiece of the evening's festivities was to be rapper Lil Wayne, also known as Weezy. Dykstra agreed to pay Weezy $125,000 to sing four songs at the party, walk on the red carpet, participate in at least five or six on-site press interviews, and conduct a meet-and-greet session with Players Club executives an hour prior to showtime.

Dykstra was cashing in at the height of Weezy mania. Born Dwayne Michael Carter Jr., he had just released an album entitled *Tha Carter III* that had sold more than 1 million copies in the first week after its release on June 10. Known best for his commercially successful single "Lollipop," Weezy was being touted as "the Best Rapper Alive" by *Time* magazine.[1]

In the article, *Time* described Lil Wayne's sound as "Redd Foxx covering Bob Dylan." The article went on to note that over a four-year period, the twenty-five-year-old Lil Wayne "morphed from a mediocre rapper with a thuggish point of view into a savant who merges sex, drugs and politics with a sneaky intellect, a freakish knowledge of pop culture and a voice out of the Delta."

To many, his look was just as intriguing as his sound. Television talk show host Jimmy Kimmel once described Weezy as a "walking museum." The perpetually stoned Weezy sported big dreadlocks and bragged about having more than $150,000 worth of gold and diamonds in his mouth—diamond-studded tooth replacements and the like.

In addition to the permanent dental jewelry, Lil Wayne sported a lot of ink. He has the words "fear" and "god" tattooed on his eyelids and several teardrops engraved next to his eyes and mouth to represent dead loved ones. He has a tattoo on the inside of his lip and a script letter "C" on his forehead between his eyes. It's supposed to be a tribute to his mom, Cita, but in an odd way, its placement reminds me of Charles Manson's swastika.

Behind the scenes, the party was falling apart. "I was so humiliated to have to explain to the event planner that gazillionaire Lenny Dykstra didn't have enough money to pay for the party," says Dykstra assistant Samantha Kulchar. "They had booked Mr. Chow's, which is only booked twice a year because of difficult city permits; carved out the time on Lil Wayne's schedule; and deployed countless people to start working feverishly on the party."

Rather than owning up to the real reason for the party's failure, Dykstra chose a convenient scapegoat: Lil Wayne. In an e-mail to a top executive at American Express, Dykstra said he wanted to explain the reason the party had been canceled.

"Late last week, we became aware of a scheduling conflict from the event planner," Dykstra wrote. "Lil Wayne was ordered to report to court in Las Vegas on drug charges. His attorney feels that he will likely be detained on that day by the authorities. Obviously, this is not what the Players Club wants to be associated with."

Dykstra went on to say that it's "almost spooky" how the Lil Wayne incident solved his problem because his instincts told him that the party was "all wrong. . . . I never felt right about the timing of this party, especially with the All-Star game going on the same week." Instead, the Players Club would plan a "monster" Super Bowl party, he said.

"Lenny just told everyone that he had to cancel the event because Lil Wayne was headed to jail, which was completely untrue," Kulchar says.

At the same time the party was imploding, Dykstra made maintaining relationships with our counterparts at TheStreet.com more difficult. After blowing off a meeting at TheStreet, Dykstra wanted to know how many new subscribers "Nails on the Numbers" had signed up. Finding out proved to be a difficult task, driving a major wedge between me and Dave Sterman, an editor at TheStreet.com responsible for the newsletter.

One Friday evening, I sent Sterman an e-mail asking for the data. He said he didn't have it. I noted that we needed to establish a regular flow of such information so that I could manage the business on my end and provide data to Dykstra when he asked for it.

Sterman responded that "Lenny kind of wants it both ways" because he didn't return editor in chief Dave Morrow's phone calls but still had "expectations of communications." I told Sterman that I wasn't involved with, and couldn't control, when Dykstra spoke to Morrow. However, that shouldn't prevent us from establishing a pipeline for the flow of essential info. I thought that was the end of it.

However, as with every e-mail I sent, I copied Dykstra. He took exception to Sterman's jabs and set out on a mission to try and get him fired. His first e-mail to Sterman was a full-on assault:

> Who the fuck are you? DAVID STERMAN? I NEVER HEARD OF YOU! You don't know when I return DAVE'S CALLS AND IT'S NONE OF YOUR FUCKING BUSINESS!!! YOU GOT SOME BALLS TO POP OFF—LIKE I SAID, I HAVE NEVER HEARD OF YOU! MIND YOUR OWN FUCKING BUSINESS!

Around this time, I started to seriously reevaluate my own judgment in regard to Dykstra and Dorothy, who had set a dangerous precedent for all of the employees by working through the night regularly and not collecting a paycheck. I had received just one paycheck since starting nearly three months earlier. It was hard to imagine walking away—I was in too deep.

I did my best to mask my personal concerns and stay positive. I still had my staff to consider. I believed in the concept behind the Players Club and saw that "Nails on the Numbers" was already a winner. I was just unsure about Dykstra and the perpetual havoc he wreaked intentionally and unintentionally on everything he touched.

When staffers asked about Dykstra's financial issues, I was honest. I told them that it was only natural to feel uneasy, but that they should concentrate on the things they could control, like their work performance. I also told them that ultimately they had to do what was best for them and that I understood if they felt they couldn't stick it out.

"At this point we believed that, although we were all having hardships with Lenny, the idea behind the company and magazine was good enough, and despite Lenny's lack of leadership, the people around him were good enough at what we did that we could turn around the company," says James Kouledianos, Dykstra's PR guy.

CHAPTER 22

GREED IS GOOD

The voice on the other end of the phone whispered, "Blue Horseshoe loves Ana-cott Steel." It was Dykstra reenacting a line from one of his favorite movies, 1987's *Wall Street*, from director Oliver Stone and starring Michael Douglas as the unforgettable white-collar creep Gordon Gekko and Charlie Sheen as young and hungry stock trader Bud Fox. The antitheme of the movie, as stated by Gekko, is that "greed, for lack of a better word, is good. Greed is right. Greed works."

The movie may have been fiction, but it drew significant parallels to Dykstra's life and my job. "The movie has a traditional plot structure: The hungry kid is impressed by the successful older man, seduced by him, betrayed by him, and then tries to turn the tables," film critic Roger Ebert writes in his 1987 review of the film. "The actual details of the plot are not so important as the changes we see in the characters."[1]

The lesser-known line Dykstra was speaking to me refers to an illegal insider-trading scheme Gekko cooks up. As Dykstra uttered those words, in my head I pictured him in Gordon Gekko's suspenders, cupping his hand around his mouth so that no one except me could hear him.

My imagination couldn't have been further from reality. "Bro, did you hear that?" Dykstra asked excitedly, returning to his normal tone. "I'm taking a shit," he said, and then started making overembellished grunting noises and laughing. I thought he was kidding until I heard Dykstra yelling at Terri, telling her to get the hell out of the bathroom.

Anxious to change the subject, I told Dykstra I wouldn't be available to work for him during the upcoming Sunday because my godson Sean was being christened. "You're Jewish?" he asked, sounding confused. "No, Lenny; he's being christened," I said. "You're a jeweler?" he asked again, using his code name for Jewish people. I explained that Sean is Protestant and I'm Catholic.

"All right, bro, how many subscribers did we sign up today?" he asked. It had become a daily question, and I began receiving intermittent updates from Dave Morrow of TheStreet. Sales were taking off, and I gave Dykstra the latest figures. He was excited, and so was I. More sales meant more money coming to our bank account.

I later learned Dykstra was using the information for something else entirely. He would have made Gordon Gekko proud. Dykstra tried to coax several friends and employees into partnering with him on a stock scheme.

"He gave me some insider information on a call on TheStreet.com," says Bill Conlin, a veteran Philadelphia sportswriter. "He said, 'We're gonna beat the number, and one of the reasons we're gonna beat the number is because I've raised so much money for 'em with the subscriptions of my newsletter.'" Translation: Dykstra claimed subscription sales of "Nails on the Numbers," nonpublic information, would push TheStreet.com stock price higher once the figures were released.

Dykstra told Conlin that if he bought $150,000 worth of a certain October 2008 option of TheStreet.com's stock, he could double his money. If that happened, they could split the winnings—$75,000 apiece. However, if the pick didn't "pop" (make money), Dykstra promised to cover Conlin's losses.

"I didn't have that kind of cash, but I went in on my own for $15,000 just before [TheStreet] reported their second quarter [earnings]," Conlin says. The option went up, but not by as much as Dykstra had predicted, and Conlin sold it for $4,500 in profits.

Conlin wasn't the only one lured by Dykstra's inside scoop. A source, whom I know from my time working with Dykstra and who wishes to remain anonymous out of fear of legal troubles, says Dykstra also promised guaranteed profits on TheStreet.com stock. "He basically said I won't lose," the source says. As with Conlin, the source says Dykstra offered to cover any losses. The source did not know anything about stocks, but Dykstra provided instructions on where to wire the money. "We gave him $17,000 and got $24,000 back," the source says.

Insider trading is a white-collar crime that is often hard to prove or prosecute. The litmus test as to whether information is considered "insider information" is fairly straightforward, says Geoff Bobroff, a former trial lawyer for the Securities and Exchange Commission. Insider information is information that a publicly held company has not released, but that if released would cause stock traders to react differently. People using this information have an unfair advantage over other market participants and are committing a crime.

It's not clear how significantly Dykstra's information would have made the stock move, but it was not public and he was trying to profit from it in an underhanded way. However, maybe because I was naïve or because Dykstra wasn't doing much personal trading at the time owing to his finances, I didn't realize until later that he was up to no good. Most of Dykstra's newsletter picks were not actual trades he was completing but rather hypothetical moves he made with pretend money.

As July 15 approached, the date we were to receive our paychecks, I received a call from Samantha Kulchar warning me trouble was brewing in California. Kulchar told me that Dykstra owed brokerage house Oppenheimer and Co. a significant sum and that he was desperate for cash.

One afternoon, she recalls, Dykstra asked her for checks from one of his closed bank accounts. "I asked why, and he basically told me to mind my business," she says, noting that he grabbed the checks, retired to his office, and shut the door. A few days later, she began receiving angry phone calls from at least three different executives at Oppenheimer saying Dykstra had bounced a $300,000 check to their firm.

When Kulchar asked Dykstra what to do, he instructed her to avoid their calls. "He kept saying, 'Just hang up,'" Kulchar recounts. "Of course, they kept calling me. I told them I work for a lunatic. I don't know what he does half the time, and I am not always involved in certain transactions."

That's when she says she received a call from one of the big bosses at Oppenheimer. He explained that Dykstra convinced two of the firm's traders to put a trade through prior to payment clearing with an "I'm good for it promise." The traders were anxious to please Dykstra in hope of winning additional future business from him.

The trade went south, leaving Oppenheimer on the hook for the losses. Kulchar says the executive told her "to convey to Lenny how serious this is and have him call me because if I don't hear from him in twenty-four hours, I will involve the Securities and Exchange Commission and he will not be happy."

Kulchar says that Dykstra intentionally wrote the rubber check to Oppenheimer and that it was commonplace for him to write bad checks both on purpose and by accident. "He's done it so many times, it's ridiculous."

Following the conversation with Oppenheimer, Dykstra began scrambling to pull together the funds. "He knew he was in trouble. They weren't going away quietly," Kulchar says. That Sunday night Kulchar told me that Dykstra would likely intercept the money TheStreet.com was sending to us and that I should be prepared.

Since I was the only authorized signer on the bank account, I contemplated avoiding Dykstra until Tuesday morning and running payroll. That would give me the chance to pay Chris, James, Dan, myself, and a handful of freelancers I had brought into the mix, most of whom were former coworkers, business associates, and friends. But I knew that approach would surely get me fired. Plus, if he was unable to reach me, I assumed he would call TheStreet and have the money sent to him directly.

So when he called, I reluctantly answered. "Listen, Chris, I need you to do something for me," Dykstra said, sounding slightly out of breath. "These two guys from Oppenheimer are going to call you first thing in the morning. I need you to wire them some money . . . the money from TheStreet." I told Lenny that was impossible because that money was earmarked for salary and needed to last us three more months. "I know, but you have to do this," he said, noting we would find some other way to pay the staff. "It's serious. We don't have a choice. Thanks, buddy."

By 7 o'clock the next morning, my phone was ringing off the hook and I had a number of e-mails from the Oppenheimer traders inquiring about the money. One of the men explained that the securities they had purchased on Dykstra's behalf had declined by more than $85,000. At the very least, Dykstra needed to cover the losses.

I told him that TheStreet.com would be wiring us only slightly more than $71,000 and that the money was not Dykstra's personal cash, but that it was supposed to fund the businesses' payroll. He apologized but reiterated that Oppenheimer might have to take the matter to the SEC if we did not pay.

Before I sent the money, Dykstra instructed me to get assurances from the men that they would not sell out of the two stocks they had purchased on his behalf and force him to take the $85,000 loss—he felt the stocks would rebound. Dykstra told me that at least one of the stocks was going to be a big winner: TheStreet.com.

The Oppenheimer brokers told me whatever Dykstra wanted to hear, and I eventually wired them the money. Oppenheimer sold out of the position, sticking Dykstra with the loss, and he refused to pay the remainder. An arbitrator later found Dykstra liable for the remaining $15,988.86.[2]

CHAPTER 23

BLOOD IN THE STREETS

I had been setting the tone in the New York office. Most of the staff told me the calm I exhibited and the faith I showed in Dykstra's businesses in the face of utter disaster provided them with a degree of comfort.

However, once Dykstra swiped the payroll money, the staff was devastated and morale was destroyed. The staff felt betrayed by Dykstra, and I felt like I had let them all down. Under the surface I resented Dykstra, and my blood would boil whenever I thought of him flying around the country on his private jet or ordering room service at the Carlyle while the rest of us lived on austerity because of him.

Chris was the first to take action. When he found out Dykstra had taken our money, he went out for lunch and never came back, informing me later that night that he had quit.

Dykstra "doesn't ever bring someone in and intentionally try and hurt them, but if he does hurt them through collateral damage, he doesn't lose sleep at night," Dorothy explains to me during an interview. "He has unrealistic expectations of how long someone should hang in there and not be taken care of."

A few days later, Samantha was given the boot. In the beginning, Dykstra told everyone that she was major league, a team player. "She got along well enough by being nice at first, but she got exposed a little each day," he later said to me, adding that she had cried when he fired her.

Samantha's departure was a deflating blow to me. As bad as things were, they would have been ten times worse without her. Samantha negotiated many of Dykstra's debts downward, kept the electricity from being shut off in Dykstra's home, helped keep the peace between Lenny and Terri over money issues, and provided an effective bridge between the East Coast and West Coast employees.

Not long after she started, she was receiving ten to fifteen calls a day, or more, from people waiting to be paid for the work they'd done for Dykstra. "These were hardworking people struggling to keep their businesses afloat," she says. "They would front the costs for Lenny because he was very convincing. He would use their resources and money, and he would stiff them completely. It was horrible—I felt like an accomplice to many bad things because I represented him."

When Samantha tried to pay someone, utter chaos ensued. If Dykstra looked at his bank balance and saw there was money in the account, he would grab it regardless of whether there were checks written against that money. "Then I would have to run to the bank to beg them to clear the check or ultimately waive the overdraft fees," she says. "I found myself speeding to the bank at times to intercept his mistakes, like some high-speed espionage scene out of a bad movie. The bankers rolled their eyes when I walked in every day and dreaded my visits."

While at the Gretzky mansion one morning, Samantha and Terri received a call from Keith Peel, Terri's brother, who served at Lenny's leisure. "Keith called and told me that I was being let go," Kulchar said. "I told him that I wasn't going anywhere until they paid me," she said, noting that included her salary, agreed-upon severance, business expenses, and the money she had laid out for COBRA payments because Dykstra did not provide health insurance as promised.

"Terri signed a check for one week's pay and promised the remainder, in writing," Kulchar reports. She took the check and went on her way. Later, when cleaning out her car, she says she found a check to Dykstra from TheStreet.com mixed in with some other papers and wrote to Terri to tell her about it. Kulchar says that because she still had not been paid, she offered to meet Lenny or Terri at the bank so that they could cash the check and give her the money.

Instead, Dykstra maintained that Kulchar was blackmailing him and Terri, an allegation he later repeated to Keith Kelly of the *New York Post*.[1] "At first I was enraged that someone would accuse me of a crime like blackmail," Kulchar says. "Then I realized, it's Lenny. He accuses everyone of blackmail, extortion, theft. It's his only defense when someone calls out his behavior."

Next in line to leave was Arthur Hochstein, the art director at *Time* who was helping Dykstra design the *Players Club*. Dykstra respected Hochstein a great deal, and they had developed what appeared to be a genuine friendship, even though Dykstra constantly complained that Hochstein "never reached for a single check" during their many dinners together.

In a carefully orchestrated e-mail to Dykstra, Hochstein went out of his way to say that, although he valued Dykstra's friendship, he felt he wasn't getting his "due professionally." Translation: Dykstra was racking up a big bill and was late paying it.

Hochstein was paid $100,000 but is still owed $98,000 for additional design work he did for the *Players Club* and items he purchased on Dykstra's behalf but was never reimbursed for, he claims. Dykstra told me that he didn't owe Hochstein a dime and that he was just bellyaching because he was jealous of the attention and money Lenny was giving to Joanne Katsch.

Hochstein didn't intend to walk away from the *Players Club* altogether, but said he wanted to take a step back from their work together so that the debt didn't run up any further and create more tension. When the money issues were resolved, he would resume a more active role, he said. He was going out of his way to treat Dykstra with kid gloves.

"I don't do timeouts," Dykstra told Hochstein. He branded his former friend just another selfish quitter who "doesn't see the big picture." A while after Hochstein "was sent to his room," he filed a lawsuit against Dykstra.

When someone says something negative to Dykstra or tries to convince him to look at things from that person's perspective, he takes that as "unbearable criticism," according to Dorothy. "I've never been able to get inside his head about what he feels because when he hires a new person, he is so upset that very first time when he can't pay them. It's devastating he can't keep that promise," Dorothy explains. "Then, when they quit over it, he gets mad at them. When it doesn't work and they react negatively and quit on him, then it's their fault. . . . I don't know that he feels any remorse."

Katsch, who usually worked from her home in Connecticut, quit a short while later and filed a hefty $630,000 lawsuit against Dykstra for missed salary payments and breach of contract. Ken Baron, an editor Katsch had brought into the mix, also walked away from the project after a very short time owing to Dykstra's repeated insults.

The bloodbath didn't end there. Dykstra had been souring on Dan and James for weeks, growing increasingly nasty and short-tempered. In one instance, Dan sent Dykstra an e-mail saying one of the sports agents on the *Players Club*'s mailing list had not received the magazine. In a shouting, all-caps e-mail, Dykstra responded, "WHAT DO YOU THINK I AM, THE MAIL BOY? YOU NEED TO LEARN WHO IS THE HEAD OF DISTRIBUTION IN OUR COMPANY."

Dan had also been out of the office too much for Dykstra's liking. He took time off to attend his younger brother's graduation ceremony in Buffalo, but extended his time there to attend the funeral of a family member who had died unexpectedly. Dykstra questioned whether Dan was telling the truth and grew increasingly distrustful of him. Less than a month later, Dan missed some more time for a preplanned trip with his girlfriend. "The kid just doesn't want to work," Dykstra complained. "Get rid of him when he gets back."

Unlike Dorothy and I, Dan and James were not as willing to "grind it out" during nights and weekends. Their attitudes had taken a hit when Dykstra swiped the payroll money. Why should they go the extra mile for a guy who made empty promises, placed himself first at every juncture, and expected them to wait indefinitely for their paychecks? Plus, with no money expected to come in for three more months, there was little reason to think they would be paid anytime soon, if at all. They were right, and Dykstra's demands on them were completely unfair, but I grew frustrated because their less than enthusiastic attitude made my job more difficult.

"I did not feel like working for an individual that did not value his employees and honor his obligation to pay us," Dan says. "He promises you the 'St. Regis–type lifestyle,' but, unfortunately, once you pull back the curtain, it is really Jamaica, Queens. . . . I was miserable. Up until that point, I had the luxury of not knowing financial hardship but now I do. . . . I had to borrow money from my parents to cover my expenses."

Dykstra was late paying him starting the first month and regularly changed his salary without as much as a conversation. At first, Dan says, his salary was supposed to be $80,000 a year. That was knocked down to $1,000 a week, or $52,000 a year, out of the blue and then raised back up to $60,000 a year when I came on board.

In early July, Dan informed Dykstra that "due to inconsistency and lack of a paycheck, I have taken on a financial burden I can no longer bear." Dykstra owed him $12,500. He couldn't take it anymore and quit on July 28, 2008. I was happy for him but sad my first friend at the company was leaving.

"Apparently, the circumstances I left on were good, in Lenny's eyes," Dan says. "He wrote me stating that the timing wasn't right, that it was his fault and not mine, and if I wanted recommendations for any future job, I could ask him for one."

Lenny also wrote to Dan, "You are a good person with integrity. Your family has done a great job raising you, as you know: I have the utmost respect for your father!" For his part, Dan felt the circumstances were anything but warm and fuzzy. "I was leaving very bitter," he says. As of this writing, Dan has not been paid his remaining salary.

For his part, James was also struggling to survive. As Dykstra repeatedly blew off media appearances and press interviews, such as scheduled slots with *Nightline* and on Jim Bruer's show on Sirius Satellite Radio, James could tell the job just wasn't working out.

"James is clueless," Dykstra complained to me daily. "I tell him to go right, he goes left." In addition to his original role, James was now expected to sell advertising for the *Players Club*. James told Dykstra that he had no experience in sales but was desperate to learn. Dykstra was unimpressed.

"Are you kidding me?" he asked James via e-mail. "What else do you want me to do? Hold your hand when we walk across the street? Find a way to produce or I have no job for you."

Another source of conflict between the two was scheduling time for Dykstra to talk with former athletes and coaches. Dykstra asked James to set up meetings with potential player reps, former players who still had ties to the game that could help bring more players into the Players Club.

James picked former New York Knicks fan favorite John Starks, ex–New York Yankees relief pitcher Jeff Nelson, and former Tennessee Titans tight end Frank Wycheck. Nelson and Wycheck, who were both involved with radio, had heard about Dykstra's recent success and were intrigued.

On a Friday night, James set up phone conversations with Nelson and Wycheck and a face-to-face meeting with Starks for the following Wednesday, as per Dykstra's instruction. By Tuesday night, Dykstra still hadn't responded to James's repeated phone calls and e-mails seeking confirmation.

Frustrated, James tagged along with me to a nighttime meeting with Dykstra at the Ritz Carlton–Battery Park. Dykstra told James the times no longer worked and directed him to reschedule the phone interviews and move the meeting with Starks to Dykstra's hotel room.

The day of the interviews, James went to work at a part-time job Dykstra allowed him to maintain at Sirius Satellite Radio. When he got out, he called Dykstra to find out how the conversations with Nelson and Wycheck had gone. "He said, 'Ahhh, I didn't talk to them. I was doing something. I didn't have the time. I'll talk to them another time.'"

When James reminded him of the meeting with Starks, Dykstra said he could no longer make it as he had to fly out of town on his private jet. Instead, Dykstra wanted Starks to meet him in fifteen minutes at a steakhouse. However, Dykstra didn't have the exact address or know the name of the restaurant, but he knew the general vicinity and remembered the name had the word "Meat" in it.

James called Starks and told him Dykstra was being "temperamental." He apologized for the change of venue and asked Starks if he could meet Dykstra right away. Starks was about thirty minutes away. In the meantime, James headed down to the streets with the partial information to figure out where the hell Dykstra was eating. Receiving some help from a doorman at a building nearby, James figured out the location, texted Starks, and headed inside to join Dykstra at his table on the second floor.

When Starks arrived, he and James ordered drinks and Dykstra chowed down on filet mignon. Dykstra gave his Players Club pitch. "It was a casual but somewhat productive meeting," James recalls. "Lenny is actually quite convincing, quite charming, when he wants to be. I understood why people did business with Lenny as much as they did."

When the bill came, Dykstra was a bit short. "The bill was about $140," James says. "Lenny went into his pocket and had a crumpled $100 bill and two singles." He turned to James and told him that he had misplaced his wallet, instructing him to pay and get reimbursement from me the next day.

Before they parted ways, Dykstra had one more task for James. "The other thing that was asked of me was to take the doggie bag of his half-eaten steak and give it to his driver." James went outside and handed the man the bag, noting that Dykstra wanted him to have it. "The driver didn't really have a reaction because it was a closed bag," James says. "I have no idea what his reaction was when he saw the half-eaten meat."

CHAPTER 24

YA GOTTA BELIEVE

"No drugs," Dykstra whispered into the phone, as I sat on the other side of the room at the Carlyle typing on my computer and trying to stay awake after yet another all-nighter. Dykstra was speaking to someone at the radio station WFAN and laying ground rules for an upcoming interview. He was adamant that he did not want to talk about steroids on the air.

Dykstra said he was friends with the opinionated host Mike Francesa from his playing days as a Met. "He used to give me tips for betting on football," Dykstra told me. He expected Francesa to shine a positive light in his direction—and boy did he need it after a string of dicey news articles.

As Dykstra prepared for the interview, I knew James's days were numbered. Not only had Dykstra asked me to arrange the interview, but he also instructed me to keep it a secret from James until he was on the air. "I don't want to hear his dopey rap," Dykstra said to me. "I can't take it."

Dykstra headed to the studio, and I rushed to my apartment to watch the interview on television, break the bad news to James, and get some shut-eye. Back in the Players Club office, James hung on every word, nervous about what might come out of Dykstra's mouth.

When asked about his reaction to the HBO *Real Sports* profile, Dykstra told Francesa host Bryant Gumbel "took a few shots" but that was okay because any publicity "is good, you know, unless you go to jail or something." James winced.

As Dykstra addled on about how his ex-business partner stole from him and how he fired his family, James cringed. When Francesa asked Dykstra if his market views were contrarian, he responded that he "put the 'C' in Contrarian." James smirked. Dykstra told listeners that the Mets were in his heart and that his most memorable moment in a Mets uniform was when he beat up on Boston pitcher Oil Can Boyd in the 1986 World Series. James smiled.

When Francesa repeatedly asked Dykstra about steroids and his curious exchange with HBO *Real Sports* reporter Bernard Goldberg, James sighed. After overhearing Dykstra's earlier conversation, I didn't think they would be talking about the juice. Those of us who had spent any time around Dykstra in private were overly familiar with his history of abusing performance-enhancing substances and his current propensity for bragging about it. In comparison, his on-air denials rang hollow.

The uncomfortable conversation between Dykstra and Francesa went like this:

Francesa: I will tell you personally, I don't really care, but let's just say it and get it over with. Did you or did you not do steroids when you played?
Dykstra: Absolutely not!
Francesa: Did not?
Dykstra: Nah.
Francesa: That's on the record—did not do steroids?
Dykstra: Absolutely.
Francesa: Why were you playing a game with [Goldberg] that night saying you did, did, didn't, did, did?
Dykstra: I saw the tape. When I watched the show and I thought I remembered telling him I didn't. I don't remember telling him I did.
  . . .
Francesa: Put it on the record right now.
Dykstra: Absolutely not. I worked hard and put my time in the weight room and because twenty years ago . . .
Francesa: So no steroids?
Dykstra: No.
Francesa: Lotta weights?
Dykstra: Hard core.
Francesa: Because you came back much bigger that year with the Phillies. You put a lot of weight on.
Dykstra: Yeah. Diet, strength, working hard, so . . .
Francesa: I don't really care, so we'll get that outta the way. No steroids. We're done with that.

Listeners were then treated to a smorgasbord of Lennyisms and peculiarly entertaining stories that mirrored the odd, aimless nights I spent working with him. There was a certain charm to his delivery, and fans ate it up. "With this magazine people doubted me," Dykstra told Francesa. "They think I'm outta my mind. Yeah, I'm outta my mind in my $400,000 Maybach and $18 million mansion. That's how outta my mind I am."

He told Francesa about his high-flying lifestyle and his struggles as a kid to break out of the middle. "My way out of the middle was baseball. . . . By the way, I don't stop in the middle anywhere either," Dykstra said. "I get in either California or New York. I don't get in the middle, no way."

Dykstra spoke about his love of lawyers and how he always surrounds himself "with any army of attorneys" that he pays $200,000 a month. "I'm an attorney nut," he said. "I'm one of the few guys that believes in attorneys and spends the money on them." He also told Francesa that he gambled heavily on the Players Club. "I pushed all my chips in here," he said, noting he had spent $5.5 million on the magazine so far.

The longer Dykstra spoke, the more nervous I became. He announced to the world that Willie Mays, whom he privately referred to as his "field nigger," was part of the Players Club. "Willie Mays is a spokesman for us," Dykstra told Francesa. "I had dinner with Willie Mays the other night and it was like, 'This is Willie Mays, best player in the world.' It's an honor." The only problem was that Mays was not, in fact, our spokesman.

Next Francesa asked Dykstra who else is part of the Players Club. "Oh, I mean everybody from Ron Darling, Keith Hernandez, you know Derek Jeter, you can just keep going and going and going," Dykstra said. "David Wright, I can keep naming these guys. Cam Neely, all the people that you see in here. Hundreds and hundreds and hundreds . . . Tim Brown is a big spokesperson."

In truth, the Players Club had just one member: Lenny Dykstra. We didn't have an army of athletes to tout the merits of the business. And there was no infrastructure set up—no preferred partners—to provide the necessary handholding to any players who wanted to join the club.

Hernandez and Darling had helped Dykstra during the early stages of the magazine, but I hadn't seen or heard from either during my entire time working for Dykstra. The rest of the names Dykstra rattled off were just athletes who had been interviewed by the *Players Club* staff or featured on the pages of the magazine. They hadn't joined the club.

Another anxiety-causing moment came when Dykstra began touting his perfect stock-picking record. "I haven't lost one," he said proudly. "There's no losers this year." By the time of his appearance, he had picked up forty-two victories and $97,200 in profits.

However, there are strict rules governing how advisers and financial firms advertise the performance of their portfolios. I didn't know the exact rules, but I worried Dykstra might be crossing the line. Although his win/loss record was technically correct, it was misleading. Many of his picks that were still in play were sinking fast. Those were not counted in the loss column because the outcomes were undetermined.

Dykstra's boasts were nearly causing me to have a heart attack. Fans, on the other hand, loved every minute of the stroll down memory lane and showered Dykstra with praise during a call-in session after the interview.

––––––––––––

There were plenty of red flags that would have sent many running for the hills, but there were equal reasons for me to believe success was right around the corner. Plus, I had grown accustomed to the chaos.

Dykstra asked me to lease two additional offices at 245 Park Avenue to house new *Players Club* staffers we would be hiring. Our deal with AMEX was coming to an end. Instead of a ragtag band of hardworking, hungry young men, Dykstra began recruiting seasoned magazine staffers with pedigrees to run the *Players Club*.

First, he tapped Kevin Coughlin, a Pulitzer Prize–winning photographer who resigned from the *New York Post* to handle the magazine's newly created photo department. Coughlin's job was to take pictures, organize a stable of freelance photographers, and negotiate the purchase of photos from agencies such as Corbis and AP Images.

"Chris, you'll like him. He's a grinder, but he's got bad fumes," Dykstra told me. He told others that Coughlin was a "gamer" who "wants to work, which is a very rare thing this day and age." Dykstra liked that Coughlin came from a "high-powered" publication like the *Post*.

I first met Coughlin when Dykstra brought him by the office one night at about 9:00 p.m. for a face-to-face meeting with the remaining skeleton staff. Coughlin was a short, unimposing, doughy, middle-aged white guy, with a shaved head and a buzzed Fu Manchu. He was anxious to step into a world of luxurious private jets and lush photographic magazine layouts and walk away from the endless daily deadlines of the *Post*.

He seemed a nice guy. Jubilance radiated from Coughlin as he sported an ear-to-ear grin while leaning against a table jutting out from the wall. The rest of us congregated around the room and listened to Dykstra tell stories about how he used to find out which umpires had gambling problems. "I would blackmail 'em into giving me better calls," he bragged.

On that night, Dykstra was extremely loose as he held court with the glowing Gotham sky behind him. It was a nice respite from the schizophrenic nature of most of Dykstra's meetings. We were hanging around BSing with each other.

After telling us that he used to rub human growth hormone on his elbows and knees during his playing days, Dykstra got down to business. "Do you guys know any editors that can run the *Players Club*?" Dykstra asked us. "They need to be big league. I'm done with this small-time shit."

After rattling off a few names that came to mind, Coughlin and I began discussing a mutual acquaintance we heard might be available. Dykstra called him and left a message. As time passed, Dykstra grew impatient, paging him repeatedly but without reaching him. Holding up his phone to reveal the numbers "911-911," Dykstra jokingly asked us if we knew what those numbers stood for. "It's the pussy line, man," he said. "That was my code. I used to bang a lot of chicks back in the day."

Dykstra continued his hunt for an editor, turning to longtime Philly columnist Bill Conlin for help with the recruiting effort. Conlin was now writing for the *Players Club* magazine and had the connections to reel in a big-time editor for us.

That editor was Neil Amdur, a sports journalism legend. Amdur, who was a few years shy of seventy at the time, had written for the *New York Times* for nearly fifteen years from the late 1960s to the mid-1980s. From there he went on to become the editor in chief of *World Tennis* magazine before returning to the *Times* as a sports editor. In 2002 he was appointed as the senior editor for staffing/national recruiting at the paper.

In an effort to woo Amdur, Dykstra invited him to his mansion and offered to put him up at the pricey Four Seasons hotel. Amdur didn't need the job but was intrigued by the project—it sounded challenging and fun. The two met and discussed everything from salary to staffing, and in a surprise move, Dykstra announced Amdur as the new editor of the magazine while on a conference call with the *Players Club*'s newly assembled ad sales staff. Caught off guard at the rapid pace and informal nature of the negotiations and proclamation from Dykstra (no contract was signed), Amdur improvised an "acceptance speech."

Amdur was precisely the kind of guy we needed at the *Players Club*. He brought instant credibility. He had connections, knew his stuff, and, most importantly, had the standing to tell Dykstra no. We hoped that Amdur's presence would finally get Dykstra to back away from the day-to-day details of the magazine and focus on being the face of the Players Club.

Once he returned to New York, Amdur dropped by our offices to meet the staff while awaiting his official start date. However, something had gone terribly wrong. Dykstra wasn't returning Amdur's phone calls or e-mails. Behind the scenes, Dykstra was rapidly souring on Amdur and the $250,000 annual salary he had promised the veteran journalist.

On the phone, Dykstra complained to me that Amdur was a "fossil" who was "trying to take over my company." He felt that Amdur would marginalize his input and run things the way he wanted to. It was clear that Amdur was out, but Dykstra refused to break the bad news, leaving him to wait and wonder.

Finally, Coughlin decided to level with Amdur, who had already assumed Dykstra was reneging on the deal. Amdur, for his part, just wanted to be reimbursed for the $1,900 in expenses he laid out for his trip to California.

Shortly thereafter, I received an ominous e-mail from Bill Conlin saying that Amdur was "shocked and disappointed by the way negotiations were terminated with no explanation." He noted that Amdur still hadn't gotten his money from Dykstra.

"I just hope you guys know what's happening to your credibility and reputation in the magazine industry," Conlin wrote. "Neil Amdur was one of the giants in newspaper sports editing and you waved him off like he was some porn mag hack."

The fifth edition of the magazine and the first we were publishing on our own was just a few weeks away from deadline, and we still didn't have an editor or any writers on staff. Dykstra owed me $34,000 in back salary and was again needlessly making enemies out of powerful people. The situation couldn't have been bleaker, and if not for the money I was owed, I would have bolted. The newsletter was still a moneymaker, and I believed that by sticking around I would have a better chance of getting paid and influencing Dykstra's decisions than by joining the crowd of "quitters."

Summoned to Dykstra's suite at the Ritz Carlton–Battery Park, I schlepped downtown for yet another midnight meeting. As I entered the room, Dykstra and two other men were sitting at a dining room table on the left and the large panoramic windows on the right revealed the Statue of Liberty with her lit torch illuminating the harbor.

I joined the men at the table and silently listened as they continued their conversation. Once they were done, Dykstra shifted his attention to me. "I've got good news for you, bro," he said with a wink and a smile and some excitement in his voice. "You're getting called up to the big leagues—I'm making you the new editor of the *Players Club* effective immediately. You've earned it." He said I understood how to work with him, and he thought that, unlike Amdur, I could bring fresh young blood to the publication. Plus, I understood the importance of loyalty—he trusted me.

I would keep my job and salary as president of Nails Investments, plus he would pay me an extra $5,000 a month to run the *Players Club*. I knew how important his baby, the magazine, was to him and was flattered he had selected me as the editor.

My plate would be very full, but from a professional and financial standpoint, it was too good an opportunity pass up. Between the magazine and the newsletter business, I would be pulling in $190,000 a year in salary plus bonus, but I would be working between 100 and 120 hours a week until the businesses were on more solid footing. Plus, very few journalists get the chance to run a publication of that prestige by their early thirties.

Addressing another pressing concern of mine, Dykstra told me that he arranged for TheStreet.com to pay us every month instead of once every three months. That was great news. I felt that my e-mails to him respectfully outlining my financial concerns—both for me personally and for the newsletter business—had sunk in.

"You need an injection of liquidity, bro," Dykstra said. "I want you to pay yourself $30,000 right away. I really owe him $35,000," he said with a chuckle, turning to the other men. "But Chris is a team player." He really owed me $34,000, but I appreciated the gesture and wasn't about to argue with the fact that I was finally getting paid!

As the other men at the table congratulated me, a great weight was lifted off my shoulders. Dykstra had come through in the clutch again, rejuvenating me and restoring my faith in him. I had previously considered quitting as soon as I got what I was owed, but once I was promoted, my outlook changed. I was thankful for the opportunity, and I felt bad for doubting him.

CHAPTER 25

HUNTING THE WHITE WHALE

By late summer, Dykstra could feel the vise tightening, which was weighing heavily on him. As his cash reserves dwindled to nearly nothing, his pursuit of the ever-elusive white whale that could rescue him from financial ruin intensified. It isn't entirely clear exactly where all of Dykstra's money went. However, he did make a number of mistakes that cost him dearly.

Dykstra got himself in a financial pickle by going overboard in his use of leverage, according to Keith Peel. "Lenny's always been the master of leverage, and that could only take him so far when the chips kind of got a little short because he was in such a high-end area in everything and he wanted to do everything first class," Peel says. "It worked in his other businesses, but he might have shot a little too deep and he went all in . . . and it kind of just started snowballing on him."

Dykstra's ultimate downfall stemmed from an inability to recognize his own limits, says Bert Brodsky, a longtime friend, business associate, and chairman of Sandata Technologies. "The Players Club is a good idea," Brodsky says. "The problem is he tried to do it all by himself." He didn't have the economic infrastructure or the management infrastructure in place, and he wouldn't listen to advice.

He could have been a great figurehead—a public face for the Players Club. However, someone else should have been running the organization. "He never understood that," Brodsky says. "I told him, 'Lenny, you don't have the skill set.' Lenny is not dumb, but he is also uneducated. . . . You can't just go from being a baseball player to the president of a company. There's something in between."

Dykstra insisted on funding the project with his own money, which Brodsky says he advised against. "He had the opportunity to raise money, and he just wouldn't do it." Brodsky says he told Dykstra they could raise $10 million in exchange for a 20 percent stake in the company, placing an initial valuation of $50 million on the company before having a single player in the club. Dykstra refused. "He is not a trusting person," Brodsky says. "He thinks everyone has an ulterior motive, and most of the people did." Months earlier, while scrambling to print the second edition of the *Players Club* magazine behind Randall Lane's back, Dykstra had turned to Brodsky for money.

Brodsky first met Dykstra through Mets pitcher Dwight "Doc" Gooden in the mid-1980s. When Dykstra, who was crashing at Gooden's apartment, needed a place of his own, Gooden referred him to Brodsky, who says many of the team's players used his office as a "security blanket."

Dykstra and Brodsky became friends, with Brodsky serving as best man when Lenny and Terri wed. "I stood up for them," Brodsky says. "I sent them to Atlantic City to the honeymoon suite."

After the Mets shipped Dykstra to the Phillies, he and Brodsky remained in contact. "I helped finance his litigation with Lindsay [Jones], and I got my money back from the insurance company," Brodsky reports. When Dykstra got into money trouble with the Players Club, Brodsky says Terri called him pleading for a loan. "It was secured by those notes that he had from the sale of the car wash."

The problem, Brodsky explains, was that Dykstra didn't really have the $41 million he claimed to have from the sale of the last two car washes—the South Corona and Simi Valley locations. "If you sell a $100 note for 2 percent interest, that note is not $100," Brodsky says, citing an example. "It's only really worth $75 or $70. But he didn't focus in on that. He would tell me he sold the property for $41 million and he took back a $23 million note at below interest, payable over ten years with interest only."

That $23 million note ended up being worth a lot less as Dykstra ended up selling it for a mere $14 million, Brodsky says. "He needed the money. He was desperate. When someone comes to you and says lend me $100, I'll give you $200 next month, that's like shylock money."

A year after Dykstra sold the car washes, he went back to the Iranian businessmen who had bought them and asked for a financial bailout, according to a later article published on ESPN.com. An attorney for the Iranian businessmen told ESPN that Dykstra agreed to retire the $23 million note if they paid off about $13 million of Dykstra's debt. They also agreed to forgive $1 million Dykstra owed them and give him an additional $1.25 million. However, according to the article, Dykstra later sued the men, claiming they hadn't paid off about $1 million of the debt.[1]

With Lenny already delinquent on one loan to Brodsky, he began hounding his old friend for more cash. "You are the only person I can count on when my family needs help," Dykstra wrote in one e-mail. In another note, he told Brodsky that "without liquidity, I'm a dead man." In one instance, he even told Brodsky that he could not go home until he secured a loan because "Terri is very upset with me."

He called Brodsky, constantly demanding the money and sending him e-mails with all sorts of propositions. He needed money to fuel up his private jet or to pay his hefty hotel bill. He needed more than $431,000 for an engine for his private jet. He needed money to print the next edition of the magazine. He was persistent and sometimes threatening.

"YOU WILL BE MAKING A TERRIBLE MISTAKE IF YOU CONTINUE TO BLOW ME OFF—AS I WILL NOT ASK AGAIN," Dykstra wrote to his longtime friend. He, of course, did ask again, urging Brodsky to call him right away or sending Brodsky e-mails with wiring instructions and dollar amounts as if he could will his old friend into sending the money. "I would say, 'Lenny, how are you gonna pay it back?'" Brodsky recalls. "'I know you want to pay it back, but how are you going to pay it back? Where are you going to get the money to pay it back?'"

Samantha Kulchar says that when she was employed by Dykstra, she did some calculations and realized that unless he came across at least $40 million, there was no way he could he could maintain any sense of financial ease until the Players Club started to make money.

The amount of the bridge loans he was seeking would merely buy him time. "I realized that even if he got the loans, he'd be right back where he started in a month," she says. "He portrayed himself to be rolling in financial stability, and he lied, plain and simple. He owed so many people so much money, it was insurmountable."

With Brodsky fading into the background and Dykstra running out of time, lender after lender balked at his hefty loan requests.

On one trip with his family to Cooperstown, New York, site of the Baseball Hall of Fame, Dykstra brought along a former member of the Bush White House who he thought would help him get his finances in order. However, he forgot one important item: his false teeth. Dykstra accidentally left them on a rented private jet that had already departed, leaving him to roam Upstate New York without his chompers.

At first, Terri Dykstra believed Lenny was on the verge of landing a big-time investor or securing an eight-figure loan. He would tell her he was going to New York or Atlanta or Boston and would be coming home with many millions in his pockets. "I somewhat wanted to believe that," she says. "Then it got to the point where I started figuring out it's never going to happen because I've heard it too many times."

Terri says Lenny would get in a prime position to land the money and then self-destruct. She says he would try to cut corners or send the lender badgering e-mails in an attempt to get the documents signed. "Any business person, when they see desperation, they back off," she says.

As each agreement collapsed, Lenny's mood swings grew wider and his behavior more troubling. "He freaked me out one day when we went through the same conversation three times," Dorothy says. "He was in such one of those down—really down—very depressed moods, and I was really worried about him. I actually called Terri and said, 'You can't leave him alone for the day.' She made Keith stay with him all day."

A while after Brodsky, Dykstra sized up J. R. and Loren Ridinger of Market America, a direct marketing company some have compared to a giant pyramid scheme. Some of Miami's most influential people, the Ridingers were on their way to running a billion-dollar company, according to *Haute Living*, a high-end lifestyle magazine.[2]

Dykstra courted the Ridingers while trying to wow us with stories about cruising on their yacht and attending a party for Loren's friend J-Lo. He also sent Loren a regular e-mail with personalized stock tips in an attempt to curry favor with her.

CHAPTER 26

ELI MANNING IS TOO COOL
FOR SCHOOL

"Eli Manning needs to be taught a lesson. I scratched him from the lineup as he thinks he is too cool for school," Dykstra wrote in an e-mail to *New York Post* reporter Mark Cannizzaro, a freelancer for the *Players Club*. Dykstra wanted Manning on the magazine's cover, but Little Brother wouldn't give the *Players Club* an interview. "I was not happy with Eli Manning's bullshit games—so I gassed his ass! *Brett Favre is en fuego right now!*"

Favre, who had announced his retirement in a teary speech only to later claim that the Packers had forced him to retire and that he still wanted to play, was a compelling story for our pro athlete readership. If we framed the story right, it could provide the perfect tie-in to the Players Club's core message of guaranteeing a secure retirement. The problem was that Dykstra hated Favre only slightly less than he hated the New York Jets. But in the end, showing up Manning won out.

The feature on Manning was banished to page 96, buried in the lifestyle section away from the other sports-related stories and in between articles about wine and Stephan Winkelmann, president and CEO of Automobili Lamborghini S.p.A.

The Favre cover was significant for another reason: it was the first time the magazine had featured a Caucasian male on the cover. "I'm no racist; I put three darkies and a bitch on my first four covers," Dykstra joked repeatedly, referring to Derek Jeter, Chris Paul, Danika Patrick, and Tiger Woods. As for Patrick, Dykstra was also taking credit for some of her success. "I made her," he illogically claimed, as if she weren't famous before she graced the cover of the *Players Club* magazine.

The Eli Manning debacle also exposed a gaping hole at the *Players Club*. We had no one qualified to design the covers. Coughlin's training was in taking and preparing photographs, not in designing magazine covers. His best attempts to figure it out understandably underwhelmed.

Because Hochstein had designed the first four editions and was no longer in the picture, Dykstra wanted to undertake a complete redesign of the *Players Club* and erase any trace of Hochstein. To do that, Dykstra had a plan: survival of the fittest. He hired several designers to create a prototype, never revealing they were in secret competition with one another.

Rowean Design was one of the contestants. The company later claimed Dykstra had stiffed it on $21,000 in fees and expenses. The winner was Space 150 and its founder and chief executive Billy Jurewicz, who was known to Dykstra as King Cock, or King C. Crazy nicknames aside, Dykstra had previously hired Space 150 to create a "one million dollar Web site" for the *Players Club*, which he was late in paying for.

In the midst of that complete chaos, I began my tenure as editor of the *Players Club*. I had a mere two weeks to pull together the huge, 144-page September edition. Whereas Doubledown had had about thirty staffers involved in the magazine in some way, shape, or form, we had just a handful.

I knew the *Players Club*, unlike "Nails on the Numbers," was Dykstra's baby, and he was much more protective of it. I just didn't anticipate how destructive Dykstra's mental paralysis could be to the editorial process. Not only wouldn't he make decisions; he also wouldn't allow others to make them either. He also shot down ideas at an unprecedented pace. If he hadn't heard of a particular athlete, he didn't want that person in the magazine, and in most of the sports he was out of touch. No articles could be assigned and no layouts could be started without his approval . . . and even then he sometimes balked.

Dykstra clearly didn't understand the time needed to put together the magazine, and he created a massive bottleneck during crunch time. I quickly learned what Clifford Blodgett, Nicole Blades, and Doubledown's editorial staffers had been through.

For example, we needed a player's wife to feature in our "Better Half" column, and James suggested the former Heidi Strobel, wife of Philadelphia Phillies pitcher Cole Hamels. He said she was dying to be featured. Eva Longoria, now ex-wife of NBAer Tony Parker, and Tanya Staal, the better half of Carolina Hurricane's center Eric Staal, had been featured in the first two issues. However, Dykstra didn't want Hamels's wife in the magazine because she was a "slut." During her appearance on the reality show *Survivor*, Strobel took off her clothes for some Oreo cookies and peanut butter. She later posed for *Playboy*.

In the front of the magazine each month, the *Players Club* ran short two-page profiles on top players in each sport. However, when it came to women's tennis or golf, Dykstra wanted only aesthetically pleasing women. He refused to put "ugly bitches," usually female Asian golfers, in the magazine. "No one wants to see that," he would say.

Most of the time I suspected Dykstra's off-color comments were more about saying something shocking than about expressing any actual prejudices. After all, he said he was friends with Elton John and Dave Morrow of TheStreet.com, both openly gay men. "It's weird. I end up hanging out with a lot of fags . . . like real ones . . . like actual homosexuals," Dykstra said to me several times. That would be followed up with a series of questions about gay acts. "Can you imagine enjoying that . . . putting a cock in your ass, pounding the fudge? They like it; they can't help it."

In a later video posted on YouTube promoting a potential Lenny Dykstra reality television show, Dykstra was shown interviewing a potential employee. "You like men or women?" he asked the guy, who said he prefers men. "I like women; I'm a normal dude," Dykstra responded, adding that he didn't look down on homosexuals. "I know for a fact nobody chooses to wake up next to another guy's hairy ass."

I didn't take Dykstra's comments too seriously. Most of the time he was entertaining and reminded me of an extreme version of Archie Bunker, the fictional blue-collar bigot played by Carroll O'Connor in the 1970s hit sitcom *All in the Family*.

However, as Dykstra's mood turned darker in the fall of 2008, his "jokes" were taking a toll on the magazine. In a feature about Lakers superfan Jack Nicholson, Dykstra insisted we pull a picture of Nicholson screaming courtside. He deemed the shot disrespectful to Nicholson because it had a "spear-chucker" in the background. He was referring to Celtics coach Doc Rivers.

In another instance, Dykstra wanted me to write an article about the "baboons," referring to tennis superstars Venus and Serena Williams. The article was to showcase their off-the-court ventures and business successes: Venus's interior design firm, Serena's line of clothing, and the pair's commercials for Oreos. However, Dykstra later instructed me to bury the article deep inside the back of the magazine.

While Coughlin handled the photos, I did my best to line up story ideas and interviews; gain Dykstra's stamp of approval; assemble a stable of writers, copy editors, and support staffers; and coordinate the workflow of the magazine. With the exception of three assignments already dished out, I had inherited a blank canvas.

One of those three pieces was from Bill Conlin, the now-disgraced journalist, who played a major role in the *Players Club*. Dykstra's relationship with Conlin stretched back nearly two decades to Dykstra's time with the Mets.

Conlin, an older, heavyset guy, says he first bonded with Dykstra over some of the nicknames Conlin gave to players in his columns, citing Jason "Friday the 13th" Grimsley as an example. "He thought that was a sensational nickname," Conlin says. "Every time he'd see me, he'd be like, 'Hey, Friday the 13th,' and he would give me that dude talk."

For the September 2008 edition of the *Players Club*, Dykstra asked Conlin to pen a feature on Jim Cramer. He promised to pay Conlin $5,000 for the article, the ungodly and unnecessarily high rate Dykstra offered to all big-name reporters writing for the *Players Club* because he wanted them salivating at the chance to write for the magazine. (A usual rate would have been a buck a word.)

Topics for the lengthy question-and-answer session ranged from Cramer's love of running and soccer to the carnage in the markets. Cramer's snarling face greeted readers on the opening spread of the six-page feature. He was wearing boxing gloves and standing in the *Mad Money* studio.

Always a compelling character, Cramer disclosed that if he were stranded on a desert island and granted one companion (from a list of five choices) by a genie, he would pass over Warren Buffett and Alan Greenspan and take Vladimir Ilyich Lenin, a Russian Marxist revolutionary. "I would kill him," Cramer told Conlin. "He caused much of what went wrong in the 20th century and spawned Hitler."

When asked what he thought was the best film in history about Wall Street and/or high finance, Cramer replied, "*Wall Street* is actually real good. *The God-father* Parts I and especially II are how business is really done in this country."

With only three articles under way and very few advertisers in the magazine, I needed to generate about one hundred more pages of content. I turned to friends and former colleagues to write and copyedit for the magazine. However, with limited funds and next to no time, I took on the bulk of the writing myself.

Probably the most interesting and difficult piece to write was "Evan Longoria: Man with a Plan." It featured Tampa Bay Rays rookie Evan Longoria, who had just signed the largest contract ever for a rookie. The contract guaranteed $17.5 million over six years, with options that could stretch the deal to nine years and $44 million.

James had gotten Longoria, through his agent, to agree to a lengthy interview with the *Players Club*. The idea was to interview Longoria, ghostwrite the piece for him, and publish it with his byline.

After speaking with Longoria for about thirty minutes, I wrote the article. It explained how finances are not a common discussion topic in the clubhouse and how Longoria heard the horror stories about athletes losing all their money. The article would be better than we had hoped—it was essentially an endorsement of the Players Club's core message, a free endorsement from one of the game's rising young stars.

Dykstra had agreed to the article initially, but after we had interviewed Longoria and received approval from his agent on the text, Dykstra changed his mind without even reading it. "We're not running it," Dykstra told me. "He's a rookie—no one gives a fuck what he has to say."

Dykstra wanted players with four or five years' experience because, by that time, they would be making a higher pay grade. But Longoria was different. He had already scored a massive deal and could speak to young players who would soon be up for those big contracts. It was an important article because those young players could turn to the Players Club in the future for advice.

Dykstra felt Longoria's endorsement wasn't big enough. "He should be sucking my dick to be in the magazine," Dykstra said, insisting we write a whole bunch of things Longoria never said. I refused, and the article became a tug of war, with Dykstra on one side and James and me on the other. When all was said and done, the six-page article appeared on page 38 with a giant subhead that read "One of the American League's Brightest Stars Shares His Thoughts on Why He Believes in the Players Club."

CHAPTER 27

BOX OF ROCKS

The September edition of the *Players Club* rolled off the presses looking pristine, and those of us who had survived the crash course were exhausted but proud. Dykstra was pleased, and Kevin, James, and I felt we had pulled off a miracle.

Coughlin, for his part, was giddy. Dykstra congratulated him on a job well done and sent him e-mails saying things like "Great job Kevin. . . . You brought in a big winner. Way to go!" He walked around the office quoting Dykstra's lines from the HBO *Real Sports* episode.

"One of the reasons I was glad to leave the *Post* at the time was that they treat people like crap," Coughlin recalls. "You can't put a price on the way you are treated."

Meanwhile, my relationship with Coughlin was complicated. Having seen the revolving door at the *Players Club*, I made a conscious decision to be professional and friendly but keep new employees at arm's length. That included Coughlin and Dykstra's new California-based assistants.

I gave Coughlin some friendly advice about surviving in Lennyland, such as telling him to cash his paycheck as soon as he received it. I also urged him to exhibit some patience and to be careful in his communications with Dykstra. However, I didn't know Coughlin well enough to determine how much I could trust him, and I suspected he didn't fully trust me either.

I wanted to level with him but feared that telling him too much might come back to bite me. I couldn't put my finger on it, but there was something about him that I knew would rub Dykstra the wrong way after a while.

In my mind, it was only a matter of time for Coughlin, and the tide began to turn just a few days later when Dykstra asked him for an unusual favor.

Dykstra wanted to borrow Coughlin's credit card to reserve a $13,000 private jet flight. He was going to fly to Atlanta to pick up a $500,000 loan, he said.

Those of us who worked for Dykstra all experienced crazy conversations like that at one point or another. I knew better. Extending Dykstra a generous grace period in paying me was one thing, but letting him charge tens of thousands of dollars on my credit card was quite another.

A few days after his phone call with Dykstra, Coughlin nervously approached me in my office, recounting the uncomfortable conversation. He was embarrassed and worried, telling me Dykstra threw him a line about his own credit cards having high limits that couldn't be used over the phone. Incredibly, he bought it. He was kicking himself for being so naïve. Kevin said that when he expressed concern about the arrangement, Dykstra replied, "You can trust me with your life, bro."

Unbeknown to Coughlin, Dykstra flew that night not to Atlanta but rather to Helena, Montana, to spend time with his son Cutter, who was playing for the Helena Brewers. A few days later, Kevin received a call from a charter jet service saying his credit card had been declined for a $22,937 authorization. Confused, Kevin told the man that the authorization was only supposed to be for $13,000. Stunned, he quickly learned that the $13,000 flight had already taken place and that Lenny had tried to use the card to reserve another flight from Helena to Atlanta.

When Coughlin informed Dykstra that using his card without his permission was a crime—credit card fraud—he says Dykstra told him to calm down and offered him a $5,000 bonus to find a way to get him on the plane. Worried that he would never see any of his pay or the $13,000 already charged on his credit card for Dykstra's first flight, Coughlin scurried to come up with the money.

From that point on, the relationship between Dykstra and Coughlin spiraled out of control. Dykstra no longer appreciated Coughlin's work ethic. He now considered Coughlin to be an unintelligent dweeb. "He's a box of rocks, man," Dykstra said to me nearly every time we spoke.

As we attempted to put together the massive 204-page October edition of the magazine, which was already behind schedule, Dykstra's main priority seemed to be to make Kevin Coughlin his personal bitch. "Everything he told me at my initial interview totally digressed," Coughlin says. "I became a photo monkey for him—a picture picker."

Dykstra set out to humiliate Coughlin in front of the entire staff and newly assembled extended network of freelancers. An e-mail exchange a few days later set the tone for the rest of Coughlin's tenure. Coughlin sent a note to me, Dykstra, James, Dorothy, and the designers at *Haute Living* with the subject line "post-mortems / S.W.O.T Analysis." The acronym stood for Strengths, Weaknesses, Opportunities, and Threats. It was publishing biz lingo, Coughlin said.

"As a new manager in this organization, I would like to get our production process down to a science, and reduce the number of very late nights to a minimum for ALL of us," Coughlin's note read. Cutting back on the late nights sounded like heaven to me, but in the back of my mind I knew it wasn't really possible because Dykstra ran a 24/7 ship. And I accepted that to a degree.

The part about being a new manager felt a little out of place. It was a small organization, and none of us threw around titles. Coughlin wasn't my boss. He wasn't James's boss. And he certainly wasn't going to tell Dykstra what to do.

Coughlin was just trying to organize the troops, but it felt like he was attempting to exert some authority. I knew that Dykstra hated it when someone appeared to be making a move—even inadvertently—without asking him first. Dykstra was very insecure that way.

That night, Coughlin received an angry phone call from Dykstra. "Let me handle the therapy," Dykstra said to him. "You pick the pictures." That was followed by a public e-mail response for all to see. "BEFORE YOU TAKE OVER MY COMPANY—I STRONGLY SUGGEST THAT YOU TAKE CARE OF YOUR SIDE OF THE STREET." The letters were huge and screamed from the page. Dykstra ended his e-mail to Coughlin with another little dig. "P.S.: By the way, save the newspaper rap, it's painful." Coughlin's time as Dykstra's shiny new toy was clearly over.

Just a few days later, Dykstra called a meeting in our New York office to discuss the editorial lineup for the October edition. Our new office manager, twenty-two-year-old Diana Lin, prepared the budget list while Kevin and James buzzed around the rooms, moving the tables together in the corner office to create a place for us to sit. Kevin laid out chilled bottles of water, pads, and pens in front of each chair. It was to be our first official editorial meeting and would, we all hoped, help get the magazine running like a well-oiled machine.

When Dykstra showed up more than two hours late, he walked into the corner office, looked around, and asked no one in particular, "What's all this shit?" Holding a stack of papers in his hand, Kevin explained we had all prepared for the meeting. "Naw, I'm not having no fucking meeting," Dykstra said as he walked out the door and into my office, telling me he needed to speak with me privately.

Once inside, Dykstra called Diana into my office too, leaving Coughlin and James in the corner office wondering what the heck was going on. He hadn't met Diana yet as I had hired her only about a week earlier. Diana, the cousin of a friend of mine, seemed young for her age, but hardworking and intelligent. After experiencing the impact of Dykstra's financial woes firsthand, I set out to hire only younger employees who were not the breadwinners for their families. I also refused to hire anyone away from an existing job. Diana fit the bill.

"You graduated from college, so you're smart?" Dykstra asked, turning to Diana, who was sitting next to him and across the desk from me. She smiled and excitedly told him about her schooling, her confidence growing. He complimented her on the documents she prepared for our meeting. "Stick with me, and you're gonna make some serious cheddar," he told her in an upbeat tone.

"He was telling me how we were going to expand and how we're going to make a lot of money together," Diana recalls. "I had high hopes."

"What are we paying you?" Dykstra continued. She told him she had been hired at $43,000 a year. "Make it $50,000. I have a good feeling about you," he said, before turning his attention to the "bozos" in the other room. Sliding the weird, drive-thru-like window open, he summoned James to the meeting.

Outside the closed window, Coughlin nervously paced back and forth, glancing in on the four of us talking. "Watch this," Dykstra said with a chuckle. "I'm going to fuck with Kevin." He then pointed to Coughlin and continued to speak, making it look as if we were talking about him. "Look at him. It's killing him."

That continued for the next few minutes until Coughlin couldn't take the suspense any longer and knocked on the window before sliding it open. "Can I join the big boy's party?" Coughlin asked in a light and joking manner. "No, we're discussing something here," Dykstra barked back in a serious, no-nonsense tone. "I'll let you know when I'm ready for you," he said, slamming the window shut.

I felt sorry for Coughlin. At the same time, I could hardly contain my laughter. I looked around the room, and James and Diana were also unsuccessfully struggling to keep a straight face. The whole situation was so absurd that it was funny and surreal. Dykstra ended the meeting and then headed out without really speaking to Coughlin at all or making any decisions about the content for the magazine.

The onslaught continued in the ensuing days.

In mid-September, Dykstra wrote to Coughlin that his inability to provide the kind of photos needed for the magazine was "getting painful" and asked, "What in the hell are you doing?" Just a few days later, in response to a note from Coughlin updating us on the status of his various tasks, Dykstra sent a lengthy e-mail with the text in various fonts and sizes.

"Today is another example of your failure to do what I asked. . . . I do not have the time to correct your work—it seems as if you don't want to do it my way. If that is the case, it's a problem. . . . You need to take your game up about three levels."

As Dykstra's e-mails grew more aggressive, Coughlin's frustrations mounted. On top of the way he was being disrespected, he was really upset with the way Dykstra was jerking Wayne McLean around. McLean was a designer who had jumped through hoops several late nights to help Dykstra with various aspects of the September edition of the *Players Club*. "I brought my friend Wayne in, and Lenny told me he doesn't need to get paid because he's black."

Coughlin also started doing research on Dykstra, digging up a CNN article from 1999 entitled "'Nails' in Jail." "Look at what a degenerate we work for," Coughlin called out to me from his office one night as he sent the article via e-mail. The report detailed how Dykstra had been arrested on misdemeanor charges of sexual battery and child annoyance for inappropriately touching a seventeen-year-old girl who worked at his Simi Valley car wash. He was released on $5,000 bail after being accused of touching the young woman inappropriately "outside her clothing."[1]

Dykstra was later cleared of the charges, with his high-powered attorney Dan Petrocelli even suggesting that Dykstra was the victim. "It's not uncommon for high-profile personalities, sports figures, to be a target for unmeritorious charges."[2]

Petrocelli said the teen had come to the car wash when she was not scheduled to work and should have been in school. "She sought him out and engaged him in conversation," Petrocelli said. "The next thing Mr. Dykstra knew, she was alleging sexual harassment against him." The district attorney in the case said he believed Dykstra was guilty of the charges but that he could not prove them beyond a reasonable doubt to a jury.

When Coughlin wasn't venting to me, he was taking his frustrations out at the gun range. One afternoon he showed up to the office with a picture of Dykstra ripped out of the *Players Club* magazine. It was riddled with holes, especially where Dykstra's face used to be. Coughlin was proud.

"I got talked to at the Nassau County gun range," Coughlin later explained during an interview, noting that he was told that he was supposed to use only authorized NRA targets, not pictures of Lenny Dykstra, at the shooting range. "This was a special job," he said he told the men. "I hope nobody kills him with a .22-caliber bullet because I'm the first guy they'll look at," he later announced with a laugh.

Eventually, Coughlin had enough. He sent Dykstra a lengthy message, noting his two Pulitzer Prizes, twenty years of experience, and the sixteen-hour workdays. He also claimed that he had kept creditors from cutting off the *Players*

Club's access to images and told Dykstra not to "insult [his] intelligence about picture selection." Lastly, he asked Dykstra to address these criticisms directly and privately, not to publish them for all his coworkers to see.

Dykstra became enraged. "I don't need all the bullshit—just photos that I can say, 'Okay, these are okay, Kevin.'" If Coughlin hadn't comprehended the gravity of the situation before, it became crystal clear after that e-mail. "Last thing: I will not be going back and fucking forth with you any longer—you either do your fucking job the right way, the way I say to do it—not you, or you will not be working for the *Players Club*. It's that simple. . . . I ask you to do a simple task and you turn it into a fucking cluster-fuck. Please ask Chris to explain what I want before you say something that eliminates you permanently."

CHAPTER 28

YER OUT

As Dykstra continued to hammer away at Coughlin and, to a lesser degree, at James, his mood continued to darken. Was he drinking again or on drugs? Was the stress just getting to Dykstra? Was he mentally ill?

They all seemed realistic possibilities, and we each had our suspicions, but the details didn't really matter. We were powerless to fix those issues. The bottom line was that something was very wrong and that Dykstra was acting really, really weird.

Up until that point, I had mostly avoided Dykstra's criticisms and bad-mouthing. However, my day of reckoning had finally come.

It was a Friday afternoon in mid-September, about six months into my tenure, and Coughlin had just received another nasty note from Dykstra when I received an accusatory e-mail from him as well, marking the beginning of the craziest nine days of my life.

I knew instinctively this was the beginning of the end. The note was written in various fonts, sizes, and colors. One section was in all capital letters, while another was all in bold. And Lenny's tone seemed to change several times within the letter.

"For some reason you want to try and do this all by yourself?" the letter began. Dykstra was claiming I purposely refused to hire staffers to help with the magazine, which of course wasn't true. Diana was already on board, I had hired a pair of freelance copy editors and had recruited prominent sports reporters from the *Houston Chronicle*, *Arizona Republic*, and *Dallas Morning News* to write for us. I also continued to manage a handful of high-profile freelance writers, including Bill Conlin, Frank Fitzpatrick, Mark Cannizzaro, Ira Miller, Art Spander, Hal Bodley, and Mark Heisler.

Dykstra said he didn't care about the cost; he wanted new staffers immediately.

He added that the reason the *Players Club* was the only one in its space was because he played to win. "Anyone that got in my way, I ran them over. I don't give a fuck!"

On the flip side, Dykstra peppered in compliments, saying my "hard work and dedication does not go unnoticed, trust me. . . . I want you to know: I have my two boys and I have my wife," he wrote in all caps. "That is the only family I have. I fired the rest of them and I am fine with that."

Lenny said that I was "a big part" of the Players Club and the $60 billion market that "we own" by ourselves. "You have hung in there through thick and thin, and for that, your day will come when you get paid off," he continued. "I just want to remind you to stay focused on you, take care of number one. Don't let feelings get in the way of making the correct business decisions. Do what you have to do to make this the best magazine in the world!"

I worked on my laptop through the night that Friday and Saturday as we raced to finalize the October edition of the magazine, catching catnaps in my apartment during the afternoons. On Sunday, Dykstra told me to take the night off. I desperately needed it.

I decided to take Rhea out for dinner and some singing. We were joined by her brother, Ferdinand, and our friend Lily. It felt good not to think of work. We enjoyed some cocktails and spirits, ate Chinese food, and did our best rock star impersonations while belting out karaoke tunes.

Before long my phone started buzzing, and I was suddenly transported back to the reality of my job. Screw it; I'll call him later, I thought to myself. But he kept calling. From my Blackberry, I sent Dykstra an e-mail telling him that I was unable to talk, but that I would call him later. He kept calling.

Finally at about 10:30 p.m., I'd had enough of the crazy calling. I stepped outside to answer his calls and make sure he wasn't having a legitimate emergency. "What is so important, Lenny? You told me I could have the night off," I said. He ignored the part about giving me a respite and instructed me to report to his hotel suite right away. He had just arrived in New York, and there was a lot of work to be done, he said.

Reporting to his hotel right away was impossible, I told him, but I did say to send any work he needed done to me by e-mail and I would handle it when

I got home. Plus, I let him know I needed a proper night's rest in order to be on top of my game on Monday, the day we were putting the finishing touches on the magazine. "If you don't want to work, I'll just find someone else who can get the job done," he said, his voice growing louder as he launched into an unintelligible tirade. "Call me as soon as you get home," he said and then abruptly hung up the phone.

I took a deep breath and went back into the room. Rhea smiled at me, but I could see the disappointment in her eyes. Dykstra's interruption had sucked the air out of our get-together, and I had allowed his intrusion. By that point she was, unfortunately, used to and reluctantly resigned to these interruptions.

We wrapped things up and headed home a short while later. I called Dykstra several times, but he didn't answer, so I went to work on the newsletter. Two hours later, nearly 1:30 in the morning, he called, telling me he needed me at his hotel right away. "I promise it will only take an hour," Dykstra said in a friendly tone. "It's important we meet face to face. I have no time tomorrow, and I want to go over a few things in the magazine with you."

I wasn't thrilled, but in relative terms, an hour seemed reasonable and Dykstra was staying nearby at a hotel called the Lowell.

Five minutes later, I was knocking on his door. A six-foot-six man with a five-o'clock shadow answered. Dykstra called him his "Russian killer" and said the guy was packing heat.

For the next hour and a half, it was just a typical hangout session with no apparent pressing business to discuss.

Fatigued and worried about the detail-oriented task I had in front of me in the morning, I began to work on my laptop. "What the fuck are you doing?" Dykstra exclaimed. I told him I was getting a head start on Monday's tasks. "You work when I tell you to fucking work," he barked. "I can't take the attitude anymore; it's brutal. Get the fuck out of here," he said, his voice growing louder. "GET THE FUCK OUT."

I explained that I was worried about finishing everything on time. "I just want to do my job," I said. Our argument was growing heated—mostly on Dykstra's side—when I looked up to see the Russian Killer staring me down as if to say, "Don't even think about it."

Dykstra eventually calmed down and resumed his aimless stream of consciousness until the sun came up. Finally, he said I could go but wanted to know how many editors I had hired since his e-mail to me two days earlier. I told him I hadn't hired anyone new over the weekend. "I want two new editors working in my office by 2:00 p.m. this afternoon." The clock was ticking.

After catching a few short hours of sleep at home, I headed to the office to discuss some pressing matters with James. Dykstra wanted him gone, and James had had enough of Dykstra as well. James and I spoke, and before Dykstra showed, James cleaned out his desk and left the Players Club for the last time.

Meanwhile, Diana called a staffing agency to line up interviews with job candidates. As it turned out, Dykstra wanted to oversee the hiring process himself and instructed Diana to set up a series of interviews starting at 7:00 p.m.

That night, Dykstra arrived early, for a change, with the Russian Killer and flight attendant Amanda in tow. As we all gathered in the corner office, Dykstra quizzed me about the magazine, the staffers, and the status of our health insurance. I told him that a friend of mine, a human resources professional, was helping us set up a payroll and benefits infrastructure . . . and she was doing it for free as a personal favor.

"Where is she?" he asked. I said that she was probably at home—it was nighttime. Dykstra began berating me in front of the entire staff. "It's funny how you have all these hidden employees. Why are they all hidden?"

They were freelancers, I said, and explained that most of them worked from home or their own offices and charged us only for the hours they worked for us. That was preferable to hiring, training, and managing a number of employees on a whim—and a lot less expensive, I explained.

Next, it was time to interview the candidates. First up was a middle-aged woman who showed up to the interview in jeans and sneakers and didn't know much about sports. She was applying for a job as a copy editor but had typos on her résumé. I interviewed her by myself and didn't think she was a good fit. Plus, we didn't need any more copy editors—we already had two.

However, Dykstra didn't understand the difference between editors and copy editors, and he wanted to chat with her. With Dykstra sitting on one side of the desk, and me and the woman on the other, he played on his computer while asking her questions like "You worked for a law journal, so you're smart?" and "Do you know who I am?"

When she responded to a real question I had, Dykstra would zone out or interrupt and ask one of his bizarre, irrelevant questions.

He hired her on the spot.

Later in the evening, we came across Kevin McCarthy, a twenty-two-year-old Long Islander who had been born the day after Dykstra's famous triple in the 1986 playoffs against the Houston Astros. Tall and thin, the recent Fordham graduate showed up to the interview appropriately dressed in a suit. Although he was still very green, I liked his enthusiasm and his knowledge of sports. After I conducted a typical job interview, it was "Lenny Time" again.

"I didn't really understand the interview questions he asked," McCarthy says of Dykstra. "He asked me whether Fordham was a coed school and stuff like that. It had nothing to do with the job." After barely looking up from behind his laptop during the entire interview, Dykstra hired McCarthy by the end of the night as well.

We had no time to check their references, bring them back for second interviews, or give them editing tests. However, as Dykstra wanted, we had two warm bodies.

At about 10:30 p.m., hours after Dykstra had departed, I was still in the office when I received a phone call. "Chris, it's Lenny," he said in a monotone. "Did I leave my laptop there?" I looked around and told him yes. I heard him talking to someone else on one of his other cell phones before he hurriedly told me he would call back.

I waited around for about an hour and then locked the laptop in a desk drawer and shut the office down for the night. On my way home, the cool September air rushed through the partially rolled-down taxicab window and brushed against my face. Relaxing! I was sitting comfortably back in the seat when my phone rang again—it was Dykstra. "Where are you?" Dykstra asked incredulously. "Why didn't you bring me my laptop?"

I told him it was safely locked up at the office and he could easily retrieve it the next day when he came to the office for a rent-related meeting with building management. "My hotel is right in your neighborhood," he yelled. "What the fuck is wrong with you? Why didn't you just bring it by?" Dykstra hadn't asked me to do so, but in truth I knew he had several other laptops with him, so I purposely didn't take it home with me, fearing that would be an excuse to summon me to his hotel and trap me there all night. I had already worked through the night four nights in a row, catching a few hours' sleep after dawn each day. I needed rest.

"You have a real fucking attitude problem," he screamed. "And I don't want to hear 'Don't fucking talk to me that way' because . . . "

I finally reached my breaking point when respect and deference no longer mattered. As the driver turned east down a dark side street, I sat in the back of the taxi engaged in a full-on shouting, cursing match with my boss. It was not a proud moment, but at least I was standing up for myself.

When I exited the taxi, I was so upset that my hands were shaking. As I walked toward my building, I looked up at my apartment windows and saw the lights were still on—Rhea was waiting up for me. Instead of going upstairs, I sat on the cold, hard cement steps outside my apartment building trying to calm down and contemplating whether I had just kissed away the ton of money Dykstra owed me.

That night, Dykstra told Dorothy that he "snapped off" on me, and she says she came to my defense. "Out of all your employees . . . of everyone I've worked with for you . . . there is no one more solid than Chris," she wrote to him in an e-mail. Dorothy told Dykstra that I was the "best asset" he had. "Plus he truly likes you too and has a great deal of respect for you as he should," she continued. "And, he understands your unconventional work habits and unreasonable hours . . . and for the most part . . . thrives. I think you should be nice to him. He has worked hard for your respect. He has mine."

The next morning, our newly expanded staff was already experiencing troubles. Because Dykstra had not paid the staffing agency, it instructed the woman who had worn sneakers to the interview to pack her things and leave. She did.

As Diana began to train Kevin McCarthy and the two ventured out to buy him a computer for his workstation with the little money we had, I prayed Dykstra would be on time for his 4:30 p.m. meeting with the building management concerning our rent.

Dykstra had promised to show up, check in hand. Our rent was seriously past due, and we needed to pay at least $59,554 to avoid having our phones and Internet shut down. Adel, the management company rep, hadn't started collections procedures or shut off our services earlier as a favor to Dykstra, but now he was concerned his own job was on the line.

By 5:30 p.m., Dykstra was still a no-show. He wasn't responding to e-mail and wasn't returning Adel's phone calls. With no other options, Adel shut our services down. Instead of finalizing the magazine for printing, the four of us— me, Diana, and the two Kevins—were left to throw all the papers and equipment into boxes, packing up the office in a hurry. We needed to take as much as possible because we might not be allowed back in.

Kevin Coughlin packed his car and headed home, while Diana, Kevin McCarthy, and I lugged heavy computers, printers, and boxes through the streets of Midtown Manhattan in search of a taxi to transport the items to my apartment. However, the United Nations, which was just a few blocks away, was in session, and many of the streets were blocked off and taxis were in short supply. Two hours later, we loaded up a cab I hailed and went our separate ways, possibly for good.

CHAPTER 29

LATE-SEASON COLLAPSE

Summer was a distant memory. It was just a few days after we had been booted from the Park Avenue offices, and it was wet outside—showers on and off all night. There was a persistent murkiness hovering over New York City, and I was mentally and physically drained.

The long hours were catching up to me physically and they felt even longer following my fallout with Dykstra. I had aged a lot since I starting to work for Dykstra, and I had packed on more than a few pounds too.

However, on September 25 I had a job to do—an important one. We desperately needed to secure a new office quickly. It was only a matter of time before people found out that we had been evicted from our old offices, and if that happened, it would be next to impossible to rent a new space.

Dykstra was at Shea Stadium for a pregame ceremony commemorating the few remaining days of the stadium. The Mets would unveil Citi Field in 2009, and Shea would be demolished. As the last game drew nearer, the Mets were welcoming back celebrities and former players to help with the countdown.

Fittingly, Dykstra, a hero in Mets lore, was standing in the outfield before the fans in the stadium's waning days—an honor to be sure. To those of us who were working for Dykstra, it was a welcomed night off from him.

On that night, I was running a few minutes late for an appointment with Diana when I received a call from Kevin Coughlin. "I called to give you a heads up," he said with a hint of exasperation in his voice. "I just got off the phone with Lenny."

Coughlin proceeded to tell me that Dykstra had accused him of blabbing about our office "relocation" to a Philly-based reporter. That was the last thing we needed in the paper—and Dykstra was still technically supposed to be negotiating a buyout of the lease.

Reenacting the phone conversation and doing his best Nails impression, Kevin shouted, "KEVIN, WHAT THE FUCK DID YOU DO?" Kevin was clearly annoyed and nervous at the accusation, but because the situation was so unbelievable, he seemed to find it almost comical. Somehow, word had gotten back to Bill Conlin that the Players Club had been tossed out after owing tens of thousands of dollars in past-due rent on the 245 Park Avenue offices. Not only did Bill send Dykstra an e-mail questioning him about the intel; he also sent a heads up to Dykstra's pal Jim Cramer.

"This confirms my mounting fears that you are tapped out and the magazine and Players Club is in dire straits," Conlin wrote to Dykstra. "If this is true and the top, award-winning writers I have lined up for you don't get paid, it will be fodder for every Media columnist in the country."

Conlin had embarrassed Dykstra in front of Cramer, and he was pissed. Someone was going to pay, most likely with his or her job.

I ended the call with Coughlin as I approached the building. Diana, dressed in a dark navy business suit, was seated inside the lobby waiting for me. Even though it was late, she had a smile on her face and was anxious to show off the potential new office space. I was thankful to have her on the team.

As we embarked on the tour of the ninth floor, my mind was preoccupied. It was only a matter of time before Dykstra called me for questioning. I knew that telling the truth wasn't good enough—the only thing that mattered was whether Dykstra actually believed the truth or not. And often, I had learned, that was a crapshoot. So I played the scenario out in my head, over and over.

Surely, Dykstra was stomping through the slushy outfield grass in front of a roaring crowd at Shea. I assumed I was safe for the moment. But I wasn't so lucky. My phone began to buzz, and it was him. I took a deep breath and answered. "Hey, Lenny," I said, trying to sound upbeat. He dove right in, shouting, "CHRIS, DID YOU FUCKING TELL BILL CONLIN WE GOT EVICTED?" In a slow and deliberate voice, I said, "Absolutely not," leaving it short and sweet. "Well, somebody did. The drama queen's stirring up shit again," he said, using his favorite nickname for Conlin.

I excused myself into an empty office before telling Dykstra where I was and what I was doing. "I'm sure it's Kevin Coughlin," he said, his voice growing louder. I didn't say anything, worried our tour guide might overhear something she wasn't supposed to and ruin our chances of renting at the building.

"Are you near a TV?" he asked, his voice leveling off. I wasn't, but before I could answer, he said, "Look, I'm walking through the outfield right now. I gotta go. I need you to find out who did this," he said and quickly hung up.

As the three of us searched for the ceremony on a TV in the lobby, Dykstra made his way toward the outfield warning track. Wearing his signature light-tan Maybach cap, dark suit pants, brown jacket—and not a hint of clothing that suggested he had once played for the Mets—Dykstra and Mr. Met, the team's baseball-headed mascot, continued with the ceremonial countdown. They ripped down a board containing the number "5"—it fell to the ground, stirring up a small gust of warning track dust. Dykstra patted the new number "4" before turning and heading off.

Back in the office, Diana and I finished our tour and went our separate ways. As I rested my head down for a solid six hours of sleep later that night, I hoped Friday would be a better day.

"Bill, you really fucking piss me off—you told Cramer that things weren't going well?" Dykstra wrote to him in all caps. The exchange was waiting for me in my inbox when I woke up. "Who the fuck do you think you are making stupid ass accusations that are complete nonsense? You should know by now Bill, don't ever underestimate me! You don't think I had it planned to leave the $35,000 a month offices after the first full year?"

Dykstra had very specific instructions for the graybeard reporter. "You better e-mail and call everyone you told these lies to—and I want to be blind copied on every fucking one of them! I am fucking hot. . . . Did you do this purposely . . . [to] try and hurt me? You really fucked up Bill."

———

A few days later, after another all-nighter at Dykstra's hotel suite, I packed my leather work bag as Dykstra got ready to head off to the final game ever at Shea Stadium. Things were still awkward between us after the shouting match a few days earlier but were getting better. I told him I was going to Shea too.

"Maybe I'll see you there," he said to me. "Only if you bring your binoculars," I replied. "I'll be in the upper deck." Dykstra asked me where that was, and I explained that the upper deck was the level of red seats at the top of the stadium. "No, you'll be my guest," he said. "I'll leave the tickets at will call for you." I thanked him and then rushed home to get ready and meet up with Rhea.

Not only did the game have historic significance as the final game to be played at Shea; it was also a big game for the 2008 Mets. On the last day of the regular season, the Mets remained deadlocked in the wildcard race with the Milwaukee Brewers. The Mets had been in a free fall and were on the verge of their second consecutive season-ending collapse.

If both teams won their respective season finales, they would face off in a single game to determine who advanced to the postseason. However, if the Mets beat the Marlins and the Brewers lost to the Cubs, or vice versa, the winning team would move on while the loser would head home.

When I arrived at the stadium's will call office, no one had ever heard of me and there were no tickets from Dykstra for me. The ticket agents at will call suggested I visit the team's public relations staff. I waited my turn in line and eventually explained my plight to the attendant. She asked me which player was supposed to leave the tickets for me, and when I told her it was Dykstra, she rolled her eyes and told me to hold on just a second while she checked on a few things. After about twenty minutes, she came back with four passes for me. I thanked her, and we entered the stadium.

I didn't love the way Dykstra had been speaking to me at that time, but I was grateful to him for providing me with a once-in-a-lifetime experience. As we walked through the Diamond Club, the Mets exclusive restaurant, and through some restricted tunnels, I realized my passes weren't for some average seats. They provided us with access to an enormous luxury suite beyond the left field fence.

As Rhea and I walked down the tunnel, I recognized the man next to me as former Mets second baseman Tim Teufel. I shook his hand and said I used to watch him play ball all the time when I was a kid. Not wanting to bother him or intrude on this special day, Rhea and I walked away. Teufel, however, was walking in the same direction and continued to chat us up. He was supernice, and meeting him was a big highlight for us. Later, when I told Dykstra that Teufel, his former teammate on the '86 Mets, had been so kind to us, he was unimpressed. "Tim Teufel is a pussy, dude," he snapped back.

As we stepped inside the suite, we were surrounded by Mets royalty who were participating in a postgame, stadium-closing ceremony. As I sat on one of the benches, I saw players I had revered while growing up. Standing just a few feet away were Wally Backman, Jesse Orosco, and Lee Mazilli, teammates of Dykstra's from the '86 Mets. On the other side of the suite were Doc Gooden, Darryl Strawberry, and Gary Carter.

I spotted Mike Piazza chatting up Todd Zeile and Robin Ventura, teammates from the 2000 National League Champion Mets, and I saw Brooklyn-bred pitcher John Franco sitting with his family just a few seats away. Even some of the real old-timers were there: Ed Kranepool and baseball icons Willie Mays and Yogi Berra. The whole thing was awesome.

While my brother-in-law and sister took pictures with the Mets legends and Rhea enjoyed the jumbo shrimp cocktail, the 2008 Mets blew the game. With the score tied 2–2 in the eighth inning, the Mets' bullpen surrendered a pair of solo home runs to the Marlins to fall 4–2, ending the season. *USA Today*'s headline read "Shea It Ain't So! Mets Fall Short of Playoffs Again."

As the 2008 Mets filed off the field, Dykstra and the other legends returned to the diamond for one last curtain call. Wearing dark pants, a tucked-in Mets jersey, and a tan Maybach hat, Dykstra touched home plate one last time and waved good-bye to the cheering crowd.

CHAPTER 30

PROPERTY OF DEADBEAT DYKSTRA

September 29, 2008, started out as an unremarkable day. Dykstra sported a 70–0 stock-picking record, with $189,100 in profits, but the central nervous system of "the best magazine in the world" was running through my cozy, 350-square-foot, prewar apartment, which doubled as the East Coast headquarters of the Players Club. Papers and printouts were scattered across my plush tan couch cushions and were piled up on my end table.

To my left was a brand new touch-screen computer packed up in its box, and to my right was the oversized office printer sitting atop my displaced coffee table. The *Players Club* had been homeless since the previous Tuesday, and boxes containing office supplies, magazines, paperwork, and equipment cluttered my already cramped apartment.

The overcast midmorning sky was dripping pockets of light into my otherwise dark apartment when my Blackberry sounded the warning bell. I stretched across my recliner, knocking a few loose papers from the couch onto the floor.

"Box of Rocks must go. Fire his ass immediately," Dykstra insisted, referring to Kevin Coughlin. With the festivities behind him, Dykstra was fully refocused on his witch hunt to find out how Bill Conlin knew we had been booted from our office. Dykstra had told me to fire Coughlin several times before, but each time I suggested that we wait, and he acquiesced. Not this time—he was judge and jury, and the verdict was in. Coughlin was guilty and had to go.

"If you don't want to be a man and do it, I'll handle it. I'll tell that motherfucker what I really think of him—that he sucks at picking photos, that he is a piece of shit," he said, his voice growing more irate. "I'll spit in his face. . . . I'll enjoy it."

I suspected Coughlin could stir up a lot of trouble if he wanted to. Although I had fired only two other people in my life, I offered to do it rather than have Dykstra needlessly insult the guy on his way out the door.

I called Coughlin, who had been up late the night before working on the magazine. "Listen, Kevin, Lenny is going in another direction," I said to him. "Just pay me," he said matter-of-factly. "All I want is what I'm owed." I told him I would do my best.

I had implemented a payroll system for the company to try and provide some structure, ensure employees got paid on time, and provide them with some state-sponsored protections. However, none of that mattered if the money earmarked for payroll never made it into the bank account, I explained. Shortly thereafter, I was able to issue both James and Kevin Coughlin their final checks, emptying the bank account. Coughlin claimed his check was missing pay from his first week at the *Players Club*. Regardless, we had no money left.

That day was significant for another reason—I made probably my biggest mistake while working for Dykstra. I realized almost immediately that I had committed a cardinal sin: I had vouched for Dykstra. My reputation and his were now more intertwined than ever.

Dykstra called me and was incensed that the press might find out he was broke. He was growing increasingly paranoid following the flare-up involving the dynamic duo—Conlin and Coughlin. That morning Conlin forwarded both of us an e-mail he had received from one of the nation's most influential sportswriters.

The sportswriter, who also wrote for the *Players Club*, said he had heard Dykstra was broke, the magazine was out of business and selling off its assets, and the writers would be getting stiffed. "If this is true, it could be a major story what with all the country's economic woes," the note to Conlin read.

Conlin had a complex relationship with the *Players Club*. He had an economic interest in seeing the magazine do well—he was being paid $5,000 or more each month. It was a king's ransom. On the other hand, he was still a reporter, and he had put his reputation on the line to bring others into the fold.

The lack of clarity on which hat he and the other writers were wearing at any given time made it difficult territory for me to navigate. Were they sportswriters covering Dykstra? If they were prohibited from writing about him, would they slip tips to their fellow journalists? What was their priority: their freelance fee or the news about Dykstra's faltering empire? And what would happen when those interests conflicted?

It was obvious Conlin didn't trust Dykstra, but he wanted to stay on the money train. Conlin had seemingly done his best to put *that* fire out. However, that wasn't enough.

"I'm tired of standing up for everyone . . . carrying the load," Dykstra shouted at me through the phone. "It's about fucking time someone stood up for me. I want you to write a letter to every one of those writers telling them Kevin Coughlin made this shit up. It's time for you to step up to the plate. Tell them that motherfucker is a scumbag."

As the call continued, Dykstra said that he had finalized a loan and it would fund within a week. At best, Dykstra was overly optimistic all the time about when the next loan, round of funding, or money source would come through. At worst, he outright lied . . . a lot. Either way, reality was a far different picture from the one Dykstra had painted, and deciphering the truth was nearly impossible. The money was always a few days or a week away from hitting his bank account, and he was always on the brink of becoming liquid.

Back on the call he wanted me to write the letter immediately to our freelancers squashing the rumors and telling them they would be paid within fifteen days. Action was needed—it wasn't a suggestion.

I refused to bring Coughlin's name into the mix but told the writers I wanted to "address some bad information" about Dykstra and the *Players Club* that had been "started by a disgruntled former employee and spread by some irresponsible members of the press." With James gone, I was acting in a public relations role as well, and I wasn't used to it.

I said that the rumors had no merit, that the October edition of the magazine would be rolling off the presses within the week, and that we had relocated the Players Club's offices as planned to a classy new residence on Fifty-third Street that met our needs better and cost a fraction of the price in rent. (Diana had lined up a new office, but we were waiting for Dykstra to give us the $31,000 for rent and deposit before we could move in.)

Saying we had planned to move might not have been completely true, but it was the company's official position, and Dykstra insisted that not paying rent was part of his plan to negotiate a way out of the lease. I didn't buy it, but I couldn't argue the point without calling my boss a liar.

In my note, I also told the writers that Dykstra personally paid a number of the reporters that Doubledown had failed to pay. Lastly, I said that Dykstra paid his writers "handsomely and in line with our freelance policy. And most importantly ON TIME. . . . Because of these nonsensical rumors, Mr. Dykstra wants you to rest assured that you will be taken care of. So, we are issuing all payments early this month."

I was a seasoned veteran at avoiding Dykstra's minefield, but I had let my guard down for a split second. I should have said no, but I didn't. I knew the e-mail was a mistake the moment I hit the "send" button. Now a handful of the best sportswriters in the world had a note from *ME* promising them payment within fifteen days. It was an overly aggressive timeline for most magazines and a nearly impossible one for us.

The gravity of the situation began to set in immediately. If Dykstra didn't pay those writers, I would have a hell of a time getting another reporting job at any reputable news organization. I might have just tarred and feathered the professional reputation I had spent the previous decade building, I thought to myself. I was screwed—I needed Dykstra to keep his word.

Things got weirder each day, descending from peculiar to outrageous. One day I found myself picking up office supplies in boxes labeled "Property of Deadbeat Dykstra" left on Kevin Coughlin's stoop; the next I was hearing about how one of Dykstra's California-based assistants quit following one of his famous farting incidents. Bending over, he asked the assistant to look and see if he had accidentally split the seam of his pants. When she leaned in to check, he cut a smelly one.

Back in New York, new staffers were also beginning to get their first whiff of Nails's wrath. With our team of three reassembled back in our new office on Fifty-third Street, Dykstra instructed Diana to secure a number of small business loans and a bunch of business credit cards.

When Diana contacted several banks, they all denied our applications because of Dykstra's debt, his legal troubles, "serious delinquency," and too many inquiries within the previous year, among other reasons. When she informed Dykstra, she became his newest target.

"My personal business is my personal business, it's that simple!" he wrote to her in bold black letters. "Obviously you were not told," he continued, switching to bold red capital letters. "I do not like people trying to find out personal information about my background." Back in bold black capital letters, Lenny continued: "You have no idea what I went through the last 10 years—or what

I am still going through. The reason that you see flaws in my personal credit has nothing to do with me." In phone conversations, he blamed his kid brother, Kevin Dykstra.

In a veiled threat, he told Diana he would address the issue this one time but not a second one. "I wasn't prying into his personal life," she says. "I was just doing what he told me to do—doing my job."

Worried about the e-mail, I helped Diana craft a nonthreatening response. She explained that she was following his instructions, was completely on his team, and even looked up to him. "I was really upset. I was hoping I wouldn't become the next Kevin Coughlin," she says. "I had a feeling I was going to be next."

Diana's note kept Dykstra at bay for a bit, but before long he was pressuring the both of us to use our own personal credit ratings to secure loans and credit cards for the Players Club and Nails Investments. He said his lawyers would draw up contracts ensuring we wouldn't be held liable for the charges. It sounded fishy, and each time he asked, we told him we couldn't do it.

———

My personal struggles with Dykstra continued as well. One night at his hotel suite—the Ritz Carlton in Battery Park—we ended up getting in another blowout over one of the articles slated for the upcoming edition of the magazine. I had pitched an article to Dykstra about a pro baseball player who had gotten injured but was making a solid comeback after being out of the game for a few years. It was the perfect article for our audience because injuries could have a huge financial impact on a player's life, I told him. We could talk about the need to save—a core motto of the Players Club. Plus, the player was smart—he understood finances.

At first Dykstra, who was groggier than usual that night, ridiculously saw the player as potential competition because he did his own stock trading, but he later gave me the go-ahead. "I don't want players thinking they can do this themselves," Dykstra said. So I agreed not to include anything about the player's stock-picking prowess in the article.

I interviewed the player, set up the article and layout, and placed it on the magazine's pages. From that moment on, Dykstra whined about the piece, complaining about the headlines I wrote and the photos we used. One photo of the player celebrating and letting out a yell after hitting a home run was awful, he said. "It looks like he is sucking a dick. We can't use this." Ironically, in a photo of Dykstra included in a feature about the final days of Shea Stadium in the same issue, he was making a similar facial expression during his home run celebration against the Houston Astros in 1986.

Dykstra bitched about the text I wrote even though he didn't read it. He was upset the player wasn't a superstar of the caliber of Derek Jeter or Lebron James. It was a nightmare. The player, the brother of a friend of mine, had been nice enough to give us his time. It would be embarrassing to me both personally and professionally to backpedal. Plus, it would be a huge waste of my already severely limited time, and, most importantly, the article was good. Dykstra didn't care. It wasn't about the magazine; it was about exerting control.

Dykstra saw the preproduction layout of the article and launched into a tirade. "What's this shit?" he exclaimed. I told him it was the article we had previously agreed upon. He began yelling. "Fuck no. I don't want it. He's your friend. That's why you want him in the magazine." I was having déjà vu. It was the fight over the Evan Longoria piece all over again.

After he calmed down, I told Dykstra that I had never even met the guy and had spoken to him on the phone only for the article, but that it was a good story for our readers. "So you're telling me it's a solid story?" he said, looking at me, his voice leveling off. "Yeah, Lenny, it's good. I wouldn't have suggested it if it wasn't," I told him. He said that he was going to trust me and the layout could stay.

When I left the hotel that morning after another all-nighter, I thought the issue was resolved, but it wasn't. A few days later, as we were mired in the intricate details of commas and periods, trying to make final adjustments to the magazine before printing the next day, Dorothy called.

"Hi, Chris, Lenny couldn't take any more details tonight, and he put me in charge of closing the magazine," she said. Closing the magazine was technically my job. I wasn't thrilled, especially after having worked on the magazine for thirty straight hours, that Dorothy suddenly had been given the final say. It was weird and just another one of Dykstra's games.

She sheepishly explained to me that Dykstra had instructed her to swap out the piece we had argued about earlier and insert a story from *Haute Living* in its place. That made absolutely no sense. Not only shouldn't we be making major changes like that at the eleventh hour, but also the story from *Haute Living* was crap. It was a lifestyle piece and didn't belong smack in the middle of the *Players Club*'s financial section. It wasn't edited for our audience, and it was too late to move all the pages around—everything had been copyedited, and this was the middle of the night. Dorothy agreed with me but said it was out of her control. "Lenny wants what Lenny wants," she said.

"Lenny can have whatever he wants, but if you replace that article, I quit," I told her. She asked if I would at least help her make the changes that night and then quit the next day. "Absolutely not," I said.

She agreed to keep the article and told me she would explain to Dykstra that the *Haute Living* article was bad. "And I'll pretend I didn't hear that little thing about quitting," she said to me, trying to lighten the mood.

I knew the end was near; I had to find a way out. But for the moment, I was stuck—I was owed too much money to simply walk away, and if I quit, all the people I had brought into the mix and all those who counted on me to get paid would have no shot at their money.

CHAPTER 31

FOOL ON THE HILL

I was sitting in the back of a taxi flying down the FDR Drive at 1:30 a.m. Dykstra had summoned me to the Ritz Carlton yet again. However, that night was different because Rhea was sitting next to me.

Earlier, Dykstra had said he would put us up in the room next to his. "Come down, bring your girl, it will be like a minivacation for you here in New York," he had told me. We really appreciated the kind gesture.

We arrived and attempted to check into our room. "I'm sorry, sir, Mr. Dykstra has no more room left on his credit card," the man behind the counter whispered, trying to be discreet. Dykstra had told me TheStreet.com was paying for the rooms, and I explained this to the clerk. He apologized again and said that if I wanted the room, I could put it on my credit card and then sort things out with Dykstra later. I certainly knew better than that.

I looked at Rhea, and she offered to go home. However, I wasn't about to do that to her—not after I had dragged her all the way downtown in the middle of the night.

I spoke with the manager and worked out a deal. He agreed to delay charging my credit card until Dykstra checked out. That way he could find out if TheStreet.com was in fact paying for the rooms. That sounded reasonable.

I handed over my credit card, but with a caveat. "I'm sure I don't have to tell you that Mr. Dykstra is an overly extravagant person," I said to the man. "I, however, am not. If TheStreet doesn't pay, you are authorized to charge my card for my room only. No incidentals, nothing. I don't want to be charged for any of Lenny's things." He assured me that would not be a problem and handed me the room key.

Rhea and I went upstairs. After checking out our room and noticing the amazing view of the Statue of Liberty, we met Dykstra. Rhea thanked him before retiring for the night. I had to stay and get some work done, he said.

I updated Dykstra on the progress of his New York staff. I had interviewed a steady stream of writers and editors to fill out the magazine's staff, but when I gave Dykstra a short list of the candidates I liked most, he was no longer interested.

We also discussed the upcoming edition of the magazine, and he told me he wanted me to write a special tribute to Paul Newman, the legendary actor who had just died. Before he lost his battle with cancer at the age of eight-three, Newman had invited Hollywood's elite to San Francisco to perform in *The World of Nick Adams*, a show based on the short stories of Ernest Hemingway. The star-studded performance would benefit the Painted Turtle, a camp for kids with serious illnesses. With Newman gone, the event would double as a celebration of the actor and philanthropist's life.

"Everyone's going to be there. I got a couple of tables," Dykstra explained. "I want you to go and write about it. You can bring Rhea—it's going to be big league." He told me he was donating the use of his Gulfstream and a second Gulfstream to usher the stars back and forth to the event. The list was impressive: Danny DeVito, Tom Hanks, Jack Nicholson, Julia Roberts, Sean Penn, Bruce Willis, Danny Glover, Billy Crystal, Warren Beatty, Annette Bening, and Edward James Olmos. "I don't really have the bullets right now, but there was no way I could say no. It's for kids with cancer."

He said I should fly back with him to California at the end of the week, where we would attend the fund-raiser and work on the magazine. However, before he left New York, Dykstra had to speak at an investment conference hosted by TheStreet.com.

———————

As Dykstra approached the podium at the conference at Chelsea Peers, I sat in the back of the room hoping Dykstra wouldn't strike out. He hadn't prepared a speech, and it was obvious as he held up a print copy of the newsletter and asked audience members why they hadn't bought a subscription yet. He rambled, bouncing aimlessly from topic to topic, telling them repeatedly they should buy "Nails on the Numbers" for only a thousand bucks a year and that he was undefeated. "One win pays for the whole year," he repeated.

He then pointed toward me, telling the audience that I was his editor and that I actually did some ghostwriting for him. Before long, he began asking me questions as if I were standing next to him. He wanted to know how many wins we had and wanted me to remind him of some of his recent picks.

As I shouted back the answers, I wanted to crawl under my chair. Dykstra was funny, but not for the right reasons. When the spectacle was over, a large group of investors flocked around Dykstra. Some were baseball fans and wanted his autograph. Others thought he was a savant and wanted to hear more of his rap.

After the conference, Dykstra disappeared onto a gigantic yacht docked at the pier, while I stood in the rain in the parking lot fighting off a cold and waiting for him to come back out. Downtown, Dykstra's flight attendants Amanda and Brit were supposed to check him out of the Ritz and meet us at the airport, but there was a snag.

"We spent the whole day in the lobby because Lenny had went to give a speech and he hadn't paid for the hotel," Brit says. "Until the authorization went through, they wouldn't release Lenny's bags. We stood there in the lobby from 9 a.m. to about 5 p.m., and then they said we could go."

When I saw Amanda later, she told me that, despite the frustrating and embarrassing episode at the Ritz, the hotel employees didn't charge my credit card. I thanked her profusely. Disaster averted, I thought. Weeks later when I received my credit card statement, I noticed some unusual charges. There were two of them—both from the Ritz. One was for $561.03 and the other $281.

I was really bummed but thought maybe I was going to be stuck paying for the room after all. However, why were there two charges? When I called the hotel to find out, I was told that the two charges were for Dykstra's livery cabs around the city.

I told the woman from the Ritz that was unacceptable, and she responded by telling me I was charged because I was part of the same party as Dykstra. "It's like when you go out to dinner with someone," she said, "if they don't have the money to pay, you're stuck paying."

I explained that I had never authorized those charges and that the hotel had committed credit card fraud by using my card without my permission. She refunded the money.

We were still on the move by 2:00 a.m. the next morning, and we were in California, having just touched down at the airport. During the flight, I learned of a new reality TV project Dykstra was supposedly working on called *'Til Debt Do Us Part*. In it, Dykstra would play a character similar to Donald Trump on *The Apprentice*, presiding over teams of two trying to become financially astute.

Dykstra also informed me during the flight that we would no longer be attending the Paul Newman event in San Francisco, the whole reason for my trip. The news was highly frustrating since Rhea had bought a new dress just for the occasion and had purchased an airline ticket because prior obligations prevented her from flying on the private jet with us. However, even more troubling, I realized I was stranded at Dykstra's mansion and was at his mercy for five whole days.

We arrived at the estate and headed straight through the mansion and out the back door to his office, which was located in a separate building on the grounds. On my way down the pitch-dark pathway, I missed a step and found myself face-down on the cold, hard brick, scuffing my hands. All I wanted was to go to sleep, but Dykstra insisted it was time to work. I had no choice but to comply.

The office was massive and had a kitchen, bathroom, dining room table, and Dykstra's command center—a desk with three adjacent computer screens and two gigantic flat screen televisions tuned to CNBC, one above the other, on the wall in front of him. Dykstra opened the French doors behind him to let some air in the office, while I set my computer up on the dining room table about ten feet from him. My section of the office was dark, whereas Dykstra's was dimly lit.

As with all the previous nights of work with Dykstra, it was not very productive. When I was trying to select a female tennis player to feature in the magazine that month, Dykstra seemed more interested in sending me crotch-shot photos of potential candidates. "Check your e-mail, bro," he said, laughing hysterically. "Look at that camel toe, bro; look at it."

———————

When the sun finally came up, it was time to call it a night. Dykstra packed his bags to head to his other home. Instead of a bedroom in the vacant mansion, Dykstra said I should sleep on a sofa just feet away from his broken 1986 World Series trophy.

With the sun beaming in on my face through the window, I did my best to try and catch some shut-eye. A few short hours after falling asleep, I was awakened by the sound of Dykstra screaming. He was dressed and on the move, asking me why the hell I hadn't answered my phone or his e-mails as he stormed into the office.

Still struggling to awaken, I told him that I hadn't heard the phone and that he had left only a little more than three hours before. Not pleased, he told me he was heading out to meetings and would be back later and that I should get to work.

That afternoon, Dykstra came storming back into the office while I was typing away on my computer. "Bro, you've got to get going. I need you out of here right away." I didn't know what he was talking about, but I began to save my work and pack up my computer. He told me someone was coming to take a look at the house—a possible buyer—and he didn't want the potential buyer to see me, as if I might somehow derail the deal.

He ushered me to the gym, a separate building on the other side of the pool. My computer was shutting down, but Dykstra couldn't wait. He kept telling me there was no time and that I had to move right away. Suddenly, I felt like Dorothy—"hidden."

Once in the gym, I got a call from Dorothy. I knew Dykstra was furious with her over a mix-up regarding some loan documents. He felt she had cost him a massive loan.

Nonetheless, Dorothy wanted to swing by the mansion to finally meet me face to face and drop off some computer software we needed for work on "Nails on the Numbers" back in New York. Because Dykstra was pissed at her, I told her to clear it with him. So she sent him an e-mail saying she was coming to the house to see me, not him.

Dykstra was infuriated, yelling at me and asking what the hell I thought I was doing inviting her over. I told him that I hadn't and that she wanted to come and deliver some software. "Have her mail it. I don't want her here," he said.

As I sat on a wall next to Dykstra's tennis court near a small grove of grapefruit trees, Dorothy vented her frustration to me on the telephone. She wondered what was so terrible about her that Dykstra barred her from the grounds. She told me she was quitting effective immediately. I asked if she would train me, Diana, and Kevin on how to create the newsletter's Stat Book, but she refused. She said her relationship with Team Dykstra was over.

———————

With Dorothy out of the picture, Dykstra and his new entourage assembled in the office. Present were Noah, who had traveled with us from New York; Ivy,

Dykstra's new flight attendant, and her boyfriend, Chris, who were staying in the guest house; and a couple of pilots. Dykstra suggested dinner, and Noah and I loaded into the Maybach while the others rode in a separate car.

While stopped at a gas station minimart on the way to pick up cigarettes, Dykstra turned to Noah and me and said his wallet was a little light and that he needed to borrow some cash. Noah, who didn't work for Dykstra but was considering helping facilitate the reality show, didn't say a word. Dykstra looked at me, and I offered a hundred fifty bucks. "Thanks, bro, I'll pay you back." When we got to the restaurant, Dykstra sat at the end of the table with his head buried in his laptop, except when he tried to flirt with the waitress by asking about her Italian accent.

After we finished our meals, Dykstra, Noah, and I headed to the counter to pay the check. Dykstra forked over $50, handed me the bill with instructions to pay the rest, and then walked out of the restaurant. I was ticked. I had just lent him enough to pay for the meal. Instead, he pocketed most of the money and milked me for more cash. I didn't want to cause a scene in front of the entire group, so I paid the bill and left.

Instead of being grateful, Dykstra made a number of rude comments at my expense on the car ride home. He was clearly ticked that I was leaving to go pick Rhea up at LAX later that night. He had asked his driver, Paul Lee, to go get her, and I told him I would be going along for the ride to make sure she got in okay.

When we arrived at the Gretzky mansion, Lee was waiting. He was a hulking, intimidating guy—a former college football player who could have served as a bouncer in a club.

He was about my height but jacked, and although he was fifty years old, he looked like he was in his midthirties. He didn't belong to a gym—he kept in shape the old-fashioned way, running a mile at 6:00 a.m. every day and pumping out pushups, a hundred at a clip. He reminded me of Michael Clark Duncan, the late actor who played John Coffey in the movie *The Green Mile*. Face to face, Lee seemed nice, but he looked like the kind of guy you wouldn't mess with.

A middle linebacker at Long Beach State in the late 1970s, Lee always had jobs, but never a career. Now he was Dykstra's driver, earning $1,000 a week.

"I was really enthusiastic about the opportunity to work with him because of what he achieved as a professional athlete," Lee recalls. "It was an opportunity for me to work with a man who played team sports at the absolute highest level in his given sport."

The job went well at first—Dykstra was nice to him and paid him after just two weeks. "I went to work for him with an attitude of gratitude," Lee says. "I was going to serve this guy to the best of my ability short of breaking the law and taking my own life."

As Lee and I pulled away from the mansion in the Maybach, he told me the gas gauge was almost on empty and we needed to stop and get some fuel. "Lenny didn't give me any money, and I don't have any of his credit cards," he explained. Under normal circumstances, I wouldn't have minded paying since we were going to pick up my girlfriend, but after Dykstra had bled me dry at dinner, I was miffed. I gave Lee $50, and he filled the car up while I sat inside.

However, the car was beautiful, and we picked Rhea up with little problem. Once at the mansion, I showed Rhea to our room, which I had claimed earlier in the day, and spent a little time with her before she went to sleep and I went back to work.

At 1:00 a.m. I walked into the office to find Dykstra sitting at his desk, busy at "work." I noticed my computer, which I had left powered on, had been used. There were a number of windows open, including one containing the video of the *Fox & Friends* episode in which Dykstra wrestled the host.

"Lenny, why did you use my computer?" I asked, intentionally sounding confused.

"No, no, Noah was using it for something," he responded nonchalantly, keeping his head buried in one of his laptops. "Ahhhhhh . . . he said he needed to check something." I dropped the subject, even though I didn't believe him. As I browsed through the other open windows, I noticed someone had gone through my e-mail.

At the top of my inbox was a new note from Dorothy that had already been marked as read. I dove in. She apologized for her earlier outburst and said she would honor my request to show the staff how to create the Stat Book images before her phone and Internet got shut off later that week for nonpayment. However, she wouldn't be able to teach us the special sauce of Dykstra's system—that needed to come from him, she said.

However, most of her e-mail was emotional venting about how she was disappointed in Dykstra but would remain loyal to him to the last. "I'd like to think he needs me . . . but that's a crock and very self-delusional, even if he has said he can't live without me. . . . He will replace me in five minutes or less . . . and not think twice about it," she wrote. "He is too resilient to really need anyone."

She said that without a miracle she would go under in a big way. "Everything good that I have tried to do for my family for the last three years will stop in a week and I have no way to fix it," she wrote. "None. Because I loaned Lenny my safety net and charged up my credit cards for him . . . so I have no fall back and I am out of time. . . . Lenny is my only hope and now I fear he is too angry to care what he has promised me . . . or too over extended to help even if he wanted to." Despite the one-sided relationship, Dorothy intended to continue fighting for Dykstra, saying that someone would have to "rip the torch out of my hands before I give up."

Two minutes after I finished reading the note, Dykstra broke the silence, asking me what Dorothy had to say. It was an awkward moment because I hadn't told him about the e-mail, but I assumed he knew because he had snooped. I was honest, telling Dykstra that Dorothy was upset about not being able to come to the mansion and that she agreed to help us with the Stat Book.

"She's being dramatic again!" he commented and then changed the subject. I worked again through the night and snuck out of the office at about 3:45 a.m. when Dykstra fell asleep, facedown on his desk. As I left, I looked around, taking in the beauty of the mountains and the gorgeous mansion. I couldn't help but think that the scenery couldn't have been in more contrast to the man living in the mansion.

CHAPTER 32

LIVING IN FANTASYLAND

I could feel the noose tightening around my neck. My savings were running thin, Dykstra owed me a lot of dough, and the economy and job market were tanking. Unfortunately, Dykstra wasn't the only one failing to make good on his obligations, making my situation even more precarious and leaving me to wonder if birds of a feather really do fly together.

Staying up until 3:00 a.m. to edit Eric Bolling's columns yielded nothing but frustration. He eventually stopped writing for TheStreet.com, and when I tried to collect for my editing services, Bolling balked. He said he had made very little money from the endeavor, as if to excuse his debt.

When I pressed him further, Dykstra intervened, telling the television star not to worry about paying me because he would take care of it, which he never did. Months later, Bolling promised to send me a check—a small check—since I hadn't been paid a single cent for editing his columns. It never arrived. I wasn't thrilled, but I knew the terms with Bolling had never been fully outlined, so I chalked the experience up to an expensive life lesson.

Tim Brown, the former NFL icon, was another story altogether. After I received initial wire payments for ghostwriting Brown's columns, there was a break in the chain. Brown was to receive $4,000 a month from TheStreet.com and then give me half. However, before long, he began keeping all the money for himself.

It started out seemingly innocently enough. When I first inquired about the delay, Brown told me he was having issues with his bank and would be switching to a new one shortly. It would take a little while, he said, but I would be paid. So I continued to ghostwrite his columns.

That short period of time turned into a few months. When I followed up with Brown, he explained there was an illness in his family and apologized for the holdup. I certainly understood. The next time I asked about the money, Brown told me he was coping with the death of a friend and that he had lost all of my contact information when his computer crashed. Again, he asked for my patience, and although I was growing increasingly suspicious, I did not want to be insensitive either.

Several months later in February, a few months after I had quit writing for Brown, I inquired about the outstanding invoices. Once again he apologized for the lack of communication and said he should be recovering some funds shortly. He claimed I would be made whole by the first week in March 2009.

Two months later, Tim Brown told me the "economic crunch has all but ruined [him] financially" and asked for more time to pull the cash together. He said he would be in touch by the end of the following week with a more definitive plan. Five months later—in September 2009—Brown said that he could apologize until he was blue in the face, but that he was dealing with some "incredibly horrific financial situations." However, he said there was good news: all the issues were being worked through, and I would get my cash.

"I know I am testing your patience but hold tight a little longer and I should be able to get this taken care of by the end of the month at the latest," he wrote to me. He never responded to my final inquiry. As of this writing, I have not been paid the $7,600 he still owes me.[1]

I wasn't the only writer in the fall of 2008 worried about getting stiffed. Conlin and the other reporters were growing increasingly anxious too. The payment Dykstra (and I) had promised them in my ill-fated e-mail was well past due, and many of the writers were tired of getting the runaround.

In typical Dykstra fashion, he refused to answer their e-mails or phone calls personally, leaving me and Conlin holding the bag. For his part, Conlin was getting "a little fucking sick" of hearing from the writers asking for their money.

When I asked Dykstra about the reporters' inquiries, he instructed me to send them all another note promising payment. "Just tell them the truth: they will be paid on Monday," he said. I urged caution and said to Dykstra that our best bet was to wait until the money had been sent and then provide an update. I had learned my lesson. After much debate, he eventually agreed.

Dykstra did, however, construct a plan he felt would keep the wolves at bay. He didn't have the money to pay all the writers, but he had enough to pay one of them. Since most of the writers were friends and talked to each other, paying one might give him some breathing room, Dykstra thought. However, his methods were a bit unusual. Instead of sending a check, wire, or money order, he stuffed $5,000—fifty $100 bills—in a FedEx envelope and shipped it out to one writer. He said he did that because the writer "wanted it so bad, I made sure there wasn't any confusion."

Despite his delaying tactics, the walls still appeared to be caving in around Dykstra. Neil Amdur, the legendary *New York Times* editor Dykstra had hired over the summer only to unceremoniously ditch without notice, was also reaching the end of his rope. Dykstra promised to repay Amdur's travel expenses but ignored every one of Neil's invoices and phone calls.

Unable to get a response from Dykstra, Amdur reached out to me and Conlin separately, venting his displeasure. When we told Dykstra, he responded with disdain. "I was planning on sending out the money to everyone—but I can guarantee you one thing: It sure wasn't the fuck because of Neil Amdur. . . . Sounds like the old miserable fuck needs $1,000," Dykstra wrote in an e-mail.

Conlin was also applying his own brand of leverage. He told me he had heard from a fellow reporter that Dykstra was on the verge of being indicted, while other much more influential reporters were getting ready to go for Dykstra's jugular. Conlin also implied I was about to be dragged down with Dykstra.

"When the shit hits the fan—and from what I'm hearing it's going to hit it big time, do you prefer Chris or Christopher?" he wrote to me. Dykstra was not amused, and to his credit, he told Conlin to back off. "Bill, you have a fucking problem?" Dykstra wrote. "You take it up with me, not Chris. . . . Are we clear? I am starting to believe the people that say you are more trouble than you are worth. . . . I am waiting for your call. I can't wait to hear the latest bullshit you have come up with this time."

As the three-ring, cross-country circus continued, things got weirder and I grew increasingly disgusted with Dykstra. In one incident at his hotel suite, Dykstra had a disturbing surprise for me. In his best Ace Ventura impersonation, he waved his arm side to side, loudly warning, "Do not go in there." Pointing to the guest bathroom by the suite's front door, he asked if I had used it recently. I hadn't.

"Oh, bro, you have no idea; I wrecked that bathroom," he said. I wasn't surprised. There was typically urine all over the toilet seat and on the floor in

Dykstra's bathrooms. And not just a little. I always assumed it was accidental, the product of Dykstra's sometimes shaky hands. However, I was wrong. Dykstra proceeded to tell me how he liked to leave a large amount of feces in the toilet bowl and a mess in the bathroom so that he could hear the shrieks of the hotel's grossed-out maids when they discovered what he had left for them.

As I walked toward the exit, Dykstra urged me to go into the bathroom to check out his masterpiece. I declined. "No, bro, I am serious; you gotta check this out," he said, before playfully grabbing me by the arm and attempting to pull me into the bathroom. "I'll take your word for it, Lenny," I said as I broke loose and rushed out the front door.

———————

While I was disgusted with Dykstra, I was also becoming increasingly disappointed with myself. My relationship with Rhea was suffering, and so was my health. Poor sleeping habits and a crappy diet were making it harder to control my diabetes. Everything and everyone had taken a backseat to Dykstra and the potential opportunity that came along with working for him. And I had allowed all of this.

However, the realization that I was inadvertently helping Dykstra scam others made the greatest impact on me and weighed most heavily on my mind. I was sickened that I had chosen to be loyal to a man who treated everyone as expendable.

By late fall, there was no question that there was a method to Dykstra's madness. He would hire someone, ride him or her as far and as long as possible and then discard that individual, paying little or none of what he had promised. Like a parasite, he would latch onto a host, suck it dry, and then move on to the next victim.

At first, my sin was optimism. Later, as things started to get more difficult for me, I still viewed my situation in a vacuum. I realized the situation wasn't good, but I thought the only one I was hurting by sticking it out was me. But as Dykstra's pattern repeated, I understood clearly that by keeping his businesses running and picking up the pieces after each business deal gone bad or employee burned, I was helping Dykstra's web grow wider.

New people replaced the fired ones. Fresh new vendors unaware of Dykstra's growing reputation as a slouch stepped in to pick up the slack. Plus, I had already brought in no fewer than ten freelancers or vendors whom I had previously worked with to help with the newsletter or *Players Club*, and those people were still owed money. That didn't include Kevin McCarthy or Diana.

I didn't want to destroy what was left of my professional reputation, and I couldn't sit idly by and let this situation get worse. However, I also didn't know what to do or how quickly I should do it.

Desperately needing a break, I told Dykstra I was taking a long weekend—to spend some time with Rhea and my parents, who were vacationing in Florida. So on Thursday night, I hopped a flight from LaGuardia to Orlando while Dykstra unexpectedly stayed in New York to try to secure a $300,000 loan.

When I got off the plane, I was greeted by sunshine . . . and an urgent voicemail from Diana. She explained how Dykstra had promised money to Joe, an employee of Legends Air, Dykstra's new California-based jet charter company. Joe called Diana to find out when she would be wiring him the money on Dykstra's behalf. She tried to be vague, as per Dykstra's instructions. However, Joe was persistent, so she told him she wasn't sure of the exact timing of the wire.

"A few minutes later, Lenny calls me flipping out," Diana says. "He's like, 'Diana, you really fucked up this time. I told you not to tell anybody. You screwed this up; you fucked up everything.'" He told Diana there would be "changes" as a consequence, and then he hung up on her.

I tried to calm Diana, who was clearly shaken, but in the back of my mind I was worried she wouldn't survive the weekend.

In my absence, Dykstra ramped up his bullying of the young New York office manager. He called her repeatedly, insisting the $300,000 loan had landed in his bank account. The only problem was the wired money hadn't settled in Dykstra's account as he claimed.

"I would tell Lenny that, and he would flip out on me," Diana says. "He kept making me sound like I was really dumb. I kept telling him, 'Lenny, I know what I'm doing. It takes time.'" Instead, Dykstra ignored her explanations and insisted she march down to the bank immediately and wire that money out to people he owed.

When I spoke with Diana, it was obvious she had been crying. I told her I would try to smooth things over with Dykstra and that she should hang in there.

Later that night while in my hotel room, I received an e-mail from Dykstra with the subject line "911-911-911" and a note inside that read "CALL ME ASAP—IT'S EXTREMELY IMPORTANT." That was followed by a phone call in which Dykstra launched into a temper tantrum.

"Diana quit on me, man," he repeated over and over. "She fucked up so bad."

Diana had explained to me earlier that once the bank closed for the night and the money had not settled in the account, she didn't feel there was anything else she could do. So she went home after 7:00 p.m.

When I finally got a word in, I told Dykstra that Diana was working hard under very difficult circumstances. "She didn't create this situation, Lenny," I said. "But she's doing her best to fix it." He erupted, screaming that he was going to fire Diana and that if I wasn't careful, he would fire me too for talking back to him. Then he hung up.

With Diana in the doghouse, Dykstra turned to Kevin McCarthy, telling the young writer, "You're the only one I can trust, bro." Upon receiving the call, McCarthy rushed to the bank. The doors were locked, and the bank looked closed, but Dykstra was inside speaking to the manager. McCarthy slipped some papers under the door and stood there waiting for Dykstra to release him for the night.

When Dykstra came out, he had cash in hand and a smile on his face, telling McCarthy he had pulled some strings. After calling Diana a bunch of ethnic slurs, including Pearl Harbor, Dykstra jumped in a waiting car and summoned McCarthy to come with him.

Dykstra asked McCarthy about his salary, and the young writer told Dykstra he grossed about $700 weekly. "He goes, 'All right' and takes out this wad of cash and counts out $700. He goes, 'How about two weeks?' and counts out another $700," McCarthy recalls. "And then he goes, 'How about three?' And counts out another $700. He gives me $2,100 and says, 'Thanks, bro, I can count on you, but you have to do me a favor tonight.'"

McCarthy was worried Dykstra was about to ask him to do something illegal, but he really just needed an errand boy to pay most of the writers and vendors, including many of the people I had brought to the magazine.

Although it was good news Dykstra was paying all those people, he didn't use a dime of the money to pay me, Dorothy, or Dan, who had quit in July.

Next, Dykstra wanted McCarthy to go to his hotel to pack his luggage while he dined at a fancy restaurant. Once everything was ready, McCarthy noticed a safe in the corner and called Dykstra, who gave him the combination.

"I open it up, and there's some watches and stuff," McCarthy says. "And then there were these balled-up pieces of newspaper in the safe. Clearly, there's some sort of drug in there." Dykstra instructed McCarthy not to open any of the balled-up papers and to put them in a separate luggage compartment.

On his way out of the Carlyle, McCarthy was stopped by one of the hotel's staffers, who asked if he was checking Dykstra out of the hotel. The man informed McCarthy that Dykstra owed more than $30,000 for his stay and asked

Kevin for his credit card to charge the payment. "I looked at them and said, 'I can't help you with that. I'll let him know, but it has nothing to do with me.'"

Trying to salvage what was left of my minivacation, I looked forward to a relaxing Saturday afternoon. Instead, I got a call from Dykstra demanding I drop everything and coordinate the printing of the magazine with Creel Printing, something that should, and could, have been done earlier in the month had his money issues not put that step in a perpetual holding pattern.

While my parents went off to a dinner show, Rhea sat on the hotel bed waiting for me to finish. I frantically placed phone calls to Dorothy and the guys at Creel, trying to delegate responsibilities so that I could make it to dinner on time, which I did thanks to Dorothy.

With checks in the mail to the big-gun writers and the folks I had brought on board, I felt a major weight lift from my shoulders. I didn't want to quit while my friends and former colleagues were owed cash.

Two days later, I knew my time working for Dykstra would be over soon. While packing my bags at 4:00 a.m. so that I could make it back to work in New York early Monday morning, I received an e-mail from Dykstra. The note instructed me not to touch the funds in one of the bank accounts that were supposed to be for our payroll.

Dykstra had previously taken a loan from TheStreet.com using the proceeds from the newsletter as collateral without telling me. That left us with virtually no income, no way to fund payroll, and mounting debts. In other words, we had to hope—however unrealistic—that Dykstra would do the right thing. However, he reneged on his promise to use a portion of that $300,000 loan to pay our rent and fund our payroll. Instead, he redirected the money to his Legend's Air employees.

In my response, I told Dykstra we were relying on the money he had promised us. Without it, I said, we would be in breach of New York State labor laws, which was very serious and something we should avoid. Dykstra had been reported to the state by previous employees, and I knew more reports could spell big trouble. Plus, I wanted to get paid.

"Are you fucking serious with me right now? Threatening me?" he responded in bold, shouting letters, as if I were out of line to suggest he keep his promise, pay his employees, and obey the law. "You sure are getting bold these days; so you are going to take me to the NY State Labor Board? You are just like the rest of them, save the threats, are you going to the newspapers next? You can join Kevin Coughlin, what a fucking joke!"

CHAPTER 33

THE BARREL-FINDER

I knew I needed off Team Dykstra forever. The only question was when. By the time I touched down at LaGuardia Airport in New York, I had a solid game plan in place. I didn't care that it was one of the worst job markets in my lifetime, I was relieved to know I would be walking out soon.

I no longer had the ability to implement even a modest amount of structure in Dykstra's companies, and since I didn't have his ear anymore, I didn't have a prayer of bringing any positive change. The situation was hopeless.

Diana, Kevin, and I felt trapped. Dykstra took our paychecks and then told us we needed to find a way to pay ourselves and the rent. And Dykstra's modus operandi was now more than obvious: if you leave, you are a quitter and therefore will never get any of the money you are owed. If you insist on your salary, you will be fired and will never see your money because you are not a team player. Considering a lawsuit? Good luck! Get in line!

Once back in our half-empty office, I summoned Diana and Kevin to the common area. I pulled up a chair, sat down, and took a deep breath. "I appreciate all the hard work you've both done, and we've been through a lot together in the last two months, so I am going to tell you something important," I said, looking at Diana and then over at Kevin. "I'm quitting. I'm miserable, and I just don't see this situation getting any better."

However, I explained that, although I had decided to resign, I wouldn't be informing Dykstra of my intentions for another two and a half weeks. My last day was to be December 1, which was a strategically important date, I explained. "Nails on the Numbers" was on track to have generated enough money to pay back the personal loan Dykstra had taken from TheStreet.com by the end of November. As such, TheStreet.com should resume sending regular payments to the Nails Investments bank account—the account used to fund payroll that I controlled—on December 1, I explained.

Because I had been caught off guard when Dykstra previously redirected our payroll cash, my counterpart in the finance department at TheStreet.com assured me he would give me a heads up if Dykstra tried to grab the money again.

If Dykstra took the money, leaving the company without any funds for payroll, I planned to quit on the spot and not wait until December. If the money was wired to the account as planned, I told Kevin and Diana that I would make sure they were paid everything they were owed first—expenses and salary. From what was left, I planned to pay myself as much as possible of the $50,000 in past-due salary for the newsletter and magazine I was owed.

Either way, I knew I would be cutting my losses, leaving a lot of money on the table. With Diana and Kevin getting first crack at the money, I knew I would be receiving only a portion of my salary. I also accepted the fact that I had virtually no shot at collecting the more than $93,000 bonus I had earned. When Dykstra hired me, he promised me 20 percent of the newsletter's sales as a year-end commission.

While waiting for December 1, I told the crew we should work hard to finish the December edition of the *Players Club* and organize transitional materials for the magazine and newsletter so that the next editors could pick up where we had left off. As aggravated as I was with Dykstra, I wanted to leave his businesses in as good shape as possible and help with any reasonable transition to new staff he might need.

"I know this is a bit unorthodox, but extreme circumstances call for unusual measures," I told them. "We're not doing anything wrong. We're doing our job and have payroll set up for a reason. We're keeping quiet and hoping Lenny doesn't steal our money again to pay for his fancy hotels or his private jet. I think we're being more than fair."

I felt somewhat relieved as Diana, Kevin, and I sat there in the middle of the office reliving crazy Dykstra war stories. Without a buffer between them and Dykstra, Kevin and Diana both knew they would be dead meat and told me they planned to resign with me.

As Kevin, Diana, and I held our collective breath hoping Dykstra would take his eye off the ball long enough for us to execute my plan, Dykstra's relationship with big-time New York book agent David Vigliano was reaching a fevered pitch.

In early October, Dykstra had told Vigliano that Bill Conlin was ready to pump out some ghostwritten pages of a planned investing strategy book. "The book is a go brother!" Dykstra wrote to Vigliano. "Heck, I am 73–0 right now in the worst Bear Market ever!" With much enthusiasm, Vigliano responded, "Hell yes, that's what I'm talkin bout! NAILS NEVER FAILS!"

However, Dykstra was in fact having trouble lining up a writer he liked. Conlin hadn't written any pages, and Cal "The Maestro" Fussman, a veteran *Esquire* writer who would later ghostwrite Larry King's *My Remarkable Journey*, also wasn't working out. Cal, who had interviewed Mikhail Gorbachev, Muhammad Ali, Jimmy Carter, Donald Trump, and Al Pacino, among others, had submitted a sample chapter of the book, which he labeled *From Nails to Riches: How a Tobacco-Chewin' Baseball Hero Made Himself a Superstar in the World of Money*.

However, Dykstra told me he felt he needed someone who understood his stock-picking system and asked me to take over the writing. At that time, things between us were souring, but I hadn't formulated my exit plan yet.

"This is going to be the first book to sell for $1,000 a copy," Dykstra kept bragging. I knew it was Dykstra's typical outlandish boasting, but I thought the book could be a success. I met with Vigliano and his staffers and quickly began writing a sample chapter. I named my version of the book *Nailing It Every Time: Ten Rules for Following Lenny Dykstra's Stock Market Success*.

By that point my writing really sounded like Dykstra, and Vigliano thought my sample chapter hit the mark. Both he and Dykstra pushed for me to charge full speed ahead on the book.

Getting usable information from Dykstra, however, was like trying to throw a perfect game in the World Series—only one person in history has ever done it. When I tried to interview Dykstra for the book, he couldn't remember much about his playing days or just didn't have the patience to retell the stories. He told me to read *Nails*, his ghostwritten 1987 autobiography, and use the stories from that book in the new book.

The initial optimism that followed my sample chapter disappeared quickly. Vigliano lent Dykstra $250,000 in May and claimed Dykstra had promised to repay the loan, plus an extra $50,000—a total of $300,000—by November 2, 2008. That date came and went, so Vigliano sent Dykstra a note, which he ignored.

More than two weeks later, Vigliano sent Dykstra another note. "Lenny, this problem is not going to go away," the e-mail read, noting that unless the money was repaid within two days, he would have his lawyers commence proceedings to collect the cash. "I hoped this would not be necessary," Vigliano concluded.

Dykstra took the e-mail as a full-scale assault. "Hey tough guy," he responded, "it will be fun to see how you hold up after you are $1.0 (million) dollars in after paying legal bills?" Dykstra said he thought the book agent was his friend but was really a "money-hungry fuck" just like the others. "But, if this is the way you want to play it—then let's get it on! BY THE WAY, YOU ARE FIRED!" Dykstra wrote. "BY THE WAY, I do need you to reimburse me for the two private jet rides AND HOTELS."

November began with some of the most favorable press Dykstra had seen in months. The *Philadelphia Daily News* ran a cover story in which the headline glowingly proclaimed that Dykstra was "born to make money." Veteran journalist Mark Kram had followed Dykstra around for a few days, accompanying him on a land-prospecting trip to New England and hanging out with him behind the scenes at TheStreet.com conference.

The article failed to mention that Dykstra was in default on more than $100,000 in property taxes on the Gretzky mansion, didn't pay his attorney fees, and had numerous lawsuits against him.

Within days, the press on Dykstra went from friendly to fierce. On November 15, the *New York Post* reported that Lenny had bounced a $6,990.73 check to Halcyon Jets for a flight from Las Vegas to Van Nuys, California, and never sent a replacement check.[1] When asked later about the $7,000 dispute, Lenny said the amount was "ashtray money."[2]

A few weeks later, Joanne's lawsuit hit the press and the *Post*'s Keith Kelly also reported that Dykstra was being "nailed on past deals." The article noted that ex-assistant Samantha Kulchar had hauled him into court and that Dykstra had been "forced out" of the Park Avenue offices. The article also mentioned that Dykstra had finally settled his dispute with Doubledown.[3]

However, the article contained a more disturbing tidbit that probably sounded small to most people but that infuriated me. The night before the article was to be published, I received an e-mail from Kevin Coughlin with an advance copy of the text and the ominous subject line "Lenny Talked to Keith Kelly, threw you under the bus."

Coughlin pointed to the article's third paragraph in which Dykstra claimed he had signed only a one-year lease for the Park Avenue office space and that "someone else" had signed a lease extension without his knowledge or permission.

Dykstra was referring to me, and now that he was in default of the rent, I became concerned he was trying to make me the scapegoat.

"You and I both know that he approved that extension," Coughlin wrote to me. "Keith was good enough not to injure the innocent by name. I came across the page while approving proofs and thought you should know."

During the same week, news broke that Dykstra had settled a lawsuit with accounting firm DDK, which claimed he stiffed them on a $138,872 bill for preparing his 2006 tax returns. Outside the courthouse following the settlement, Dykstra chomped on Twizzlers and took potshots at his enemies.

The most entertaining and slashing comments were reserved for DDK. The accounting firm "folded like Mitch Williams in the ninth," Dykstra said, referring to his old Phillies teammate, who fifteen years earlier had given up the World Series–ending home run to Toronto's Joe Carter.

Dykstra's hatred for Williams dated back to that ill-fated series and persists until today. Right after Williams gave up the home run to Joe Carter in Game 6 of the 1993 World Series, Dykstra reportedly walked past the dejected pitcher, snickering, "Guess there won't be a Game 7, will there?" That off-season Dykstra and Curt Schilling publicly lobbied for the team to dump Williams.

By 2008, Dykstra's public criticism of Williams had intensified. In a March 2008 interview, Dykstra told 610 AM WIP host Howard Eskin that Williams was a "barrel-finder," implying that Williams's pitches had somehow found their way to the barrel of most hitters' bats.

"We did go to the big dance . . . until Mitch Williams kept hitting barrel after barrel," Dykstra said. When asked how Williams had found so many barrels, Dykstra said the pitcher had made a habit of throwing pitches 85 miles per hour "down the cock."

Dykstra told Eskin that the Carter home run was just one of many that Williams had given up. "Mitch Williams is a joke. Why do you want to talk to me about him? It's painful, dude. He brings up bad memories. . . . I don't like him."

Williams's response to Dykstra's 2008 jabs? "He's the most common sense– void person I've ever met in my life," Williams said. "He makes no sense whatsoever. . . . You could have a better conversation with a tree."[4]

Williams described Dykstra as a "savant with a bat in his hand," noting that "he wrote a check his ass couldn't cash." Speaking with *Angelo Cataldi and the Morning Team* on Philadelphia's 610 AM WIP sports radio, he also said he wouldn't give Lenny "$3 to walk across the street and put it in the bank for me."

Not only was Dykstra tough to talk to, but Williams also predicted doom for his former teammate. "Lenny won't have two nickels to rub together in three years," Williams said, according to the *Reading Eagle*.[5]

CHAPTER 34

OUTTA HERE

Just minutes after verbally bashing Mitch Williams, Dykstra stopped by our new offices. "You and I are gonna dance before long," he said to the receptionist with a wink, followed by a stare. "You know what I mean."

We continued into our office, where Diana and Kevin were waiting. It was awkward because the three of us knew we were quitting. The mood was tense and the weather gloomy outside. Dykstra sat in Diana's seat in front of the windows and commandeered her computer, sending Kevin out on a mission to pick up an audio recorder.

While browsing through an edition of *Haute Living* magazine, Dykstra came across an advertisement for a private jet charter service he recognized. "They owe me money," he exclaimed, pointing at the ad.

"Lenny had me look up the number, and he called them as a prank," Diana recalls. Posing as a potential customer, he asked what kind of planes they had and inquired about their charter services. Turning more aggressive, Dykstra shouted, "I have a judgment against you." He cursed at, and argued with, the woman for a minute and then hung up.

Turning to Diana and me, he lifted one eyebrow and said, "Watch . . . wait" and pointed at the phone with a smile. A few minutes later, the person called back, wanting to know whom she had just spoken to. Dykstra gave Kevin McCarthy's name and traded barbs with her before cursing at her and hanging up again.

Then he asked Diana to dial the company one more time, and he took the phone from her. Dykstra told the woman on the phone that if her firm didn't pay up immediately, he would swing by and take one of their planes in lieu of payment. "Fuck you," he screamed and hung up, never revealing his name.

Following the call, Dykstra told Diana that he had a very important task for her and that she better come through this time. "He said, 'We're gonna get these guys' and asked me to find a bounty hunter. I said, 'What about a collection agency?' and he said, 'No, I want a bounty hunter.'"

The jet company was not Dykstra's only target. He had sent Dorothy packing, apparently for good. That week he also threatened to replace me yet again. I was still in the office at 11:00 p.m. one night when I received a call from him demanding I report to his hotel suite. I explained that I needed to go home to take care of some personal tasks, like paying bills, and asked if it would be all right if I came by early the next day, at, say, 5:00 or 6:00 a.m.

"Man, I need another editor. I must be working you too hard," Dykstra said sarcastically. "This is pathetic. I'm tired of this bullshit." He then began to complain about the magazine's suddenly unacceptable articles before abruptly hanging up.

Kevin was also about to get his first beanball from Dykstra. The Saturday after Thanksgiving, McCarthy received an urgent call. Dykstra was back in New York City and desperately wanted to get into our offices but didn't have a key. He demanded McCarthy, who lived in Huntington, Long Island, about an hour and a half away, hop on a train immediately to hand-deliver his key.

When McCarthy suggested Dykstra call me or Diana since we lived closer, Dykstra responded, "I don't trust them. . . . You're the only one I can trust."

"I thought he was trying to do some covert operation," McCarthy recalls. He wanted no part of it and told Dykstra he was attending his brother's engagement party. "I just didn't want to do it and didn't think it was fair, so I told Lenny that excuse," Kevin says. In reality, McCarthy had promised to help his dad clean the garage and knew Dykstra wouldn't accept that reason.

Dykstra tried to tempt McCarthy with a "C-note," and when he declined, Dykstra begged him to get one of his friends to make the trip. McCarthy apologized but said it wasn't possible. "'If there is no key, you can stay home permanently. You better come through for me,'" Dykstra told McCarthy.

After McCarthy got off the phone with Dykstra, he called to ask for my advice on how to handle the situation. I told him to enjoy the weekend with his family and not worry about Dykstra's threats. After all, we would be quitting in just a few days anyway. If he got fired and I was still working, I would make sure he got paid.

Hours later after helping his father take items out of storage from among the rafters in the garage, McCarthy noticed his cell phone had a barrage of missed calls and several "911" texts. "I called Lenny back, and he was like, 'Where are you, bro? . . . I told you I needed you.'" McCarthy reminded Dykstra of his family obligation, but he found that unacceptable.

"If you like your brother so much, you can spend a lot more time with him," Dykstra told him. "You're done. Take a seat on the bench. Don't come back to work for a week, bro." Instead of outright firing McCarthy as he had during their earlier conversation, Dykstra commuted McCarthy's sentence to a week-long suspension. "He told me to take a week off. I didn't," Kevin recounts. "I knew there was work to be done."

———————

A little more than twenty-four hours after McCarthy was told to ride the pine, Dykstra called me. "Hey, buddy," he said with some step in his voice. "I just got into town for a major league meeting with Barclays today. They're going to be our new financial partner."

He was in an unusually good mood and spoke with a swagger he hadn't shown in months. But that didn't matter anymore, at least not to me. I just wanted to run out the clock, and the end was only a few days away. I could taste it. I was still disgusted with the way he had tried to manipulate Kevin over the office keys, and I wondered whether he would let me in on their "secret" conversation. He didn't mention it, and I acted as if I hadn't heard about it.

As I sat on my couch, I knew the drill. That wasn't the break we were all waiting for or that Dykstra had portrayed it to be. In all likelihood, Barclays was no more our financial partner than AIG, Commonwealth, or the Hartford had been before. The meeting might have gone well, but a lot of ground still needed to be covered before any formal partnership was forged.

"I've got some good news, bro. I'm bringing you in some help," Dykstra continued. "I got this guy from Hurst. Loren Feldman's going to come in and help you edit the magazine. You can work side by side with him." I knew Dykstra had reached out to some of his Philly sportswriting connections to try and land us a seasoned pro to help with the magazine.

Feldman fit the bill, as he had more than twenty years of experience in the magazine biz. Dykstra tried to play it cool while telling me about Feldman. He still needed me, and I had come through for him a bunch of times. "You'll still stay my senior editor, but Loren will help free you up to work on my book. We have to strike while the iron is hot on that," he said, noting his undefeated stock-picking record once again.

I was relieved Dykstra was hiring someone qualified to pick up the slack when I resigned. He continued, explaining his short-term plan. "The kid [McCarthy] can take over some of the 'Nails on the Numbers' work. This will take some of the pressure off of you so you don't have to do as much." In addition, Dykstra boasted that another new exec, "Jason," was going to "take the *Players Club* to the next level." (Jason's asked that his real name not be used, and I have honored his request because he is looking for a job and doesn't want his name associated with Dykstra.)

Shortly after meeting with Dykstra for the first time, Jason was unexpectedly front and center representing the Players Club in an important business meeting with Barclays. He wasn't even technically on the team yet, but he spoke about how he planned to transform, monetize, and revolutionize the Players Club's Web site and technology.

Dykstra was impressed, and when it came time for him to return to California, he insisted Jason come with him to finalize their contract. When they touched down outside of LA, driver Paul Lee was waiting to usher the men to the virtually vacant Gretzky mansion.

Back in New York, while I was working through a draft of my resignation letter, Dykstra called. "Listen, Chris, I need you to do something for me right away," he said in a low and hurried voice. "It's really important." He was clearly shaken as he told me to look up Jason on the Internet.

"This guy was in my house. He's a fraud. . . . He has another identity to avoid paying child support or something. He's a bad dude, and he's lurking around my backyard," Dykstra said, telling me he had discovered suspicious paperwork while snooping through one of Jason's bags.

The bag in question really belonged to the livery cab driver who took the men to Teterboro Airport in New Jersey, but was accidentally placed with Jason's luggage, explains Paul Lee, Dykstra's personal California driver. "I know this now, but we didn't know it at the time."

Scared, Dykstra stayed at his other house and sent Lee to dispose of Jason. "Lenny told me to 'just get rid of him. Get him off the property. I don't care where you take him; just get rid of him,'" Lee says. "At this time, I was believing the guy was an imposter . . . trying to take advantage of a celebrity or a stalker."

Meanwhile, Jason had been waiting at the Gretzky mansion all day, oblivious to the drama going on and waiting to go to dinner with Dykstra. Instead, Lee brought Domino's Pizza to the mansion to share with Jason while conducting an investigation.

"I asked the guy a couple of questions, and he tells me his experience and how he's traveled all around the world," Lee says. "So I go to the bathroom and call Lenny and tell him that the guy sounds legit. What [Jason] said didn't correlate with any of the things Lenny told me about the guy. Lenny goes, 'No, no, no, I looked through his bag, and he's not who he says he is. Get rid of him, Paul.'"

Lee confronted Jason about the mystery bag and purported alias paperwork. "He didn't know what the heck I was talking about," Lee recalls. The men finished their pizza, and Jason retired to his room. Lee called Dykstra again to express concern that they had made a mistake.

"Lenny goes, 'Get him off of the property, and get him off now. . . . Do your job.'" Lee, who was a driver, wondered when "bouncer" had been added to his job description. Nonetheless, he went to Jason's room and told the much smaller man that Dykstra wanted him to leave.

Stunned, Jason asked to speak to Dykstra. "I said, 'No, you don't need to call him. Let's just do this.' [Jason] thought I was gonna hurt him. I quickly assured him I wasn't going to do that but told him to just pack up his things," Lee recalls. "I apologized as much as I could and dropped him off near the freeway right near a Barnes and Noble in a shopping center. That's where I left him."

Later that night, Dykstra called and explained that Jason wrote him a note asking what the heck had happened. With the bravado of a television detective like Kojak or Columbo who had just caught a criminal mastermind red-handed, Dykstra snickered as he described how he had confronted Jason and given him a swift kick back to the middle.

On December 1, I awoke expecting the money from TheStreet.com to be in our bank account. It wasn't, but my counterpart at TheStreet assured me $37,000 had been sent and that the wire just needed some time to process. The amount was less than I had hoped for because some of the money was used to repay the loan Dykstra took from the company.

We kept quiet until the wire arrived, and then Diana ran payroll immediately. She and Kevin were paid everything they were owed. I got $25,000, which covered ten weeks of back pay owed to me from "Nails on the Numbers." It didn't include my final three weeks' pay for the newsletter or any of the money I had been promised to edit the *Players Club*. I left $2,000 in the account for freelancers who hadn't yet submitted invoices.

In all, including the year-end sales-related bonus I had negotiated when beginning my work for Dykstra, I walked away with Dykstra still owing me more than $119,000. That figure doesn't include any of the outlandish bonuses Dykstra dangled in front of me that I never expected and wouldn't have felt comfortable receiving.[1]

When the money finally hit each of our respective bank accounts, we were ready. As I fired off my resignation e-mail at 5:00 a.m. on Thursday, December 4, I couldn't believe the craziest adventure of my life was coming to a crashing halt.

In my note, I told Dykstra I had no choice but to resign. "Persistent payroll and healthcare issues, the problems arising from mixing of your personal and business funds, the regular verbal abuse I and the other employees on the team have been subjected to and the dishonesty in your business dealings make this decisions cut and dry for me," I wrote. "I simply cannot continue under these conditions and am not willing to risk my reputation any further or open myself up to any of your legal troubles."

I told Dykstra I ran payroll, but that I was still owed quite a bit. "Sure, part of this is about money," I wrote to Dykstra. "I'm asking you to make good on what you promised me and the money I worked so hard to earn. That was the deal. I enjoyed the job but also worked hard to improve my own personal situation."

Because I am a professional and out of respect for all the hard work Dykstra put into the magazine, I said I would ensure a smooth transition to a new editor. I also alerted Dykstra that I had finished the work on the revised December edition of the magazine. Lastly, I told Dykstra I finished that morning's "Nails on the Number" column.

"I wish you and the *Players Club* great success and despite the reasons for my resignation, I have enjoyed many parts of my employment and appreciate the many positive things I learned from you," I wrote. "However, the negatives were too great for me to ignore—they impact my personal life, health and well being in a way I cannot accept."

I had learned a lot from Dykstra—such as how to push myself harder than I had ever before and not to accept the status quo. Much of what had made Dykstra a successful ballplayer translated to the business world. It was just that his lack of discipline and ethics overshadowed his positive attributes.

As I hit the send button on my e-mail, I couldn't help but feel disappointed that the optimism and excitement of just a few months earlier had devolved into such an ugly mess. However, each time I felt disappointed, I tried to remember how, toward the end of my tenure, I cringed every time my phone rang, worried Dykstra might be on the other end.

Dykstra's response to my resignation further wiped away any remnants of nostalgia I was feeling. In a nine-page, rambling, and often repeating e-mail written in a rainbow of colors and varying fonts and sizes, Dykstra said I was "chicken shit" because I didn't resign face to face, like a man, even though we were on opposite ends of the country. "You . . . need to keep your mouth shut— if you want to believe you had it so tough—then cry on Diana's shoulders."

He said my e-mail was cowardly and the column I had written for the newsletter that morning sucked, and he asked how long it would take for me to turn into another Kevin Coughlin. "This is your decision—that is fine," he wrote. "But do not lie! Do not pull another Kevin."

Dykstra also repeatedly insisted that I had control issues. "You would not hire a staff—the staff that you did hire were hidden—very weird?" he wrote, referring to the freelance writers, editors, and printers I had lined up on short notice.

He had cut and pasted several portions of my original e-mail into his response, providing my point and his counterpoint. "There are numerous statements that you make in your e-mail that I completely disagree with. In fact, there are many false statements that are false," he wrote.

"For you to accuse me of 'regular verbal abuse' is a fucking joke," he noted during another counterpoint. "I have talked to Diana three times in my life— and the kid—I don't even know his name—I have talked to twice in my life! . . . If you want to throw away a career for a couple of kids I have never talked to— that is your call; but don't start making up stories."

He also repeated several times that I had I quit and was not fired. However, when a person works but doesn't get paid, what's the difference, really? "How quickly you forget: you were without a job, no way to earn a living—and I hired you and paid you quite well I might add!" He repeated this section several times, failing to mention that he hadn't actually paid me regularly and still owed me a ton of money and that the reason I had quit my secure job at *Ignites* was, in part, to work on HIS newsletter. Giving me a job wasn't an act of charity on his part.

For all the bluster and insults, the one thing that was not surprising was that Dykstra accused me of stealing. I had learned from my time working for him that such accusations were commonplace, especially when someone quit.

"This is very upsetting you did this behind my back—as you literally put together a game plan to steal my money," he wrote. "This is my money—you had no right to steal it." I hadn't stolen anything—I had run payroll. Heck, the money was wired to a business account where I was the only authorized user. Dykstra wasn't even listed on the account but had instructed TheStreet.com to send the money to it.

Dykstra told me I was responsible for paying the office rent and that I should do so immediately. He also demanded that I upload all the *Players Club* magazine files to the printer.

The first part of the note was followed by a huge amount of blank space before another several paragraphs appeared down below, closing with the following line: "You are not in control anymore and it kills you."

I didn't respond.

CHAPTER 35

CRASH LANDING

My life was my own again, and the fog of the previous months began to melt away. When I wasn't catching up on sleep, I was receiving a steady stream of congratulatory phone calls and e-mails from former Dykstra employees welcoming me to the club.

Dykstra, on the other hand, had quickly lost a slew of staffers. Just a few days earlier, Dorothy told me she had said good-bye to Dykstra for good, writing him that it was time for her to "fly." She said she didn't know how Dykstra had talked her into lending him money, but that she was clearly in a "pickle" and he didn't seem to care.

However, as bad as things were, she vowed not to sue him. There would never be a "Dorothy vs. Dykstra" case on the docket, she said, noting she wanted to walk away maintaining a "tiny glimmer of affection" for him.

In typical Dykstra fashion, he replied that she was "clueless" and that he actually did her a favor by taking her money because the market would have "shredded" her. Lastly, he said he must have been wrong when he thought she was a true "believer" after watching him "dismantle" all of the "fools" before her. Before signing off, he told her to join the crowd that had underestimated him and lost.

Days after the terse exchange, Dorothy ran back to Dykstra with arms open wide. He needed her to run the newsletter, and she was more than willing. "The one thing that's enabled me to stick around is that I just let things go," Dorothy later told me. "I know that he has issues with anger and just snaps off and says stupid things, and he does it often—I just don't let it bother me."

Despite the fact that he had previously bragged to people that he was going to "make her eat shit and like it," Dorothy told me that she and Dykstra later formed a pact in which he promised to never fire her if she promised to never quit. "Since he got that little agreement, he is the one who always reminds me about it," Dorothy says. "I think he takes comfort in knowing I'm not going to go away."

———————————

Things remained quiet for me for about a week until I received a call from *New York Post* reporter Keith Kelly. He was working on an article about Dykstra and had heard about the New York staff exodus.

In the interest of making sure he got the story right, I agreed to confirm facts he had heard from other sources. However, I wasn't interested in getting into a public pissing match with Dykstra—I was suddenly unemployed and looking for a job. Plus, I thought back to how Dykstra had threatened me with his legal might during our previous correspondence.

"I want to make this clear right now: if you or your two kids make up some lies and talk to anyone—there will be a lawsuit," he wrote. "If you or the other two ex-employees say one word to hurt me, my family or my brand, the Players Club, I will have my attorney use all legal recourse."

However, I told Kelly that if Dykstra bad-mouthed me, I wanted to defend myself on the record. Sure enough, my old boss couldn't resist playing the victim. He told Kelly I was "delusional" and not only denied owing me money but claimed I owed him. His response was so crazy it was laughable.

On December 17, the *New York Post* ran an article entitled "Dykstra Drops the Ball." It noted that he is "tough as nails when it comes to paying his staff or vendors" and contained part of my response to his accusation that I owed him. "That's beyond ridiculous," I said. "How could an employee owe an employer money?"

The article noted the *Players Club* had had four printers and three editors already and that Getty Images had suspended Dykstra's account after more than $40,000 in unpaid bills. Dykstra also announced Loren Feldman, the editor he planned to hire to help me, as the editor of the entire magazine. The only problem was that Feldman hadn't accepted the job and would never end up working for Dykstra. He was the first of at least five editors who would be "hired" and fired or quit between December and April—making it eight editors in the first year of the publication.

After the *Post* article, Conlin sent Dykstra a note saying he thought the article was accurate. "You live in an 8,500 square foot mansion, but right now you might as well be in a 10 x 10 room," he wrote. "I think the no-sleep, relentless pursuit of more millions, more toys, bigger mansions, more lux Gulfstreams, and all the rest, have moved you to the verge of a breakdown. I seriously hope you can fight your way out of the deepest count of your life. . . . In the week of Bernard Madoff, you're just a C-List deadbeat."

Dykstra shot back. "You crossed the line!" Dykstra wrote to Conlin. "The *Players Club* has never been better. . . . You dumb mother fucker!" With their relationship fracturing rapidly, the final edition of the *Players Club*, which I had prepared before quitting, printed in late January.

Bill Conlin wanted to know if the rumors were true. Had Dykstra really flown to the south of France to hawk corporate jets with "Miss America and Miss Universe?" he asked, referring to flight attendants Amanda and Ivy.

Indeed, they were true, Dykstra said, telling Conlin he planned to auction off the world's first Rolls Royce Gulfstream G550. The starting bid would be an outrageous U.S. $70 million, he claimed. Dykstra planned on "walking through Customs with a fistful of hundreds! ZING!"

However, that trip to France was anything but pleasurable for the flight crew. They flew with him to Nice, France, where he told Amanda he had rooms for the flight attendants at the fancy hotel he was staying at. He also repeatedly told them he had bought them dresses for a special event one evening, according to Amanda.

Once the plane landed, Dykstra disappeared. Ivy and Amanda were stranded at the airport with no way to get hold of him. "His phones didn't work," Amanda says. "We didn't have rooms, and we didn't have any money." Realizing only *HE* would be living large in the luxurious hotel, Ivy and Amanda managed to wheel and deal their way into the same hotel as the pilots.

Later in the six-day trip, they were left to sleep in the airport as Dykstra's bad behavior and financial troubles caused problems. "We got to the airport early one morning, stayed there that night, the next day, that night, and then left the next morning," Amanda says.

After arriving on the planned date of departure and wasting the day waiting for Dykstra to come up with the cash for the flight, the pilots informed Dykstra late that night they needed to return to their hotel to get some rest. "Lenny starts talking shit to them, saying, 'I'll get new pilots. Just leave. I don't need you,'" Amanda recalls.

Eventually, Dykstra got a credit card he could use and told the pilots he needed them to fly the plane right away. They said they couldn't. After waiting around all day, they were too tired to fly—it was a safety issue.

The pilots, however, agreed to take Dykstra, Amanda, and Ivy back to the United States the following morning. With the pilots at the hotel, Dykstra and the girls stayed at the airport that night. The private aviation portion of the airport had a small lounge for pilots and another for passengers. The lounges had couches, a computer, and a refrigerator with some drinks.

"All our suitcases were there," Amanda says. "We took blankets off the plane. We slept on the couches, and Dykstra stayed in the pilot's lounge working on the computer." Dykstra also borrowed Amanda's cell phone, racked up a $1,400 bill, and never gave her the money for it, she says.

The next morning, Amanda realized something smelled fishier than usual. The pilots were very late. "They were going to fly Lenny home, but he started being a dick to them," Amanda says. "They said Boo," Dykstra wrote to Conlin, describing the pilots as deer in the headlights. "Bunch of fucking pussies!"

Another pilot, Mark Malone, called the castaway crew to say that Dykstra's pilots had ditched him and boarded a commercial flight back to the United States. The entire second day was a wash as Dykstra sought new pilots. He wanted to find a company that would pay for everything up front and bill him later. However, owing to the time zone difference between France and America, he was having trouble.

As Ivy and Amanda slept on the couches for only a few hours at a clip, the airport personnel began to get annoyed that Dykstra had turned the lounges into his own personal makeshift hotel room. "Basically, the people in the airport were like, 'What the fuck are you doing? Why is your passenger here?'" Amanda recalled.

Finally, they found someone to help. "The guy was a fan of Lenny," Amanda says. He set them up with hotel rooms while new pilots flew from the United States to France. The first thing Amanda did was take a shower.

"Everybody needed it. My hair was nasty," Amanda says. "I'm sure Lenny needed it. It was pretty gross, actually."

When the new pilots arrived, they checked out the plane, and then Dykstra and the entire group took off. Pascal Jouvence, cocaptain on the flight home, says he didn't know what had happened to the previous pilots and didn't care. "In aviation, lots of things can happen," he says. "My mission was to bring the airplane back and try to get the plane under management for the company I was working for."

Once the nightmarish trip was over, Dykstra's battles with pilots and his flight crew intensified. Back in California, Dykstra and Jouvence nearly came to blows. Jouvence was at the airport in Camarillo preparing to take Dykstra, a pair of new Players Club executives, and flight attendants Amanda and Brit on yet another flight.

"Pascal was running around all day trying to get the right things so we could fly," Amanda says, noting Dykstra was already seated on the plane, waiting for it to take off. During a phone call, Dykstra and his pilot, who was in the terminal, got into an argument over who should pay for the plane's fuel. Jouvence told Dykstra he had to pay for it, and Dykstra demanded Jouvence charge it on his company's credit card.

"I said, 'No, I can't; that's not the deal,'" Jouvence recalls. "I saw the contract, so I knew exactly what was happening. When Lenny knew I wasn't going to use the company credit card, he went after my personal credit card." When Jouvence refused, Dykstra went berserk.

He began cursing at Jouvence and calling him all sorts of names over the phone. "He went off on Pascal, telling him to go back to his country and learn to speak English," Amanda recalls. "He said, 'You fucking idiot; you are raping me,'" Jouvence says. For her part, Brit was "so embarrassed" to be associated with Dykstra because of his comments. "You just don't say something like that to someone."

Jouvence had had enough. He hung up the phone and ran up the stairs of the jet to confront Dykstra. "I said you have to learn to respect the people who work with you," he recalls. "I told him I got him out of the shit he was in with the FAA. I took care of that, and he was going to have to learn some respect, or I was going to leave." During the flight home from France, Jouvence learned the plane didn't have the proper paperwork to fly over the Atlantic Ocean, and they all got in a bit of hot water with the regulator, he claims.

When Jouvence stood up to Dykstra, things went from bad to worse, says Brit. "Lenny jumped up like he was going to fight him," she says, noting he also let out another round of cheap shots.

Jouvence claims Dykstra tried to take a swing at him. For her part, Amanda says she didn't see Dykstra throw a punch but did notice him cock his fist back in preparation to hit the pilot.

However, before things got any more out of hand, the new Players Club execs jumped in between the men. "Part of me thinks Lenny did that in front of those guys to show off," Amanda says. She also says she thinks that Dykstra was only overly aggressive with Jouvence because he knew the other guys would step in and break it up, which they did instantly.

For Brit, the altercation with Jouvence was a real eye-opener: Dykstra was becoming a very different person from the man she had met just a short while before. "He was kind of changing," she says. "He started out really mellow, really nice, and then he was just nasty." She always had an uneasy feeling about Dykstra, and the incident with Jouvence confirmed it. "That's when it set in my mind that Lenny was a jerk. And this was before I realized he was scamming people."

Jouvence was hardly the first or last crew member to get into a crazy dispute with Dykstra. He fired pilots who refused to purchase fuel on his behalf. In other instances, Dykstra asked employees or friends for their credit card information so that he could reserve private jet flights, promising the cards would be used only for an "authorization" and would never be charged. Then, if he needed to, he would charge the card and worry about the consequences later.

While the flight crew was desperately trying to survive the turbulence created by Dykstra, his driver, Paul Lee, had his own potholes to contend with. By December, he was miserable.

The workload was more demanding, and Dykstra became increasingly unreasonable and nasty. "I was hoping against hope he would be the hero I saw in the World Series hitting home runs and pushing his team on to victory," Lee says. "What I saw was the antithesis of that person."

Dykstra was no longer just acting crazy; he was pushing Lee to break the law. Behind in his payments for the $400,000 Maybach and with repo men trying to take back the car, Dykstra had specific instructions for Lee: protect the car at all costs. "I had to get creative at that point," Lee says. "I hid the car, not really realizing I could get in trouble for doing that. I was just trying to keep my job."

Next, Dykstra wanted Lee to find a way—any way—to get him a Rolls-Royce. "He told me, 'Take care of your fucking business right now and get that Rolls-Royce, or I'm gonna start looking for somebody else.'" Lee called in a favor and got a dealership to send a Rolls and driver to pick up Dykstra, who stiffed the guy on the tip.

At the same time, Dykstra told Lee to unload the Maybach. When Lee asked for the paperwork, Dykstra said he didn't have it because the car dealer had screwed him. That's when Lee claims Dykstra gave him the number of someone in the Russian mafia and instructed him to call.

"He wanted me to sell it on the black market, and he wanted me to give him $100,000 and I could keep $50,000," Lee says. "He said these words out of his mouth: 'Sell it to someone that will chop it up and send it overseas.'" Once overseas, the car could be reassembled.

"I think he was setting me up to be a fall guy on that," Lee says. "If the authorities came around asking about the car, who do you think was going to be thrown under the bus?"

Lee also says Dykstra tried to use him as his own personal goon. "He wanted me to put hands on Mark Malone. I would have been arrested for that," Lee says. "When I put those two occurrences in my mind, it makes me upset."

Not surprisingly, Dykstra and Malone, a pilot, were involved in a dispute over money. Malone had paid to fuel up Dykstra's plane but hadn't been reimbursed and was owed for his piloting service.

"Lenny fired him without paying him," Lee says. "Mark Malone was putting it all over the Internet and writing letters to certain people and letting it be known how Lenny was treating him. Lenny didn't like that," Lee says. "He tells me, 'He needs to stop saying this stuff, Paul, and I need you to stop him from saying it. Go to his house and stop him.'"

Lee recalls the conversation like this:

> **Dykstra:** Mark Malone needs to be hurt.
> **Lee:** Um . . . what was that?
> **Dykstra:** He needs to be hurt, or he needs to be in jail.
> **Lee:** Do you want me to call the police?
> **Dykstra:** No, don't call the police, but he needs to be hurt.
> **Lee:** Are you telling me to put my hands on him?
> **Dykstra:** I can't tell you that, but he needs to be hurt, and you need to do your job.

The message was clear, and Lee set out to meet with Malone. "At this time, Mark was very suspicious of me, and I don't blame him," Lee says. "I asked him to please do me a favor and quit writing the stuff about Lenny. I told him it's making my job a lot harder." Lee said he had no plans to assault Malone but told him about Dykstra's instructions. Malone agreed to cool it with the Internet postings.

The next time Lee saw his boss, Dykstra inquired whether he had "stopped" Malone. Lee reported that he had talked to the guy and that Malone had agreed to back off. "Then Lenny got mad at me for talking to the guy, saying 'That guy's gonna get you fired. You shouldn't be talking to him.'"

When Dykstra wasn't asking him to break the law, he was having Lee jump through figurative hoops purely for his amusement. Over the Thanksgiving holiday, Lee says Dykstra gave him a few days off to visit his mom. The very next day, Dykstra phoned him at 8:00 a.m., asking why the hell he hadn't shown up for work? "I drive all the way back, and Lenny doesn't need me there for any reason. He just wanted me at his disposal. He did that at Christmastime too."

However, the final straw came when Dykstra began flaunting his money while refusing to pay Lee and bad-mouthing his friends. "He shows me a suit that he just paid $10,000 cash for while he owes me $7,500," Lee says.

"I think Lenny viewed me like an old shovel. You use it and use it until you can't use it anymore, and then you discard it. He uses people like tools, like they're nothing," Lee says. "He hadn't paid me. He hadn't paid my friends. He was bad-mouthing my friends, telling me they're lazy. . . . I knew it was time to quit."

———————

After that, Lee, Mark Malone, his son Miles Malone, and two other ex-employees filed a claim against Dykstra with the Labor Board. As the five jilted workers waited for proceedings to begin, Dorothy walked in. She told them Dykstra had called her the night before and sent her in his stead.

"I couldn't believe she would show up and represent this guy who she said hadn't paid her in a year and a half," Lee says. "She tells us Lenny has absolutely no money."

Malone says Dorothy didn't really dispute that Dykstra owed the money, with the exception of Lee's phone bills. "Dorothy basically said, 'Lenny just doesn't have money.'" When Malone asked Dorothy about a $200,000 check Dykstra had just received, he says she replied that Dykstra already had plans for the money. "She said, 'Well, he's going to put a new kitchen in. He likes fancy things. It's going to cost a lot of money.'"

In my May 2009 conversation with Dykstra, he marked that day as a rousing victory even though it apparently had not gone well for him. He also miscounted the number of employees. "There were eight employees that tried to say they were owed money and tried to write me all these letters and filed shit at the Santa Barbara court," Dykstra told me matter-of-factly. "All fucking eight of them they threw out. Oh yeah, dude, they're scumbags, dude. People are just piling on trying to get free money. And so all those people got smoked."

Regardless of the outcome of such hearings, Malone says Dykstra's victims are likely out of luck. "Those of us who are owed money probably won't ever get it because he will have to have it first, and he's going to have a hundred reasons why he needs a new kitchen or a new this or a new that," Malone says.

"I was hoping the district attorney, the FBI, the IRS, or the attorney general would go after him," Malone says. "I think all four of them have legitimate reasons. I just want him shut down and behind bars."

CHAPTER 36

NAILED BY THE NUMBERS

With the Players Club teetering on the brink of extinction, Dykstra's old nemesis Randall Lane hit the headlines once again at the end of January 2009. His company, Doubledown Media, was toast.

It was a far cry from a year earlier when the economy had been starting to tank. Then Lane was touting the company's dominance in the luxury advertising market to the press. Whether Lane's claim was genuine optimism or public posturing, the company's situation was drastically different from Lane's portrayal.

As 2008 came to a close, Lane and the company's management had been desperately trying to find a cure to Doubledown's mounting financial woes. First, they cut head count. If Lane had kept me on after the company's divorce from Dykstra, as he claimed he would have, I surely would have been one of the casualties.

Doubledown also implemented salary cuts of up to 50 percent, with the highest-paid employees taking the largest reductions.[1] Some sales staffers reportedly saw their salary eliminated altogether and were left to work on commission only.

The tanking economy eventually contributed to the company's approximately $3 million loss during the year, Lane claimed, noting that many of the company's advertisers and business partners were behind in paying their invoices. He said that Doubledown was owed a "substantial seven-figure" bill, according to a Reuters report. As the economy and Doubledown's finances grew worse, a unit of HSBC pulled its credit line from the company.[2]

The legal dispute with Dykstra wasn't the cause of Doubledown's ultimate downfall, but it didn't help either, according to Doubledown CTO Todd Tarpley. However, it certainly led to some hard feelings.

"I have known Randall for a long time, and I am severely disappointed in his poor judgment and his abominable behavior," says Rachel Pine. "Randall Lane loaned his investors' money, his employees' money, his vendors' money to Lenny Dykstra without their input . . . to a guy who is a chronic deadbeat. . . . It boggles the f'n mind!"

For his part, Tarpley has a different perspective on Lane. "When the company went down, he was accused of all sorts of evil deeds, like living it up while refusing to pay his freelancers and vendors. He didn't intentionally set out to scam anyone or rip anyone off. . . . A lot of the issues for which he was blamed were the result of overoptimism, not greed," Tarpley says. "That said, Double-down owed a lot of people money, and I felt very bad for those people, and I was infuriated by the company's failure to address it. And that was [Lane's] responsibility, and he knows it."

The new year didn't start out much better for Dykstra, as "Nails on the Numbers" suffered a crushing, self-inflicted blow. Dykstra's perfect stock-picking record came to a crashing halt when Amdocs, a company he had picked in June, expired, worthless, during the third week of January.

Dorothy and I had seen the disaster coming months ahead of time and had urged Dykstra to take decisive action. The stock price was in a steady free fall, and Dykstra's pick looked worse and worse as he moved closer to the options' expiration. Instead of cutting his losses and ruining his perfect record, Dykstra ignored our pleas and aggressively bought more Amdocs options to rapidly lower his average purchase price and try and force a big win.

His initial recommendation required less than a $13,000 commitment. As the pick reached expiration, Dykstra called for readers to put more than $200,000 into Amdocs. To put it another way, Dykstra initially called for buying 10 Amdocs options contracts. By expiration, he called for readers to buy 1,160 contracts.

On January 16, 2009, the options expired worthless, meaning anyone left holding the contracts at time of expiration lost all his or her money. As options near expiration, they are often harder to unload because no one wants to be left holding the bag.

However, once the options expired worthless and Dykstra's perfect stock-picking record was ruined, he attempted to rewrite history and hide his massive loss. At first, he posted a loss of $21,550 for the pick, acknowledging a loss, but not too big a loss. Then he erased the loss altogether from his scorecard.

"He retroactively went in and pretended he sold," wrote Adam Warner, an options expert and former writer for TheStreet.com.[3] Warner followed the Dykstra situation on his blog, *Daily Options Report*. "Not only did he pretend-sell, but he did it at the best possible price. Two weeks later in fact."

In an article entitled "What's Up DOX?" Dykstra later attempted to explain away the confusion surrounding the pick. "I pride myself on transparency so, even though the whole issue is one which I am terribly upset about, I will nonetheless address it here," he wrote. Dykstra's e-mail explanation was more than 3,000 words, longer than some chapters in this book.

He let Dorothy, whom he referred to only as an "assistant" and not by name, explain that when the pick was first made, she made an error when calculating whether Dykstra had actually purchased the initial ten contracts. He was trying to get off on a technicality. His process called for him to keep purchase orders on his picks open for one week, meaning he would attempt to buy the pick at the price he set for one week. If he wasn't able to, he canceled it.

The Amdocs pick was not "purchased" on the day the column was published, but it was filled within that one-week window. Dorothy says Dykstra later claimed he shortened that one-week window to just a single day prior to making the Amdocs pick. I know for a fact Dykstra never changed the time frame during my employment, and I quit months after he had picked Amdocs.

"He's absolutely positive he changed that before he changed it," she says. Dorothy also noted that a more technical issue might have skewed whether Dykstra was actually able to purchase the Amdocs contracts or not.

Dykstra claimed that owing to Dorothy's error, the entire pick, including all the subsequent times he averaged down, should be wiped away, even though he told readers about the error only after the pick resulted in a massive $201,350 loss. "No one was checking my work and no one complained," Dorothy wrote.

Dorothy further claimed that not many readers followed Dykstra's advice to buy Amdocs. It was an exercise in throwing as many excuses against the wall as possible and seeing if one stuck.

"Nails on the Numbers" did run a column in late 2008 outlining three potential courses of actions for the Amdocs pick for readers. Dykstra told readers they could stick with the pick and hope for a win, sell now and take the loss, or roll the trade out into a longer position to buy themselves more time. "I didn't offer the readers a CLEAR set of specific instructions," the note explained. "I told them to pick what would be most beneficial for their own personal tax situation." However, the column did note that simply sticking with the pick without action was "too risky."

A few weeks prior to expiration, he advised those who wanted to "live on the edge" to buy 580 more contracts of Amdocs options. Even if a true win wasn't possible, he said, readers could potentially regain some lost ground.

Dorothy then claimed that once the Amdocs options expired, she sought TheStreet.com's advice on how best to reflect the pick on the Stat Book. She thought the best course of action would be to show a $20,000 loss, and she said TheStreet.com agreed.[4]

"The very next day, two people wrote into TheStreet.com and complained that we didn't record the entire loss," the note continued. "They demanded that we re-score it. I was not about to simply accept this in light of all that had occurred."

TheStreet.com noted it was revising the "Nails on the Numbers" portfolio to reflect the most conservative accounting of the Amdocs pick. The site changed the scorecard to include a $201,000 loss. It also blamed Dykstra, saying he had provided all the previous data on Amdocs. Warner wrote on his site that the letter was TheStreet.com's way of telling people thinking of suing over the foolery to go after Dykstra, not TheStreet.

Dykstra, however, wasn't about to go along with TheStreet.com's accounting. He still maintained the original "Nails on the Numbers" site I had helped create all those months earlier, and with Dorothy's help, he regularly posted a version of the scorecard minus the massive Amdocs loss on that site.

"Though we had done our best to assist people who did buy, in the end, I went back to the fact that [the Amdocs pick] didn't fill originally and on that basis, it really never belonged on the scorecard in the first place," Dorothy said.

In the end, Dykstra just acted as if the pick had never existed. "It's such an obvious crock," Warner told me.

Initially, he started following Dykstra's picks for amusement. However, he quickly realized some major problems. "Lenny's system is inherently dishonest. It was really just a system designed to generate a win/loss record and then go get interviewed by a magazine. There are a handful of articles that say he's got this great winning record without looking at how he cheated." Warner notes that even the most gifted trader couldn't go 92–0 without some "smoke and mirrors."

Warner, who was a member of the American Stock Exchange for more than a decade and the author of the book *Options Volatility Trading: Strategies for Profiting from Market Swings*, has a handful of complaints with Dykstra and his system. "One loss wipes out fifty to one hundred gains," he says. "That's what makes the record kind of silly."

Additionally, the Amdocs trade wasn't the first losing pick Dykstra tried to weasel his way out of, Warner says. In late 2007, before I joined Doubledown,

Dykstra stopped writing for TheStreet.com to focus on the Players Club. At that time, he had a handful of picks still in play. He didn't provide updates, and many readers claimed Dykstra left them in the lurch with losing picks.

"He walked away with some bad ones and came back six or seven months later, never resolving the bad ones, and just starting over," Warner says.

Lastly, Warner says Dykstra's system had no capital requirements, meaning there were no limits on the amount Dykstra could hypothetically invest. "If a pick goes bad, he just keeps buying it and buying it," Warner asserts. "To have a real system, you need to have a fixed amount of capital you're working with so you see your return on it." He said there was no realistic way for readers to mimic Dykstra's picks unless they had an "unlimited amount of money."

In the ensuing months, Dykstra continued to pick up more wins while failing to recognize his Amdocs pick. "You can't say you're 115–0 and not be 115–0," he later told radio host Dan Patrick in July 2009. "You go to jail for that shit."

CHAPTER 37

MINI-MADOFF

For months, Kevin Coughlin had been seeing red. He wanted Dykstra behind bars or in a pine box. He even started a blog dedicated to covering the ongoing craziness in Lennyland. He sent antagonizing e-mails to Dykstra, taunting him about his 1999 arrest and his marital and financial troubles. In one e-mail, Coughlin even offered to give Dykstra a job picking up dog shit in his backyard.

Dykstra later told me that Coughlin "is on a mission," and I couldn't disagree. "It all starts with that fat fucking Kevin Coughlin," he said.

Finally, in mid-March, Coughlin got his revenge. GQ published "You Think Your Job Sucks? Try Working for Lenny Dykstra," a 4,400+ word article from Coughlin about his brief stint on Team Dykstra. The piece, which contained an illustration of Dykstra's face with a pig snout drawn over his nose, painted Nails as a racist, homophobe grifter and downright asshole.

In addition to recalling how Dykstra misused Coughlin's credit card, Coughlin described "the strange, time-sucking vortex that is working with Lenny Dykstra" in precise detail. He explained how editorial meetings featured Dykstra's "long, leisurely fart(s) for the amusement of his employees" and how he enjoyed rubbing a $500 tie on his crotch, laughing at the resulting embarrassment of those in the room.

Dykstra, of course, said the article was filled with lies. But I knew it was true, and so did many others. It was extremely damaging and sparked a backlash, with some professional sports teams refusing to allow the *Players Club* to be delivered to their clubhouse.

ESPN picked up the ball and ran with it. Reporter Mike Fish penned a massive, 8,500+ word article entitled "Dykstra's Business: A Bed of 'Nails'" and a more modest 1,700+ word follow-up a few weeks later entitled "Financial Woes

Still Hammer at Nails." Unlike Coughlin, Fish didn't have a perceived ax to grind, making his account all the more damning.

From the outset of the article, Dykstra was clearly a little batty, even falling asleep during one interview session. While showing the reporter the Gretzky mansion, Dykstra spotted a bat—"the flying variety—balled up in a corner. . . . He ducks beneath it with his hands clasped on his head, playfully screeching."

The article talked about Dykstra's "street cred"—the endorsement from Cramer—and featured Dykstra boasting that he made his newsletter readers $250,000. Unlike his earlier backing of Dykstra, Cramer declined to comment for the ESPN article, saying, "The old interview game . . . hasn't been all that productive for me of late."

It was true. Jon Stewart, comedian and host of *The Daily Show* on Comedy Central, had been taking Cramer to task for his misguided perspective on Bear Stearns and several other stocks that imploded in the wake of the market collapse. Stewart had done a bit about how CNBC was complicit in the massive destruction of wealth during the market collapse because the network was in bed with the industry it should have been objectively covering.

Cramer took issue with his inclusion in the clip and responded publicly, leading to a war of words that featured Cramer on *The Martha Stewart Show* pounding dough while pretending it was Jon Stewart. To which Jon Stewart responded, "Mr. Cramer, don't you destroy enough dough on your own show?"[1]

The feud culminated with Cramer appearing on *The Daily Show*. "I understand that you want to make finance entertaining, but it's not a fucking game," Stewart told Cramer. "I can't reconcile the brilliance and knowledge that you have of the intricacies of the market with the crazy . . . I see you do every night." Cramer tried to strike a repentant tone and said he could have done a better job at rooting out wrongdoing during the financial collapse.

When ESPN came calling, Cramer just wasn't going to stick his neck out again for Dykstra other than to say he had made several good stock picks.

For all the outlandish anecdotes in the ESPN article, it also provided a rudimentary road map of Dykstra's scheming ways. The article noted that Dykstra's private jet was grounded in Cleveland after he failed to pay for $227,000 worth of repairs and upgrades to the inside cabin. The Gretzky mansion was nearly emptied out of furniture, and Dykstra owed more than $400,000 in back taxes on his two estates in Lake Sherwood.

Dykstra had been sued twenty-four times in the previous two years and a whopping eighteen times in the previous six months, ESPN revealed. That, of course, didn't include all the people like me who got ripped off but decided not to sue.

"After thumbing through a series of lawsuits that stretches from coast to coast and chatting up his business associates, you wonder if this aspiring financial Pied Piper is, indeed, living in a fantasyland," Fish wrote. "You wonder if anyone this side of Bernie Madoff has ticked off more people—business partners and family, alike—than Lenny K. Dykstra."

Fish's article was a treasure trove of information for the public—a mixture of well-known legal battles, lesser-known disputes and details, and a handful of shady characters. "I let him basically hang himself," Fish tells me of his interviewing tactic. "I was up front about the questions I had, but I let him go through the whole spiel and try and schmooze me and give me all the nonsense. I asked questions, and he would dodge them or give me some smart-ass answer."

Fish went on to note how Lenny bounced checks, screwed partners, and stiffed employees, lawyers, and vendors. Dykstra had an excuse for each incident, claiming to be the victim each time. "One of the things I don't let people do is suck me out of my money," Dykstra told ESPN for the Fish article. "They think they can take advantage of athletes, dude. . . . I rip their heart out."

Another disturbing nugget in the article dealt with Marilyn, Dykstra's mom. According to Kevin Dykstra, Lenny called up their mom and asked her to put a $23,000 private jet flight on her credit card. Lenny was stranded in Cleveland, unable to get his plane out of hock. Even though Lenny and Marilyn had barely spoken since the fight over Kevin and the car washes, she gave him her credit card. Lenny never paid her back, and she has since passed.

After Fish's initial article, he received a flood of e-mails and calls from people claiming to be victims of Dykstra, prompting a follow-up. That article noted that Dykstra was fired by TheStreet.com and that his lawyer quit over nonpayment.

———————

Around the same time, Terri Dykstra filed for divorce.

"I couldn't go down with him," Terri tells me. "I've kept things together no matter what for a long time, but I just couldn't do it anymore because of the fraudulent things he was doing. . . . He did so many things I still don't know about." Lenny later told Dan Patrick on his radio show (July 2009) that it was as if someone "brainwashed her. . . . Now it's all about the fucking money."

Terri asked the courts to award her more than $40,000 a month in child and spousal support. Dykstra, however, said that his finances were in "extremely dire straits" and that the only income he had was his baseball pension, which totaled $5,700 per month.

"They don't call me Nails for nothing. . . . If I have to live in the street, if I have to eat grass, I'll do whatever I have to do to get this thing over with and get it done the way it's supposed to be done," Lenny later told Dan Patrick. One of those "whatever it takes" measures was keeping two sets of books—one showing his businesses were prospering and the other showing he was broke. Lenny bragged to many associates that he was hiding money from Terri.

To support herself and their child Luke, Lenny asked the court to advise Terri to get a job. She was "healthy and should start looking for work even if it's on a part-time basis." Terri, who hadn't held a job in more than twenty-three years, didn't like that suggestion.

She also filed for a restraining order, which was eventually denied, after Lenny sent her a text message stating, "PLAYING MR. NICE GUY IS OVER," according to the *Ventura County Star*.[2] She also claimed Lenny threatened her via voicemail, saying that the "war is ready to begin and I play . . . dirty." Lenny said Terri's allegations were lies.

The final straw, Terri tells me, was when Lenny took cash from their son Cutter. For months I had heard that Lenny got his hands on part of the signing bonus Cutter received when he was drafted by the Brewers. Terri confirms this during an interview with me. She also told Stephanie Hoops, a reporter for the *Ventura Star*, that Lenny claimed to have invested the money.

"It's like with Cutter, I kept telling [Lenny] it's black and white, right in front of my face," Terri tells me during the interview. "I see what you did with his money, and you're telling me you invested it." Terri recalls that when she confronted Lenny, he insisted he had worked out a deal with their son. "I know [that's] not true," she says, noting sarcastically that Lenny's idea of a deal is to spend all of Cutter's money and then maybe try and get it back for him some day. "That's Bernie Madoff for God's sakes."

Several employees confirm that Dykstra messed around with Cutter's money. Cutter, however, later denied the allegations in an interview with the Dino Costa radio show.[3]

Samantha Kulchar, who worked for Dykstra at the time Cutter was drafted, said that Lenny kept trying to get Cutter's money without his or Terri's knowledge. In one attempt, he tried to push Kulchar to bribe a notary to falsify documents giving him access to Cutter's cash. Dykstra "basically wanted me to find a notary public, who I would ask to perform an illegal act and sign off on one of us signing Cutter's name. And have the notary fake it."

Kulchar refused, and Dykstra eventually gave up on that plan, she says. Next he sought to get his hands on Cutter's checkbook. When Kulchar told Lenny that Terri had it, he sent her on a covert mission to retrieve it. Terri, however, purposely changed the bank account's password and didn't share it with Kulchar or Lenny.

When he couldn't find the checkbook, Dykstra sent Kulchar to the bank to try and talk her way into getting him the cash, she says. Kulchar told the bankers the money was for Lenny, and they refused to release the funds because neither she nor Lenny was an authorized signer on the account. When Kulchar delivered the bad news, Lenny went ballistic, screaming that Terri "blocked" him from the account.

"The next thing I know, Terri is crying and there are red circles around her eyes," Kulchar recalls. Lenny finally pulled it off. He got the cash, a six-figure payout.

Once that happened, the mood in the house turned really bad, really fast. "Terri would not speak to Lenny," Kulchar says. "She was in bad shape." If anyone asked where the money came from, Terri instructed Kulchar to simply say. "You know Lenny; he always pulls it off." When Kulchar asked what the money would be used for, she says Terri didn't know but guessed Lenny would use it for another flight on a private jet.

Several other employees and business partners witnessed questionable activity involving Cutter's bank account. Amanda the flight attendant says one businessman sought to return money Lenny had given him after their deal fell apart. The man issued a check to Cutter since the money had come from Cutter's account. However, Lenny insisted the man reissue the check to him, not Cutter, she says.

Dorothy has quite a different perspective on the whole sordid scenario. "The fact that his dad took the money and put it into the *Players Club* isn't really that bad of a thing," she says. "His dad honestly didn't think he was spending his money to lose it for him. He thought he was creating a dynasty that would be something Cutter could inherit and that Luke could inherit."

Dorothy offers up another excuse for Dykstra's behavior. Cutter is "twenty years old. He doesn't need half a million dollars in his bank account or $300,000 sitting in his bank account," she says. "How many twenty-year-olds do you know that have that kind of money laying around that would do something responsible with it?"

CHAPTER 38

BYE BYE BROMANCE

It was a late, sunny Sunday afternoon in May 2009, and I was carrying my clean clothes from the laundromat to my car when I noticed I had a voicemail from Dorothy. She said she would "jump for joy" if I would rejoin Team Dykstra.

It had been only two days since I had received the surprise phone call from Dykstra I detailed in the Introduction to this book. During that conversation, Dykstra told me that he was jacking up the price of the newsletter from $995 to $2,900 a year and that he was going to begin investing money for others.

"I've got a guy in New York where we can use his Series 7 [license]. . . . He's a real fucking goofball. . . . We can tell him what to do," Dykstra told me. "He's actually pretty smart, but he's so painful. You can take him in such small doses. You literally just have to go, 'ARRRRGGHHH.'"

Not only did the idea sound shady; I also knew Dykstra couldn't keep his hands out of the cookie jar. There were other parts of our phone call I also couldn't reconcile. "You know that everyone got paid that worked for me," Dykstra said to me. "The only people that didn't get paid are the people that didn't deserve it."

When I told him that I, in fact, was still owed quite a bit of cash, he insisted he had seen something somewhere that said I had been paid something. "Now, I don't know what our deal was because you started doing more stuff—started doing more than the newsletter," he said. "Listen, man, if anybody's owed money, man, I'm never one to run away from it. If there is some money that you feel that you're owed or something, that's not a problem. I mean I've always been reasonable when it comes to that kind of stuff."

It sounded good, but I knew Dykstra just didn't have the bullets to pay his debts, and by May 2009 my eyes were open wide to Dykstra's modus operandi.

A lot had changed in Dykstra's world too. He hadn't published the *Players Club* in months, and rumors were circulating that the magazine had folded. Yet he remained defiant. "One of the things that's not happening is the *Players Club* is never stopping," he told me. "You don't put $10 million dollars in it and let it just die. I mean, that'd be like fucking running into a wall full speed—you just don't do it."

His big-gun writers were gone, including Conlin. "I gassed him, and I told him to take a hike 'cause I didn't need him anymore," Dykstra said. "Oh, Conlin, dude, he's such a pussy. I've been really fucking with Conlin, telling him how good the magazine is, and how nobody misses him, how he's a fat piece of shit. He started cussing at me in German. Oh, dude, the guy went fucking crazy."

Of all the carnage, however, the fallout with Cramer was the most dramatic. "When TheStreet.com let Lenny go, they wouldn't articulate the reason why," Dorothy explains during an interview. "That really bothered him because they wouldn't tell him why, so he didn't have an 'in' to get around it. They just turned him off, and I'm not sure why."

When Dykstra needed Cramer to go to bat for him the most, his friend and fellow superstar remained firmly on the bench.

"You were the one that e-mailed me and said 'we miss you, we want you back writing for TheStreet.com,'" Dykstra wrote to Cramer in a lengthy email that he later shared with me. "LOYALTY IS HARD TO FIND THESE DAYS—I WAS ALWAYS LOYAL TO YOU—I STILL AM LOYAL TO YOU—PLEASE REMEMBER THAT."

When he didn't hear back, he forwarded the note again with a message at the top in big bold red letters:

JIM, I SENT THIS EMAIL A COUPLE DAYS AGO—AND HAVE NOT RECEIVED A RESPONSE FROM YOU—SO I AM SENDING THIS EMAIL AGAIN. PLEASE EXTEND ME THE COURTESY OF AT LEAST ACKNOWL-EDGING MY EMAIL.

Instead of respect, he said he got a one-liner from Cramer that simply read "I am reviewing this with the new CEO, Daryl Otte." Needless to say, it was not the response Lenny expected. In fact, it was worse than no response at all—it was an insult. There was no "I'm sorry things worked out this way, pal" or "Best of luck to you, Lenny. I'm still a fan.' It was cold, unemotional proof that Cramer had indeed read Lenny's pleas and wasn't going to help his old friend.

Dykstra usually rolled with the punches. If someone didn't want to do business with him, then he would say, "Fuck 'em; they're quitters" or they just didn't "get it." However, with Cramer he was crushed. "That's all I got back," he said, the hollow air of disbelief in his voice. "That's it, after all that shit."

That day Dykstra also fired off another e-mail correspondence to me that he thought was the "funniest thing of all." It was from the "fag" Dave Morrow, editor in chief at TheStreet.com. "This is Morrow's decision from what I understand, but I think Cramer was involved in it," he said.

The subject line read "The response to your emails and phone calls." Cramer handed Dykstra's e-mail over to Morrow, and it had obviously been run through all levels of the company's management. Morrow ignored Dykstra's smears and focused on the meat of the matter: business and money.

Morrow said TheStreet.com retained all rights to the newsletter and if Dykstra tried to fight the company, he would lose. He also needed to stay away from the customers—as per his contract—and endorse his replacement, Jon Najarian. If Lenny didn't, his final payout could take a hit, Morrow warned.

That was a huge pill for a proud guy like Dykstra to swallow, but it paled in comparison to the kick in the teeth Dykstra got next. "This correspondence to you has been coordinated with Jim Cramer and the management of TheStreet.com. . . . You must cease and desist from any additional contact with employees of the company including Jim Cramer and me," the note read. "Further calls and correspondence will constitute harassment and require additional legal action by TheStreet.com, which we do not believe is in anyone's best interest. Thank you again for your past contributions."

The next time I spoke with Dykstra was shortly after I had received Dorothy's voicemail. He was upbeat and in the mood for revenge, telling me he was "gonna take TheStreet apart" and that its management was in serious trouble. "I have a really good attorney, and he says they got a real problem with that case, and I believe him."

The conversation was much shorter than our previous one, but there was still time to bounce around for a bit before he asked me whether I had considered his proposal. "I was thinking maybe you'd have time to write. You could bang those columns out quick. It could be some extra money for you," he said. Although I wanted to still believe in Dykstra, I knew better. There was no going back.

He still owed me a lot of money, but arguing about it wouldn't have done either of us any good. He simply didn't have the cash, and even if he did, there was a long line of people much more powerful than I was with expensive lawyers waiting to recoup their losses. It was a lot of money for me, but for my own sanity, I had to let go of the idea of ever recovering it. I wasn't going to sue.

I politely declined Dykstra's offer. "Why don't you think about it, dude? You could get your rhythm going on the columns and pick up a couple grand a month, you know, or something man. Don't shut the door. We'll talk," he said before he hung up the phone.

Dykstra and I spoke only one more time after that. He was still friendly, but much more direct. "Cut and dry, I can pay you like $4,000 a month," he said, adding that if I wanted to work with him, I should let him know. "All right, bro, good talking to you," he said quickly. "Okay, buddy, bye."

CHAPTER 39

WEIRD CAT

HBO *Real Sports* planned a follow-up segment on Dykstra, so I flew out to California for the June 10, 2009, taping and for inclusion on a six-person panel of ex-employees and business partners. Kevin Coughlin and Samantha Kulchar were among the group.

The pinnacle of the episode centered on a planned meeting between reporter Bernie Goldberg and Dykstra at his mansion, When Goldberg arrived, Dykstra was nowhere to be found. Seeing that the front door was unlocked, Goldberg let himself in and searched the nearly empty mansion.

"After twenty-five minutes, the elusive Mr. Dykstra surfaced. And we began something vaguely resembling a conversation," Goldberg stated in the episode. With Dykstra sitting at his desk and Goldberg standing over his shoulder, the reporter remarked that it seemed as if Dykstra was "broke" and owed "everybody and his brother money."

Obviously annoyed, Dykstra asked whom he supposedly owed. Goldberg mentioned the magazine printer, alluding to Creel Printing. "Fuck that printer. . . . The printers are criminals," Dykstra responded. Goldberg then mentioned a flight attendant. "Fuck that flight attendant. . . . They all think that they can come here and steal my money. . . . I don't owe anybody anything. These cases are all bullshit," Dykstra said.

The interview took a curious turn after that as Dykstra pulled out a picture of Klaus, a German shepherd he said he was buying for $10,000. "That's a world champion," Dykstra said. "That's the only dog I'll buy."

Goldberg proceeded to ask Dykstra how he responded to all the people who thought that "once upon a time you were flying high and now you're broke." Dykstra whipped out a wad of cash and began counting it in front of the camera.

"It still looks like I'm flying pretty fucking high. And by the way, I'm flying high-er."

Dykstra came off looking more than a little crazy—like a demented recluse. "I don't know what makes Lenny tick," Goldberg tells me during an interview. "I'm not anything resembling an expert, but he's a weird cat. That's a very unscientific way of describing it, but he's a weird cat."

For her part, Dorothy thinks the piece was a fair depiction of Dykstra. "I don't think it made Lenny look overly foolish, but on the other hand, things could have been a lot different," she tells me.

The piece had a lot less bite than it should have had. It didn't focus on his serial scamming and in some weird way portrayed Dykstra as a victim of the economic crunch. That angle also provided *Real Sports* with a convenient way to explain how it got the story so wrong the first time.

"I called up my colleagues who were involved with the [original] story, and I said, 'I want to know one thing: was all this bullshit going on while we did the story?' and thank god the answer came back no," Goldberg says to me. "I'm not Nostradamus here, I'm just a journalist." He notes that the original segment filmed in March 2008 and news of Dykstra's troubles started surfacing in the fall.

"I'm not a mind reader. I saw his house. I saw his jet. I saw his car, and I spoke to Cramer, who told me, 'He's one of the top five stock pickers.' I did a story on it. . . . I would have had to have subpoena powers to know things at that point," Goldberg says. "I'm not saying this defensively or anything, but at that point nobody was suggesting Lenny wasn't for real. As a matter of fact, Lenny was for real; it's just that a whole bunch of things happened. . . . Hey, that's not my problem."

CHAPTER 40

THERE'S NO PLACE LIKE HOME

With virtually no other realistic option to keep his growing list of creditors at bay, Dykstra sought to shield the remnants of his crumbling empire by filing for Chapter 11 bankruptcy protection. At that time, he said he had more than $31 million in debts and assets of less than $50,000.

"Chapter 11 is like putting a sniper on top of a roof and gun down all those people that are piling on," Dykstra told radio host Dan Patrick, noting that people were trying to get hired by him just so they could sue. When asked how he planned to emerge from bankruptcy, Dykstra later told CNBC reporter Jane Wells he would get the *Players Club* back on track and would be starring in an upcoming reality television show. When she probed him further about his plan, he told her he would simply "follow the yellow brick road. It's a good roadmap."[1]

With his bankruptcy "snipers" in place, Dykstra set the stage for his next battle: the Gretzky mansion. His first opponent? Fireman's Fund Insurance Company. Dykstra claimed water damage in the Gretzky mansion and demanded the insurer give him $10 million to repair it.

"We went up there and shot the video of removed fixtures and torn-up floor boards all trying to explain where he claims the water damage was coming from," said CNBC's Jane Wells. "Of course it came out in the bankruptcy hearings that [Fireman's Fund's] claiming that [Dykstra] basically vandalized the house."

The *Ventura County Star* later reported the ex-ballplayer removed lighting fixtures and a La Cornue oven and cooktop, which the Gretzkys had installed for $51,750.[2] "He took out fixtures throughout the house," says Jeff Smith of Index Investors, one of the lienholders on the house. "He took out the stoves and appliances. . . . That was against the law—he wasn't supposed to take any of those things."

Dykstra admitted to removing some items for safekeeping, but denied selling them and claimed a bunch were stolen. He also pawned a bunch of his baseball memorabilia shortly before officially declaring bankruptcy, including his 1986 World Series Championship ring and trophy. Combined, the ring and ten other items fetched more than $162,000 at auction.[3] All of the items should have been sold with the court's knowledge and the money used to pay creditors, not line Lenny's pockets.

By the end of 2009, reports surfaced that the Gretzky mansion was "unshowable" and was "littered throughout with empty beer bottles, trash and dog feces and urine among other unmentionables," a source told the *Wall Street Journal*. The article also noted there was "raw sewage escaping from the main drain line left undone."[4]

Because of the destruction, Dykstra was barred from the exclusive gated community, and security was instructed to keep him and his associates out.

Before long, Dykstra's bankruptcy was converted from Chapter 11 reorganization to Chapter 7 liquidation. The court appointed a trustee to oversee the liquidation, which Judge Geraldine Mund said was in "the interest of creditors and Mr. Dykstra, even if he doesn't think so," according to a CNBC report.[5]

Well after the trustee had been appointed—in May 2010—Dykstra was caught selling memorabilia on Craigslist.[6] A picture of a smiling Dykstra holding the framed photos appeared in the post and was accompanied by the headline "Lenny Dykstra (Personalized) Framed Picture (He'll Even Call You)." He wanted $3,200.

The trustee, Arturo Cisneros, later claimed Dykstra had lied in court and repeatedly acted in a "fraudulent and deceitful manner." The judge agreed, saying she was concerned about "the truthfulness of some of [Dykstra's] statements," and she noted his "litigious attitude and unrealistic hopes."[7]

Aside from all the items "disappearing" from the estate, the main point of contention between Dykstra and Cisneros remained the Gretzky mansion itself. Dykstra claimed Washington Mutual (WaMu), which was later bought by J.P. Morgan, tricked him into a loan he couldn't afford. He said a WaMu rep promised him a $17.5 million loan to buy the Gretzky mansion, but later scaled that back to just $12 million. To make up the difference, Dykstra contends the rep said he could get a piggyback loan from First Credit for $8.5 million, according to the *New York Daily News*.[8]

Dykstra's monthly payments were to be $135,434 despite his having income of just $125,000 a month. He says the WaMu rep promised the package would be refinanced two months after he closed on the purchase of the mansion, but that never happened. As a result, he was forced to sell promissory notes he received from the sale of the car washes in order to pay down the smaller loan.

On his own, Dykstra filed a $100 million lawsuit against the company. Shortly thereafter, the trustee dropped the claim and reached a settlement that called for the bank to pay the estate $400,000, according to Reuters.[9]

Dykstra, refusing to adhere to the settlement, went on the warpath, saying he was going to ask a judge to make an example of J.P. Morgan. He even accused the bank of destroying his marriage. "They dismantled what this country's built on—the American family," Dykstra said during a March 4, 2011, interview with John Clark of NBC10 in Philadelphia. "We didn't just get divorced all of a sudden, no—look at the timing of it. When you're paying $180,000 a month . . . I don't care who you are. I was set up to fail."

Dykstra's battle with Cisneros reached a head in August 2010, when it appeared Dykstra was down to his last strike. "Lenny Dykstra has proven that, to quote Yogi Berra, it ain't over 'til it's over," CNBC's Jane Wells writes in an article. "On a day that lawyers for JP Morgan Chase said was 'really, really, really gonna be Mr. Dykstra's last chance' to make any case for himself in bankruptcy court, it really, really, really wasn't."[10]

Wells explains how Cisneros resigned out of the blue and Dykstra's lawyers accused the man of failing to disclose the extent of his relationship with J.P. Morgan Chase, the mortgage holder on the Gretzky mansion. The exact cause of the resignation was not immediately clear. Dykstra vowed to emerge victorious and said he would get the Gretzky mansion back.

Dykstra also revealed the SEC had investigated him for nine months in relation to the allegations Randall Lane made in his book and didn't find any wrongdoing. He also warned that the people piling on were going to get hurt. "They're going to have to pay me for the damage they've done," he told Wells. "You can't just go around making comments like that when they're not true. . . . You mess with Nails, you get the hammer."[11]

With Dykstra's life disintegrating, *Ventura County Star* business reporter Stephanie Hoops met with him at a "really dark bar at this really expensive hotel" for a story she was doing entitled "Ex–Baseball Player Lenny Dykstra Tries to Cope with Personal, Professional Losses."

At that point, Dykstra's financial mess had become clearer. Hoops noted that by early 2010, he was facing nineteen lawsuits and had $37 million in debts and just $24.6 million in assets.

In the story, Dykstra claimed his life had become a "nightmare." He said that he was homeless, that he often wondered where his next meal would come from, and that he was fighting for his life. Dykstra later told the *Los Angeles Times* that he was a "wanderer . . . like Gandhi."[12]

Earlier reports noted Dykstra was living in an office at a local airport in Camarillo. However, he hadn't paid for that office, and when the leasing company tried to kick him out, he reportedly said that the only way he would be leaving was if the sheriffs dragged him out. In subsequent news reports, Dykstra claimed to be living in his car and even on the streets.

When Dykstra showed up to meet Hoops, his "suit was all rumpled," she tells me. "It didn't look like it had been pressed in a long time. He looked like a homeless person dressed up for a meeting."

However, if he were truly living on the streets, a couple of things didn't make sense:

1. Dykstra was using an expensive laptop computer.
2. Dorothy was with him claiming to be his employee.
3. He was staying at a fancy hotel.

"I thought, 'How could he afford a secretary if he's homeless?'" Hoops recalls. "I was completely confused."

She offered to buy him a drink, and he ordered one and dinner on the paper's tab. Throughout the night, he kept making jokes about how Hoops and her cameraman weren't drinking, saying that life on the streets drove him back to the bottle. When I worked for Dykstra, he called alcohol "the devil" and I never witnessed him taking a single drink.

Dykstra's frustration was also apparent, Hoops says. He castigated a young waiter for several minutes for not bringing a drink prepared to his specifications. "He thought that people didn't notice him anymore, and it was like he was blaming the waiter for the fact that he was no longer getting the attention that he used to get," Hoops says. "I remembered feeling really uncomfortable—so uncomfortable that I pulled the waiter aside to apologize before I left that night."

In November, Dykstra officially lost the house. The Gretzky mansion was sold at auction for $760,712. Index Investors, the second lienholder, placed the winning bid, assuming about $12 million in debt and taxes owed on the six-and-a-half-acre compound.[13]

"I've done business with a lot of people in the Los Angeles area, and Lenny was the worst of them all—he was definitely the ace of spades," Smith of Index Investors says. "He was a god at one point, and his celebrity still lives on. Now he's a pathetic motherfucker."

CHAPTER 41

NAUGHTY NAILS

With the Players Club on hold and his other businesses withering on the vine, Dykstra switched directions entirely. He started a new business called Predatory Lending Recovery. In the months prior to Smith's taking possession of the Gretzky mansion, when it was clear that Dykstra would lose the property for good, Predatory Lending Recovery's Web site showcased how Dykstra supposedly won it back from the greedy banks.

It simply wasn't true. However, Dykstra promised to help others who were down on their luck to stay in their homes . . . and he would make a little money while doing so. He said it was the reason God put him on this earth.

"These banks are destroying families. . . . Right now they're walking around with impending doom," Dykstra said on the *Alex Jones Show* on February 24, 2011. "I can help people save their houses. Their life isn't over. Right now they're all waiting for the electric chair."

Victorya Moreno helped with the new business—the former gymnast and diver accepted a job to be Dykstra's personal assistant. One day Dykstra told her to organize a party at the Gretzky mansion. "He said that he had won it back," Moreno says. "His lawyer at the time said he legally had the right to be there."

That lawyer, Michael T. Pines, was making waves in Southern California by recommending that his clients break into their former homes and reclaim them from foreclosure. Pines has since gotten in trouble with the state.

With little more than twenty-four hours to prepare for the party, Moreno raced around, putting almost $4,000 in expenses on her credit card and attempting to ready the mansion, which was in "disastrous" condition. For his part, Dykstra uprooted a Sotheby's "for sale" real estate sign that had been placed on the property at the direction of the court.[1]

He reportedly spent in excess of $50,000 on the party, and Terri helped sneak him past security at the Sherwood Country Club, according to the *Ventura County Star*.[2] Inside the mansion, there was a strange mix of guests at the party, including Dorothy, Terri, and "prostitutes and drug dealers," Moreno says.

After the party, Dykstra and Pines had a falling out. Dorothy blamed Pines for directing Dykstra to go against the judge's orders, according to the *Star*. However, Dykstra thought better of breaking into the house again, she told the paper. Later, in court documents Dykstra referred to Pines as a "scumbag" and said the lawyer promised to get him $250,000 but never did. Pines is "letting a lot of people down and he's doing it again and again and again," Dorothy told the *Star*.[3]

However, Moreno has a very different recollection of Dykstra's postparty conscience. He instructed her to hire movers to remove all remaining items from the property. He told Moreno to rent a storage unit in her name and hide all of the items there.

She was also in charge of hiding items that had previously been snuck out of the mansion and stored at Lenny's residence at the time, an apartment in a high-rise at the Wilshire corridor in downtown Los Angeles (Wells Fargo was attempting to foreclose on the building's landlords and evict Dykstra, who hadn't paid rent in months). Those items included antiques and expensive artwork that Dykstra valued at between $80,000 and $150,000, Moreno says.

Before long, Moreno and Dykstra were at odds. He owed her thousands of dollars, refused to return a car she had rented for him in her name, and, she would later find out, stole her credit card information to make thousands of dollars in unauthorized charges. Moreno filed a police report.

Following her departure from Team Lenny, Moreno says the ex–major leaguer harassed and threatened her, forcing her to file for a restraining order. She claims that Dykstra had at least five different people, including his drug dealer and a "fake private investigator," call her. They accused her of stealing from Dykstra and threatened to "come into my home and get me."

Dykstra told Moreno she was "on notice" because he had reported her to Reggie Maeweather, a former captain with the Los Angeles Police Department. Dykstra accused Moreno of stealing his pants, a laptop, and $30,000. Moreno denies stealing anything.

Dykstra was also pissed that Moreno closed the storage unit account. Moreno claims she told Dykstra and Dorothy to get his things out, and when they didn't, she left them outside the unit but on the property. Dorothy claims Moreno stacked them in the dumpster.

Dykstra wrote an e-mail to Moreno about the "sickening act [she] pulled at the storage facility" and claimed that many of his items were now missing and that he believed she had taken them. He said that if all of his items and money were not returned, he would turn the case over to Maeweather and that she would "go to jail for a long time."

While Dykstra was supposedly leading the charge of a middle-class crusade against the greedy banks, he was simultaneously preying on some of the most vulnerable casualties of the financial meltdown.

Twenty-nine-year-old January Yumul was desperate for a job in a hopeless economy, unaware she was heading into a trap on Saturday night, September, 11, 2010. Shortly after she replied to a job listing on Craigslist seeking an executive personal assistant for "Mr. Kyle," she received a call from Nathan, one of Mr. Kyle's employees.

January needed to report to Mr. Kyle's residence on the Wilshire corridor that night for an interview, Nathan told her. Mr. Kyle was scheduled to leave town on a private jet just a few hours later, but he wanted the role filled before he left, so the interview had to be at that late hour. "I'm a smart girl, and I kind of knew something was wrong," Yumul explains. "I was just desperate. I was really broke."

For starters, Nathan wanted to know her nationality (she's Filipina), age, and weight, saying he didn't want to look bad in front of his boss by bringing in a fatty, or someone sloppy looking, for an interview. He also said the pay was $65,000 a year, not $85,000 plus benefits as advertised.

Nathan offered Yumul a few "coaching tips," telling her that Mr. Kyle would offer her an alcoholic beverage and that he didn't like to drink alone. Nathan told her that Mr. Kyle was an ex-athlete and that he had some injuries she might have to attend to. "Then he said that if I really wanted the job, I should bring massage oil and offer him a massage," Yumul recalls, saying she shrugged off that suggestion.

"I was so stupid for even going," Yumul says.

Upon arrival, Yumul learned that Mr. Kyle was really Lenny Kyle Dykstra, a former baseball star she had never heard of. As expected, Dykstra offered her a drink, and she took a bottle of Coors Light, which she opened herself and nursed all night. The six-hour interview was bizarre. In addition to the salary being reduced again—this time to $4,000 a month in cash ($48,000)—Dykstra asked Yumul to use her credit card to buy him a car. He offered her a $5,000 bonus, saying he was getting a large sum of money at the end of the week.

He bounced randomly from topic to topic, showing her YouTube videos of himself, and at one point even got up to shave, saying he needed to "freshen up." At other times, Dykstra played loud music instead of talking, telling Yumul that he used song to express himself because he was not good with words.

At about the five-hour mark, Nathan said it was time for Dykstra's massage. "I was thinking maybe he would roll up his pant legs and I could work on his circulation and his calves," Yumul says. She wasn't so lucky. Dykstra retreated to the bedroom, summoning her a few moments later. When she entered the room, Dykstra was lying facedown on the bed and there was an industrial-sized bottle of baby oil nearby.

"I massaged his legs, and it was really nasty," she says. "I was just trying to rationalize that it was a medical need." Dykstra kept asking her to massage higher up on the leg until she was massaging his butt.

"After that, he turned over and said, 'Let's do the front,'" Yumul recalls. "I was very careful not to go up to the crotch area. He kept encouraging me to 'go further up, further up.'" Yumul nervously talked the entire time to distract herself from the creepiness of the situation. She then cut the rubdown short, telling Dykstra she believed she had demonstrated her massage capabilities.

Dykstra hired her on the spot and asked her to stay over in a spare bedroom, but she said she had to go home. To her surprise, Dykstra told her to come back the following day to meet Dorothy. He wasn't leaving town after all. "There was no flight," she says. "It was a ploy."

When she got home in the early morning hours, she looked up Dykstra on the Internet. "I felt really sick to my stomach." She texted Dykstra that she couldn't give any more massages and that she needed to be paid up front. In typical fashion, Dykstra scolded Yumul for her lack of loyalty and told her to enjoy her life "in the middle."

Yumul was just one in a long line of young women who were lured to Dykstra's apartment under the guise of a job interview but who were subject to unwanted sexual advances, according to several former employees. "A lot of people were afraid to say no," says Peter Neil, who worked for Dykstra in 2010. He claims to have witnessed Dykstra pulling this scheme on at least half a dozen prospective female personal assistants in the final days before he quit.

Citing law enforcement sources, *TMZ* later reported that a forty-seven-year-old woman responded to a Craigslist ad for a housekeeper position, but instead got a naked Dykstra demanding a massage during an interview. The woman left immediately, flagged down a cop to file a police report, and lined up hotshot attorney Mauro Fiore Jr. to handle a potential lawsuit.[4] Through his attorney, Dykstra called the allegations "total garbage" and said the incident "never happened," according to the *New York Daily News*.[5]

By late 2010, Dykstra had his routine down to a science, several employees say. He would use various aliases to post jobs on Craigslist, such as Mr. Kyle, Mr. London, Jack Forsch, and Thurston Denning, according to these employees. "He tried to think of these high-class names, and his references were coming from *Gilligan's Island*," Neil says.

The script was the same almost every time. He would tell the women that if they were hired, they would either become millionaires or get fired. He would play Kid Rock songs and video clips from his favorite movies. "He would show them these ridiculous Ben Affleck monologues on YouTube from the movie *Boiler Room* and Alec Baldwin from *Glengarry Glen Ross*," Neil recalls.

"He usually asked for blow jobs on interviews," says Moreno. In fact, he told several of his employees to list "blow jobs" as one of the requirements in the official job postings.

Whether Dykstra told the women he needed a massage or simply wanted to give them a "tour" of the apartment, nearly every interview ended up in the bedroom. Most of the girls came out of the bedroom and went "running for the hills," says Tricia Dunning, Dykstra's former maid, who claims he also sexually assaulted her.

On the day Dykstra allegedly attacked her, he was interviewing a young, attractive, professional-looking black woman for the executive assistant job, Dunning says. The woman emerged from the bedroom, yelling that Dykstra was a sick bastard. "She's standing there gathering her stuff and he's telling me, 'I don't like niggers. They're like animals,'" Dunning recalls.

Then Dykstra turned his sights on Dunning, whose job duties also included chauffeuring hookers to and from Dykstra's apartment and going to doctors to try and get him the drug Adderall.

After demanding that she "finish [him] off," Dykstra gave Dunning a T-shirt that he said would look cute on her and offered her cocaine.

"He sat down, and he railed out four long lines," Dunning says. "He did two and told me to go ahead. I said, 'No thank you. . . . I'm a drug addict in recovery.' I have three years under my belt, so I was very adamant about saying no to him."

"I told him the drugs are a sensitive area for me. It's my weakness. I lost my kids. I was homeless for eighteen months. These drugs took me down to where I don't want to go again."

Dykstra backed off and told her to clean the bedroom. While she was tidying up there, Dykstra entered, shut the door behind him, and demanded a massage.

He pushed her onto the bed, she says, and told her to massage his legs. While she was rubbing his calves, Dykstra told her he was taking off his pants and demanded a blow job. "He grabbed me by my neck and pulled me down," Dunning says. "I told him, 'No, no,' and I started crying. He saw me crying—I know that he did. He pushed my head down and made me do that, and he kept telling me that I'm going to see God. I kept trying to stop, and he pushed my head down more. When he was done, I left."

Dunning says she was too ashamed "to tell anyone at first and too broke to walk away from the money he owed her. In what she says was a major mistake, she went back to work the following week in an attempt to collect her unpaid wages and to try and gather some evidence—a piece of paper that she says Dykstra wrote that described the "disgusting" sexual deeds he expected from some of his assistants.

Dunning went to the police after Dykstra attacked her again. She says the detectives told her it was a "he said, she said" scenario and because she went back to work after the first incident, it seemed as if she were okay with it. Prosecutors ultimately declined to file charges.

The *Los Angeles Times*, citing a filing, reported that Dunning told investigators she "needed the job and the money so she went along with the suspect's requests rather than lose her job." It also noted that she sent him text messages asking for her money and her job back. "I didn't do that act by will, thinking that I was going to get paid or that it would help me get paid faster," Dunning claimed. "He did that to me by force."

For his part, Dykstra denied the allegations. "If she was assaulted on Saturdays, then I'm a . . . ballerina dancer on Sundays," he said, according to the *Times*. "This is a maid. That's not even worth commenting on, are you kidding me?"[6] He also told the paper that Dunning attempted to coerce him into buying drugs for her.

Although Dunning made a handful of questionable decisions, ex-employees like Peter Neil say it's very plausible she was targeted by a "predator" like Dykstra. "You could just tell she was a really good person, very kind, and just trying to get her life together and doing pretty good at it," he says.

Plus, Dunning isn't the only alleged victim. A year earlier a woman named Jackie Massaro said she had been attacked by Dykstra. Scott Weston, Dykstra's personal driver at the time, says he remembers that night well.

Dykstra was meeting with a high roller from Las Vegas who had flown into town for the get-together. Dykstra hoped the man would provide a big-time loan, but the meeting didn't go as planned. When the men went to dinner, Dykstra began drinking, and Weston says the booze didn't mix well with whatever medication Dykstra was apparently on, leaving him "not all there" mentally.

After giving the restaurant an IOU because he didn't have money to pay his bill, Dykstra and Weston dropped the businessman off at the swanky Four Seasons hotel. Dykstra supposedly reserved a room for his potential business partner and promised to fly the man to Vegas first thing the next morning on his private jet. However, there were two major problems. First, Dykstra's jet was still grounded in Cleveland for nonpayment. Second, the Four Seasons was all booked.

"Lenny goes, 'Let's just take him there anyway. We'll just dump him,'" Weston recalls.

On the way back to the Gretzky mansion, the conversation turned to Jackie Massaro, Dykstra's new estate manager and personal assistant. Dykstra instructed her to report for work that night and offered to let her stay in a spare room at the Gretzky mansion since she lived three hours away in San Diego.

"He was talking crap," Weston says, adding that Dykstra said he was going to "fuck her" and "have her suck my dick." When they arrived at the house at about midnight, Massaro had gone to bed already. Dykstra was enraged. "He's sitting in his office, and he goes, 'Where is that bitch? She's sleeping? She needs to earn her keep and work.'"

Dykstra demanded Weston march upstairs and wake Massaro, but he refused, and Dykstra dismissed him for the night. "He was going on and on," Weston says. "It didn't surprise me or make me think anything bad was going to happen because he always talked shit like that." In retrospect, he believes Dykstra wasn't joking.

About a half an hour later, the confrontation between Dykstra and Massaro began. She claims Dykstra yelled at her to get to work, but when she questioned what kind of work he expected at such a late hour, he told her to get the "fuck out of my house. It's not going to work out. Just leave," according to a lawsuit later filed by Massaro.

Massaro returned to the bedroom to pack her belongings when she claims Dykstra assaulted her. "So you have nowhere to go? Give me a blow job, and you can stay the night," Dykstra allegedly said to her. Massaro scolded him, and that's when she claims Dykstra grabbed her breasts and tried to throw her down on the bed. She screamed as she broke free from his grasp and fled the house, according to the lawsuit. On her drive back to San Diego, she reported the incident to the police.

"He had this assistant that accused him of attempted rape," Dorothy tells me during an interview. "It was within two weeks of him taking his first drink," she recalls, noting she believed Dykstra had been sober for years. The police later questioned Dorothy about that night, and she informed them Dykstra had been drinking heavily. "But that doesn't mean he attacked the woman," she says.

Dorothy says Massaro is lying. "I had the telephone records that prove that when she alleges he attacked her, he was actually in the back talking to me," Dorothy says. "I know that Lenny likes to do multiple things at once, but I don't think he could quite pull that one off."

According to Dorothy, Massaro first claimed Dykstra only said something inappropriate to her. The next time they spoke, Dorothy says, Massaro claimed Dykstra touched her. During a third conversation, Dorothy says Massaro accused Dykstra of pushing her down on the bed.

"Each time when she called me, she just wanted money to make it go away," Dorothy says, adding that Massaro said she wouldn't report the incident to the police if Dykstra paid her three months' salary. "Before her conversation with me, she had already reported it. So she was just trying to extort money. She didn't know him long enough to know that he's not the kind of guy that pushes women or even ever gets violent with them."

Unlike the ever-loyal Dorothy, Weston believes Massaro. "Lenny is a crazy motherfucker, but when I saw him with alcohol in his body mixed with whatever pills he was taking, he was even crazier," Weston says. "It was not good."

CHAPTER 42

WINNING WARLOCKS

The world was going to know the truth about Lenny Dykstra if Monica Foster had anything to say about it. A few days before Christmas 2010, Foster set up a blog and posted a lengthy video blasting Dykstra over an alleged scam conducted by the former big leaguer.

Foster, a self-described "computer nerd, turned stripper, turned cam girl, turned porn star," is the author of the book *Getting into Porn—The Handbook: A Simple Guide on the Porn Industry* and has starred in porno flicks such as *Not the Cosbys XXX* and *Flava of Lust*. She claims that on December 13, 2010, she was Dykstra's escort and victim.

She advertised her services on an escort-client matching Web site and was contacted by Dykstra, who was using a fake name at the time, she says. They had agreed on $1,000 in cash for three hours of "drinks and conversation," and she went to meet him at his hotel. When she got there, she claims Dykstra was snorting some sort of drug.

When it came time for payment, Dykstra couldn't find his cash, so he asked if he could pay by check. Although she preferred cash, Foster says she accepted the check, which bounced. Foster later posted a copy of the check on her blog. Dykstra avoided her calls and messages, and when she finally was able to get a hold of him, he hung up on her.

"Being that I most likely have little to no chance of ever recouping my losses from Lenny Dykstra I have decided to tell the truth about what happened the morning of Dec. 13, 2010 at the Avalon hotel in Beverly Hills," she wrote in a blog post. "Lenny Dykstra WILL NOT EVER do this to another young woman if I can help it."

She also noted in her video post that making such waves could cause her legal problems. However, she said she didn't "give a flying fuck" because she wanted to make sure he didn't hurt anyone else. "This situation left me in the position of not being able to go home to visit my family for the holidays," she wrote.

Although she denies having any sexual interaction with Dykstra, that was more than likely an attempt to avoid admitting to illegal activity. I can't imagine Dykstra paying to talk to a girl for three hours.

"I know many people have called me a 'hooker' and a 'stupid dirty whore' and have said that I possibly may be incriminating myself, but in actuality I'm not because I didn't do anything illegal," Foster wrote on her blog. "I'm simply a young woman trying to make it in this world as an artist and an author who has chosen to do what she has to in order to get by WITHOUT being on welfare or any other government assistance."

Since she began her crusade, Foster says she has been contacted by several other "working girls" who claim Dykstra did the same thing to them. One of those women posted a comment on Foster's Web site, saying, "James London," one of Dykstra's known aliases, set up a meeting through an escort-matching site, but when she got there, he didn't have the money to pay her. He asked her to accept a check, and when she said no and left, he texted her with verbally abusive language. She also says he swiped one of her credit cards.

In the days following her blog post, Foster spoke with a few news outlets, continuing to keep the heat on Dykstra. She told RadarOnline that he was "a coward" and that she was not afraid of him. "I know in his eyes, he just screwed over a hooker and he thinks he can just treat people like crap because he was once a big name."[1]

When Dykstra finally responded to the allegations, it wasn't pretty. RadarOnline asked him about Monica Foster, and he went into a "profanity-filled tirade." "Fuck that whore," Dykstra reportedly said. He said he had never met Foster and that she had set him up by forging a check from a bank account that had been closed for years. "Do you think I stop for one second to even think about it? I don't know her, are you kidding me?" Dykstra said, according to the site. "This is some fucking black whore trying to make money off of me."[2]

Foster fired back, claiming Dykstra was upset she had exposed his scheming ways. "If he wants to be a bitch, he is fucking with the wrong ho! . . . That white son of a bitch is just doing this because I am a woman and I am black."[3]

As Dykstra's downward spiral continued to play out in public, Foster and some media outlets couldn't help but note the similarities between him and Hollywood megastar Charlie Sheen, who also made headlines for bizarre behavior and blowups with prostitutes. Perhaps not coincidentally, Dykstra and the chief warlock and Vatican assassin had reconnected in early 2011. It was later reported that the two were going into business together selling cigarettes over the Internet under the brand NicoSheen.

Amid rumors that Dykstra was actually living with Sheen and his goddesses, Sheen organized what he dubbed as the "ultimate VIP baseball excursion." The party bridged past and present baseball stars with fictional ones and brought them all together for a private screening of *Major League*, the 1989 movie starring Charlie Sheen as ex-inmate and bad boy relief pitcher Ricky "Wild Thing" Vaughn. Dykstra was reportedly tutoring Sheen on the baseball locker room rap in preparation for a possible new *Major League* movie.

Gathering at Sheen's private theater were Dykstra, Hall of Famer Eddie Murray, six-time All-Star Kenny Lofton, well-traveled infielder Todd Zeile, and big-bearded San Francisco Giants closer Brian Wilson. Pete Rose was reportedly invited as well but couldn't make it. Sheen picked some of the guys up on his private jet, including Wilson, who was in Arizona at his team's spring training camp.

Sheen invited David S. Ward, the writer and director of the movie, to introduce the film. He also allowed the boys to try on Babe Ruth's World Series Championship ring from 1927, which he had won at an auction, according to the *Hollywood Reporter*.[4]

Following the party, Dykstra and Sheen seemed inseparable. They partied on yachts and made joint and individual radio appearances gushing about each other. In various interviews, Dykstra said Sheen was "*en fuego*," "a fucking genius," a great father, a rock star, and "the most normal, humble, good-natured guy."

"Charlie Sheen and I are great friends. I've been over Charlie's house probably the last ten days," Dykstra told John Clark of NBC10 in Philadelphia in early March 2011. However, he denied living with Sheen, saying he had his own place, a $10 million house formerly owned by Macy Gray, the R&B singer known for her raspy voice and her hit "I Try."

"I'm a survivor. Whoever thinks I'm living at Charlie Sheen's—that's just more media bullshit. Okay, drama, just built up," Dykstra told Clark. "Nah, I'm his friend, man. I'm his friend."

What wasn't in dispute was that as Sheen imploded in front of America and threw away a lucrative role on top-rated television show *Two and a Half Men*, Dykstra was right by his side, cheering him on and singing his praises. In late February 2011, the two appeared on the *Alex Jones Show*, a nationally syndicated radio show with a right-wing, conspiracy theorist host. Sheen's supposedly anti-Semitic remarks about *Two and a Half Men* cocreator Chuck Lorre on the radio show prompted the cancellation of the remaining episodes of the sitcom for the season.

For his part, Dykstra defended his friend on the show. "In my world, you're a winner or a loser. Right now, Charlie's winning, and he helps me win because he stays in attack. We don't have time for whining and crying and poor me's."

In subsequent interviews, Dykstra said CBS would be crazy to fire Sheen and that, although he didn't know what Tiger Blood or Adonis DNA was, he insisted the actor was clean and sober. "Look, we all know about the past. Charlie right now is focused. He's on point. He came off medicine hard, okay, and when you do that . . . there's a reaction," he told John Clark. "People have taken a lot of the things he's made as jokes and taken them to be serious."

Sheen was eventually sacked from *Two and a Half Men*. Dykstra used the increased publicity to throw more mud on his detractors and further promote his businesses and crusade against J.P. Morgan. He told John Clark that he hadn't ripped off anyone and that the only people bad-mouthing him were "derelict losers, whores, degenerate(s) . . . disgruntled employees [and] people that had an ax to grind." Dykstra again took a shot at Kevin Coughlin without mentioning him by name, calling him an art director who didn't know anything about art. Coughlin was actually a photo editor, and Dykstra never understood the difference.

"At the beginning when I ran my companies, I tried to be nice to people when I'd fire them," Dykstra told Clark, while wearing plaid clothes that looked like they came from the Salvation Army. "I adopted a new rule. . . . It's very simple. You fuck me once, I put you on probation. You fuck me twice, I put you on death row. You fuck me three times, I execute you. Now execute in the way I fire you. No feelings. No tears. There's no crying in baseball. . . . I'm not friends with you; you work for me."

In the end, he said that when he is back on top and his former employees come back wanting to "suck my dick," he will say to them, "Go fuck yourself."

He also told Alex Jones that he was winning against J.P. Morgan and promoted his Predatory Lending Recovery business, but he failed to mention that he actually had lost the Gretzky house. Speaking on Eric Bolling's television show, he reiterated that he was a victim and said he could get his house back if he wanted to.

However, he did tell John Clark that he was a serious thorn in the side of the bank. "Don't be surprised if I'm not assassinated by one of these banks one of these days," Dykstra said. And he couldn't resist telling the world his stock-picking record had improved to 205–0, failing to mention his major loss.

CHAPTER 43

THE HUSTLER

The parking lot of Galpin Ford, a mega car dealership in California, swarmed with undercover police officers, some posing as car salesmen. Video equipment and other aspects of the sting operation were in place as well on April 13, 2012. All were waiting for their target: Dykstra.

Two days earlier, the ex-ballplayer had contacted Galpin saying he wanted a Mercedes E-350. However, Dykstra didn't know his secret was out. One of his buddies, Robert Hymers, told the police how he had helped Dykstra dupe the dealership out of three cars already by using forged financial documents.

To get the Mercedes, Dykstra went back to the same trick. He sent Galpin a bank statement showing he had more than $30,000 in the account. However, that too was a fake. The account had less than $20 in it and wasn't opened until almost a week after the date listed on the so-called statement.

"We talked to him over the phone to try and entice him, and he never came in," says Los Angeles Police Department detective Juan Contreras. After the police set the trap for a second day to no avail, they took the fight to Dykstra. "We responded to his house and arrested him there."

Contreras, who had been a street cop during the LA riots and had encountered many members of notorious gangs, such as the Bloods and the Crips, says Dykstra is a "total sociopath" and among the top three most egregious criminals he's come across in his twenty-four years on the force. "I've met a lot of gang members that have more ethics than this guy," he says.

The arrest marked a major turning point in the case for Contreras, who says he repeatedly ran into "blocked walls" because of "reluctant prosecutors" and Dykstra's celebrity status. "We're talking about the city of O. J. Simpson and Robert Blake. Nobody wants to lose."

The first crime report Contreras received relating to Dykstra was from a limo driver. "When I spoke to him, I felt so bad. . . . You could tell he wasn't making a lot of money." Dykstra dangled a hefty bonus in front of the driver if he could borrow the man's credit cards. "The poor limo driver, he got sucked in—I think he lost anywhere from $30,000 to $40,000 on two cards," Contreras says. "With that limo driver, I tried really hard, but [prosecutors] didn't want to move forward with it."

Contreras quickly learned the driver's case was not an isolated incident. In the ensuing weeks and months, he uncovered at least eighteen victims of Dykstra's scams—mostly housekeepers, pilots, drivers, and personal assistants. He investigated the crimes and worked hard to build a case against Dykstra, but prosecutors still were not interested.

Finally, Dykstra messed with the wrong guy: Alan J. Skobin, Galpin's general counsel and one of five commissioners for the LAPD. "Dykstra and his cronies had defrauded Galpin," explains LA County deputy DA Alex Karkanen. "Alan Skobin was trying to get the case filed, but apparently the case had been presented to two other DAs, and nobody had done anything."

That's when the Dykstra case fell in Karkanen's lap. He and Skobin were both attending the same luncheon, and they began talking about Dykstra. After their initial chat, the well-connected Skobin excused himself to make a phone call. Minutes later, Karkanen received a phone call from his "boss's boss's boss" with marching orders. He was on the Dykstra case.

News broke on April 15, 2011, that Nails was in jail. The LAPD's Commercial Crimes Division arrested the "defiant" Dykstra and his pal Chris Gavanis for the car scam. Dykstra reportedly had cocaine and ecstasy on him when he was picked up.

"If I hadn't arrested him . . . I think he would have been dead," Contreras says, adding that Dykstra's toenails were completely black when he was arrested. "The guy wasn't a healthy man."

In addition to the drugs, Contreras says the police found Serostim, a synthetic growth hormone, at his residence. "We recovered the hypodermic needles from inside the refrigerator with a little vial of Serostim that he was injecting himself with," Contreras says.

The police traced the Serostim to an HIV patient who, they say, had a legitimate prescription for it. That individual told them the Serostim had been stolen, but Contreras says it's not clear whether the valuable hormone had actually been swiped or whether the patient had sold it.

Once Dykstra was in custody, the Department of Justice filed unrelated bankruptcy fraud charges against Dykstra, accusing him of stealing or destroying more than $400,000 worth of property that belonged to his estate and should have been used to pay back people he owed. Dykstra later pleaded not guilty, and when the judge asked if he understood the charges, he responded, "I don't understand it, but I understand them."[1]

Dykstra's lawyer contends that no fraud was committed and that the root of the case is simply a dispute with the court-appointed bankruptcy trustee. If convicted of all thirteen counts, Dykstra faced more than eighty years behind bars.

The car case took an unexpected twist the following week when the district attorney declined to press charges against Dykstra at that time. "In light of the federal charges filed against Mr. Dykstra, LAPD investigators and prosecutors will have additional time to complete a complex and multifaceted investigation," a spokeswoman for the DA's office said, according to the *New York Daily News*.[2]

The Feds forged ahead. Prosecutors asked the court to deny Dykstra bail and to keep him in jail, but by midweek, he was sprung. Dorothy had reached out to friends and family, including Lenny's brothers, his mom, uncle, and stepsisters, to pull together the $150,000 bail.

TMZ reported that even Charlie Sheen chipped in. "The rendition-guilty trolls that kidnapped my dear friend Nails clearly forgot that he's a fellow Vatican assassin and his best pal is a warlock," Sheen told the outlet.[3] Dykstra's lawyer told the *New York Daily News* that Sheen had nothing to do with the bailout.[4] The paper also noted that Dorothy had signed a promissory note for $75,000 to help bail Dykstra out.

When speaking to friends and family, Dykstra maintained he did nothing illegal and that he was arrested because J.P. Morgan and former trustee Arturo Cisneros had exerted their influence with the FBI and the LAPD to stop him from shining more light on their "criminal" ways. He continued his sob story in a plea to fans in a May 10, 2011, op-ed piece in the *New York Post*. He said the grand theft auto charges that he had originally been arrested for were dismissed, and he accused the authorities of stealing the Ford Flex the cops say he fraudulently leased.

"Are they allowed to steal it when they brought no charges? Are they allowed to shuffle me from jail to jail in what was left of my street clothes that they made me wear for seven days without even being permitted to take a shower?" Dykstra wrote in the op-ed.

Are they allowed to then lock me up in a cell at three different courthouses, on three different days, and not even let me see a judge? Are they allowed to physically and mentally assault me and tie me up like I was some kind of animal 'because they thought it was funny?' Are they allowed to torture me to the point where two nurses happened to be walking by and saw me—came to my rescue—took my blood pressure and registered it at 180 over 120?[5]

Additionally, Dykstra said he had had $100 million in assets when first filing Chapter 11, but that it was stolen from him by corrupt bankruptcy attorneys. "I didn't make bad investments; every company that I have ever created or owned was and still is a winning company," he wrote. "Over the last two years, they have basically stolen everything from me—my family, my kids, my homes, my cars, my businesses, my reputation, my money, my life. . . . But what they can never steal is my HEART and my FIGHT—and at the end of the day, I will win and I will win big!"

The car-related case was not dropped, as Dykstra claimed, and Los Angeles prosecutors eventually took him back into custody and charged him with nearly two dozen felonies, including multiple counts of identity theft, grand theft auto, attempted grand theft auto, filing a false statement, and possession of a controlled substance.

The scam stretched well beyond Galpin to several dealerships and involved a handful of players—some willingly, others unaware—including Dorothy, Chris Gavanis, Robert Hymers, Jessica Costa, and Wilberto Hernandez.

Dykstra created fake documents showing his Predatory Lending Recovery (renamed Home Free Systems) was a legitimate and profitable company. In reality, it was a shell . . . a front. "He was presenting these financial documents that said he had millions of dollars in the bank," Karkanen, the DA, says. "He was making this stuff up, and it was all bullshit." The company Dykstra claimed he had started to help save families in foreclosure was merely a tool to scam others.

He faked paychecks, salaries, and titles for himself, Costa, and Gavanis and used the forged documents to try and lease luxury cars from various dealerships. But because of Dykstra's track record as a deadbeat, they needed a clean credit rating. So they stole the identity of Wilberto Hernandez, a friend of Hymers who had met Dykstra once, and used his Social Security number and credit score. They said Hernandez was their financial officer and cosigner.

Hymers, whom Contreras characterized as a nice, intelligent, mild-mannered, "churchgoing guy" who lacked street smarts, was an accountant with Ernst and Young at the time. He also did work for both Dykstra and Hernandez on the side, storing Hernandez's private information on his laptop. During one late-night work session at the Intercontinental Hotel in LA, Hymers fell asleep, and when he awoke, the laptop was gone, according to *Sports Illustrated*. Dykstra claimed a prostitute stole it after threatening him with a Taser, and Hymers reported the theft to the police.[6]

"He did not have common sense, and Lenny saw that and just manipulated that poor guy," Contreras says. Luckily for Hernandez, a personal credit repair consultant, Dykstra was turned away when he presented his stolen information at dealerships in Pasadena and La Crescenta.

Hymers, Gavanis, and Costa were victims as well—not as Hernandez was— but still victims, according to Contreras. They "were part of the scheme, but they were taken advantage of as well," he says. "They were each desperate in their own separate way. They got sucked into his web. . . . He destroyed their lives."

For his part, Hymers, who was twenty-seven at the time, was seduced by Dykstra and his lifestyle. Hymers enjoyed hanging out with movie stars like Sheen and had high hopes of making boatloads of cash from the business ventures they discussed.

Hymers was so blinded by Dykstra, like many before him, that he jeopardized his own finances. The ex-ballplayer talked the young man into getting a loan and giving him the money. He used his Mercedes as collateral. "Lenny, of course, said he was going to pay him back double," Contreras says. "He never saw that money, and Hymers lost that car—it was repossessed."

After Dykstra struck out using Hernandez's information, he turned to thirty-year-old Chris Gavanis, who was broke but had a solid credit rating. Dykstra enlisted Gavanis, who Contreras also says is a "nice guy," in his scheme. "He was out here from Pennsylvania. He had no mode of transportation. Dykstra promised him the world, and he got sucked in." That promise not only included a car, which Gavanis desperately needed, but also a future job at Home Free Systems making big bucks.

Using Gavanis's credit and Dykstra's phony documents, they were able to dupe Galpin Ford. Gavanis drove off the lot with a red Ford Mustang, while Hymers took a gray Lincoln MKS and Dykstra the black Ford Flex.

Jessica Costa, thirty-five at the time, was another alleged employee of Home Free Systems. Listed as the company's sales director with a salary of $120,000, the mother of five told Contreras that, although she knew Dykstra, she had never worked for the company and never received a paycheck. However, Costa's name was used on a credit application Dykstra presented to fraudulently lease a Porsche 911 in the fall of 2010. Its current whereabouts are unknown. Costa told *Sports Illustrated* that Dykstra forged her signature on the documents presented to the dealership, although the publication said the signature appeared to be hers.[7]

Costa pleaded guilty to fraud and was sentenced to ninety days in prison, which was later commuted to ninety days of house arrest. Hymers and Gavanis have pleaded no contest and are awaiting sentencing.

CHAPTER 44

DOROTHY, IN LOVE

When Contreras first tracked down Costa and showed her the pay stubs from Home Free Systems bearing her name, she pointed the finger at Dykstra's biggest coconspirator: Dorothy Van Kalsbeek. Contreras later served a search warrant at Dorothy's house. She was abrasive, Contreras says, as the police grabbed every computer under her roof. "On Dorothy's computers were the same fabricated documents that were [also] on Lenny's computer," he says, mentioning the fake pay stubs.

However, unlike Gavanis, Hymers, and Costa, Dorothy was never charged. "I wanted to go after her, but the powers that be just wanted the big fish," Contreras says. "They wanted Dykstra. . . . Everything revolved around him."

Karkanen says the DA's office thought about filing charges against Dorothy, but ultimately decided against it. "If there had been better evidence against her, we probably would have," he says. "There is a difference between what you know and what you can prove in court."

Both the police and the DA's office were convinced Dykstra did not have the computer skills to create the forged documents. "Dorothy made them all, but being able to prove that was a very difficult story because the only witnesses to her criminal activity were Dykstra and her."

Many former Dykstra employees blame Dorothy for her role in his crimes, saying she is an enabler. Terri Dykstra thinks she is just sick. "I think the key is Dorothy," Terri told me in a 2009 interview. She says that Dykstra told her Dorothy suggested the two of them could run off and get married. Other ex-employees say Dykstra relayed similar claims to them as well.

Dykstra "was the one who was getting everything and [Dorothy] was the one who was facilitating it," Karkanen says. "And she was doing it because she loved him, and she still does. . . . It's a freakish, weird relationship, but she is totally in love with Lenny Dykstra."

CHAPTER 45

NO SURRENDER

Many of the 1986 Mets were gathered in Palm Beach Gardens, Florida, in late February 2012. Dykstra was among them—granted permission by the judge to travel to the Sunshine State.

This was not a happy gathering. Hall of Fame catcher Gary "The Kid" Carter, Dykstra's teammate with the magical '86 Mets, had lost his battle with brain cancer at the age of fifty-seven. His baseball family—as well as his real family—congregated to mourn his loss and pay respects.

These were dramatically different circumstances from just a few years earlier in 2008 when many of the Mets—including Dykstra and Carter—smiled and waved good-bye to a cheering crowd after the final game at Shea Stadium. By early 2012, Carter was gone and Dykstra was convinced he would be next.

For months Dykstra kept telling friends that a fortune-teller had foreseen his fate—and it wasn't good. Dykstra, who turned forty-nine in February 2012, would not live past the age of fifty-two. In Florida, Dykstra told Wally Backman, his Phillies and Mets teammate, that "someone's going to get me" and that he would be dead within five years, according to reporter Bob Klapisch.[1]

Backman was concerned about his friend and his deteriorating condition. "Just listening to Lenny speak—he was practically incoherent," Backman told Klapisch. "He was whispering, mumbling. . . . It was sad to see what'd happened to him. It broke my heart. . . . I just hope Lenny makes it."

In court in California, Dykstra's bizarre behavior continued.

When Dykstra and his attorney would go to the back of the courtroom to talk—within earshot of the judge, prosecutors, and pretty much everyone else—he would often get belligerent, cursing at the top of his lungs and yelling, "You motherfucker, you stupid fucker."

However, when it came time to discuss a plea deal with Karkanen, Dykstra was a totally different person. "I laid it out for him, and I gave him a couple of options as to what he could plead to," Karkanen says. "I said, 'You can either have a three-year lock, which means you have to stay in prison for three years, or you can have what is called a four-year lid, which means the judge can sentence you up to four years but you can always ask for probation.'"

From that point forward, Dykstra tried to turn on the charm, complimenting Karkanen and asking for his advice. "He's obviously not an intellectual, but he's not an idiot either," Karkanen says. He warned Dykstra, "Hey, I'm not your buddy; I'm the DA. I'm the guy trying to put you in jail."

That didn't deter the ever-persistent Dykstra, who called Karkanen's office. "My secretary thought it was some guy named Larry, and he convinced her to give him my personal cell phone number, so he calls me up. I told him, 'Look, you can't call me. I'm not your pal.'"

Dykstra eventually took the deal—the four-year lid. He agreed to plead no contest, which is like admitting guilt because he is not contesting the charges. In exchange for Dykstra's accepting the deal, the DA agreed to drop twenty-one of the twenty-five charges,[2] reducing Dykstra's potential jail time from a maximum of twelve years all the way down to four years or less.

With sentencing approaching, Contreras and Karkanen prepared an extensive PowerPoint presentation for the judge. It contained as much damaging information as they could find, including his "three darkies and a bitch" comment and excerpts from a video they pulled from Dorothy's computer showing a belligerent Dykstra talking about, among other things, firing his mom.

"When we delivered that PowerPoint disc to his attorney, the very next day he files a motion to withdraw his plea," Contreras says. "We knew right then and there it was all because of the PowerPoint presentation. He knew it was just going to be too damaging for him."

Dykstra wanted to duke it out in front of a jury. "I did not commit a crime, and now I have the evidence to prove it," Dykstra told the *New York Daily News*. "They locked me up in maximum security like Hannibal Lecter. . . . What happened to innocent until proven guilty?"[3]

He added that the prosecution had not investigated the case properly. Dykstra was "so full of bullshit . . . it's hard to tell where the bullshit stops and the insanity begins," Karkanen says. The judge denied Dykstra's request, and on March 5 it came time to face justice.

When Contreras, Karkanen, and Dykstra arrived in court, the place was packed with reporters and television cameras. The attorneys huddled with the judge in chambers, and when they returned, the judge cleared the courtroom. "She goes, 'I want everybody out of here,'" Contreras recalls, noting that only he, Karkanen, Dykstra, and Dykstra's attorney were instructed to stay.

The judge asked to see the PowerPoint presentation and was "appalled" by its content, Contreras says. "In my opinion, after the judge saw that, it was over. . . . She said we couldn't show it again. . . . [Dykstra's] attorney claimed character assassination, but everything spoke for itself."

When it finally came time for Dykstra to address the court, Karkanen worried he might strike a repentant tone and curry favor with the judge. "I was concerned that he was going to stand up and say, 'I was on drugs. I messed up. I'm really sorry. I'm embarrassed by my behavior,'" Karkanen says. If Dykstra had done that, Karkanen thinks he would have had a "decent shot" at getting probation.

"I do have remorse for some of the things I've done," Dykstra said. "But because I wasn't a perfect person am I a criminal? Everyone wants to make me out to be a monster."[4] He added that had the judge granted his request to withdraw his plea, he would have been proven innocent. Karkanen said Dykstra "basically rambled on about how the police were assholes and how all this was bullshit and how this wasn't really a crime and he wasn't really a criminal."

Judge Cynthia Ulfig sentenced Dykstra to three years in jail, noting that he knew what he was doing. "Even if he's sitting in jail, he'll still think he did nothing wrong and that everybody screwed him," Terri told me years before the sentencing. Dykstra received credit for about a year's worth of time already served.

Andrew Flier, Dykstra's attorney, said that the sentence was unfair and his client was targeted because of his celebrity status. "No way this wasn't a probationary case," he said. "To give him state prison is outrageous. I find it disgusting."[5]

Karkanen's office debated expanding the case against Dykstra to include indecent exposure charges and intentionally writing a rubber check to porn star Monica Foster. However, in the end, Karkanen's office decided to keep the case "clean," meaning they focused mainly on the core of the charges—the car crimes. However, other law enforcement agencies were not yet done with Dykstra. His serial Craigslist scamming and indecent exposure attracted attention.

Contreras said while investigating the car theft case, one of Dykstra's personal assistants told him about a woman who had answered a Craigslist ad in January 2011 posted by James London, one of Dykstra's aliases. The assistant said that "something happened," and although he didn't know the details, he knew something was wrong.

He gave Contreras the woman's phone number, and Contreras invited the woman, whom he dubbed Jane Doe, to the police station to tell him what had happened. Once there, she recalled how while she was sending out e-mails at Dykstra's Wilshire penthouse, he snatched her purse and started rummaging through it. "Obviously, he was going to grab her credit card or her Social Security Number or whatever," Contreras says. When she questioned Dykstra, he told her she would get her purse back at the end of the day, and then he put it in the bedroom.

A short time later, Dykstra summoned the woman to his bedroom. She asked what he wanted, and he told her to cup her hands. "He grabbed baby oil and put baby oil in her cupped hands and says, 'You're going to give me a massage,'" Contreras reports. "She goes, 'No, I'm not.'"

He went to a nearby dresser and grabbed a knife—it looked letter-opener-only sharp. Dykstra pointed it at her throat and threatened her. He laid "down on his bed, face up, naked and demanded her to rub his upper thighs around his genital areas," Contreras says. "And she did it because he still had the knife by his side. He was forcing her to rub his genitals. She said he was erect. She was uncomfortable."

She continued to rub him up until he fell asleep, and then she grabbed her purse and bolted out of there. "Jane Doe was lucky—that could have been really bad," Contreras says. "Everything was escalating. I don't know if it was his drug use or something else, but something wasn't right. He was getting more violent."

In April 2012, Dykstra pleaded no contest to charges of lewd conduct and assault with a deadly weapon relating to the Craigslist massage scam. He was sentenced to 270 days in jail and placed on probation for three years. The authorities have also limited his use of social networking sites. The jail time in the case will run concurrent with his sentence for the car fraud case.

CHAPTER 46

NAILING NAILS

As Dykstra sat in jail, awaiting a conclusion to the federal charges, his "perverted pastime pleasures" took an odd twist, according to *TMZ*.

"We're told Dykstra sometimes puts a sheet over his head—for fun—pokes a hole around the waist area, and sticks his 'baseball bat' through the hole . . . for the amusement of anyone who dares to look," the celebrity news outlet reported.[1]

However, at other times during his ordeal, Dykstra struck a much more repentant tone. "I really for the first time understand humility," Dykstra told the *New York Daily News* during an interview in late 2011 at The Hills rehab center. "It's not everybody else's fault. It's not a coincidence that I'm here. It happened because I was using drugs and alcohol . . . The way I lived my life helped me in baseball. But when you're spending $28,000 for a bottle of wine and liking it? Nothing was ever enough. The punishment gods said, 'You know what we're going to do? We're going to put you in fucking jail. We're going to put you in the cooler because you have to pay for some things.'"[2]

On Monday, December 3, 2012, it was time to face the music . . . again. This time he was to be sentenced for his bankruptcy-related crimes. He originally faced up to eighty years behind bars if convicted of all charges but had accepted a plea deal that knocked that number down to a max of twenty years. However, prosecutors in the case were seeking a much lighter thirty months behind bars.

During the hearing, deputy federal public defender Hilary Potashner had a surprise to reveal. She told the court that Dykstra was "beaten to a pulp" in April and had his teeth knocked out while in jail, according to an Associated Press account.[3] *The Los Angeles Times* reported that Dykstra suffered a bloody nose in an altercation with prison guards while in custody.

Steve Whitmore, a spokesman for the sheriff's department, which runs the jail, denied that Dykstra's teeth were damaged but did confirm to the outlet that there had been an incident at Monterey Park Hospital. "Dykstra became agitated and assaulted a [medical technician] and a nurse," Whitmore said, according to the *Times*. "Deputies then used force to restrain Dykstra."[4]

When all was said and done, U.S. district judge Dean Pregerson issued a six-and-a-half-month sentence to run concurrent with Dykstra's other jail sentences. He had taken Dykstra's substance- and alcohol-abuse history into account. In addition, Dykstra was ordered to perform 500 hours of community service and pay restitution of $200,000.

"I'd like to first apologize to the court, to the government, and to my family for my past conduct," Dykstra said to the court, according to the *New York Daily News* account. "I don't think I'm a bad person, but I made some bad decisions, and I'm paying for them."

Dykstra said he was looking forward to a "new start" and planned to stay active in the community and take his community service seriously. "I'm looking forward to opening up a new chapter." Then, dressed in prison garb, he was led away, giving a thumbs up to Terri, Cutter, and other friends and family who had shown up to support him.

As for Bill Conlin, he was awarded the 2011 J. G. Taylor Spink Award at the Baseball Hall of Fame induction ceremony in Cooperstown, New York. Months later he resigned from his post at the *Philadelphia Daily News* in disgrace after he learned the *Philadelphia Inquirer* was about to publish an article accusing him of molesting four children between the ages of seven and twelve in the 1970s. Additional victims came forward following the news, bumping the number up to seven. Reports indicate that Conlin will not face charges because the statute of limitations has expired.

EPILOGUE

Probably the saddest aspect of this cautionary tale is that not all that long ago Lenny Dykstra, regardless of how you feel about him, had the foresight to recognize a potential problem in others that he couldn't see in himself. The Players Club, ironically, set out to help players prevent all the problems Dykstra faces today—prison, divorce, bankruptcy, and the destruction of his family unit.

When I think back over this whole ordeal, one anecdote sums up what Lenny Dykstra, my childhood hero, has become.

Former Mets pitcher Dwight "Doc" Gooden, who has a history of alcohol and drug abuse, was participating in the VH1 television show *Celebrity Rehab* with Dr. Drew Pinsky, trying to get his life in order. Dykstra showed up unprompted, unannounced, and attempted to break Gooden out of the facility.

"He thought that I had been hypnotized and [Dr. Drew] got me in there and was holding me hostage," Gooden said on WFAN's *Boomer and Carton* show. "He tried to come in with two guys to get me out of there."[1]

When Gooden told Dykstra he wanted to stay and finish his treatment, Dykstra grabbed Gooden's bags and loaded them into his car, telling the former pitcher to call him if he changed his mind and wanted to leave.

The end result was Dykstra essentially taking Gooden's belongings and leaving. "I love Lenny," Gooden told the *New York Daily News*. "Deep down, he's a really good guy."[2]

Ron Darling, another pitcher on that '86 Mets team who helped Dykstra with the Players Club, saw it this way. "He's a complicated man who somehow lost his soul," Darling told reporter Bob Klapisch. "Let's hope when Lenny pays his debts to society that we judge him hopefully on his future good acts," said Darling, "not his lost years."[3]

NOTES

Chapter 1

1. Chris Jones, "The Game," *Esquire*, March 1, 2003, http://www.esquire.com/features/the-game/ESQ0303-MAR_GAME.

Chapter 2

1. NHL.com, http://www.nhl.com/ice/player.htm?id=8447470.
2. LostHockey.com, http://web.archive.org/web/20080602071719/http://www.losthockey.com/profiles/leswick_jack/jack_leswick.cfm.
3. Obituaries, "Tony Leswick; NHL All-Star on Red Wings," *Los Angeles Times*, July 9, 2001, http://articles.latimes.com/2001/jul/09/local/me-20367.
4. Drake was scouting for the Kansas City Royals organization when I interviewed him.

Chapter 3

1. "Lenny Dykstra Compares Himself to Gandhi," interview with John Clark of NBC10 in Philadelphia, March 8, 2011, http://www.nbcphiladelphia.com/news/sports/Raw_Video_Lenny_Dykstra_Compares_Himself_to_Gandhi_Philadelphia-117546328.html.
2. "Bride, Ballgirl Bring Life to Wrigley," *Chicago Sun-Times*, August 5, 1986.
3. "Unsinkable Lenny Dykstra: Former Garden Grove Star Has Hustled into the Hearts of Mets Fans," *Los Angeles Times*, August 21, 1986.
4. MTV, 1986, http://www.youtube.com/watch?v=OzHwiDZ3pgQ.
5. Bruce Newman, "Great Scott, What a Show," *Sports Illustrated*, October 20, 1986, http://sportsillustrated.cnn.com/vault/article/magazine/MAG1065355/index.htm.
6. "Unlikely Hero Wins for Mets," *New York Times*, October 12, 1986.
7. Newman, "Great Scott."
8. Scott would go on to win the series MVP award despite playing for the losing club.
9. "Mets Top-Heavy Choice," Associated Press, October 17, 1986, http://www.chron.com/CDA/archives/archive.mpl/1986_273575/mets-top-heavy-choice.html.
10. "Boyd's Troubled Trail Leads to Hospital," *Chicago Tribune Wires*, July 19, 1986; Leigh Grossman, *The Red Sox Fan Handbook* (Cambridge, MA: Rounder Books, 2001).
11. WFAN interview with Mike Francesa, July 25, 2008.
12. Ben Walker, "Real Mets Finally Show Up for Series, Defeat Boston 7–1," Associated Press, October 22, 1986.
13. Stan Hochman, "Evans: Fumbled Homer Was Really a Corker," *Philadelphia Daily News*, October 23, 1986.
14. "Red Sox Fall Again; It's Even," Associated Press, October 23, 1986.
15. William E. Geist, "About New York; Gritty Dykstra Gets Gritty City Valentine," *New York Times*, October 29, 1986, http://www.nytimes.com/1986/10/29/nyregion/about-new-york-gritty-dykstra-gets-a-gritty-city-valentine.html.

Chapter 4

1. Joseph Durso, "Mets Pick Up Wilson's Option," *New York Times*, November 16, 1988, http://articles.nytimes.com/1988/11/16/sports/baseball-mets-pick-up-wilson-s-option.html.
2. Joseph Durso, "Santana, Dykstra, Fernandez Sign," *New York Times*, March 7, 1987, http://www.nytimes.com/1987/03/07/sports/santana-dykstra-fernandez-sign.html.
3. Joseph Durso, "McReynolds Loses in Ruling on Salary," *New York Times*, February 18, 1987, http://www.nytimes.com/1987/02/18/sports/mcreynolds-loses-in-ruling-on-salary.html.
4. Ira Berkow, "Dykstra Is Struggling to Keep Starting Spot," *New York Times*, March 29, 1987,

http://www.nytimes.com/1987/03/29/sports/dykstra-is-struggling-to-keep-starting-spot.html.

5. Michael Martinez, "New Met Casualty: Dykstra's Morale," *New York Times*, July 8, 1987, http://www.nytimes.com/1987/07/08/sports/new-met-casualty-dykstra-s-morale.html.

6. Joseph Durso, "Dykstra Displays New Look," *New York Times*, February 25, 1988, http://www.nytimes.com/1988/02/25/sports/dykstra-displays-new-look.html.

7. WFAN interview with Mike Francesa, July 25, 2008.

8. Mark Hersch, "Plenty of Nothing," *Sports Illustrated*, October 10, 1988, http://sportsillustrated.cnn.com/vault/article/magazine/MAG1067843/index.htm.

9. "Viola Leads the Mets Already—in Salary," *Deseret News*, August 2, 1989, http://www.deseretnews.com/article/57825/VIOLA-LEADS-THE-METS-ALREADY-IN-SALARY.html.

10. WFAN interview with Francesa.

11. Joseph Durso, "Dykstra Makes Noise but Mets Roll to Victory," *New York Times*, June 24, 1989, http://www.nytimes.com/1989/06/24/sports/dykstra-makes-noise-but-mets-roll-to-victory.html.

12. At the time, Terri had another child, Gavin, whom Lenny adopted.

13. "Dykstra and Phillies Agree on 1990 Pact," *New York Times*, November 15, 1989, http://www.nytimes.com/1989/11/15/sports/sports-people-baseball-dykstra-and-phillies-agree-on-1990-pact.html.

Chapter 5

1. "Lunching Senator Finds Too Much Salt in Dykstra's Language," *St. Petersburg Times*, January 1, 1994.

2. Robert McFadden, "Giamatti, Scholar and Baseball Chief, Dies at 51," *New York Times*, September 2, 1989, http://www.nytimes.com/1989/09/02/obituaries/giamatti-scholar-and-baseball-chief-dies-at-51.html.

3. Claire Smith, "Free-Spirited Lenny Dykstra Belly-Flops to Earth," *New York Times*, May 23, 1991, http://www.nytimes.com/1991/05/23/sports/baseball-free-spirited-lenny-dykstra-belly-flops-to-earth.html.

4. Bob Klapisch, "Dykstra's Downward Spiral Ongoing," Fox Sports, March 6, 2012, http://msn.foxsports.com/mlb/story/Lenny-Dykstra-New-York-Mets-jail-time-fall-from-grace-030612.

5. "Bullpen Cost Phils a Title and Dykstra MVP Trophy," *San Diego Union–Tribune*, October 25, 1993; Jennifer Frey, "If Only Dykstra Could Pitch in Relief," *New York Times*, October 24, 1993, http://www.nytimes.com/1993/10/24/sports/world-series-if-only-dykstra-could-pitch-in-relief.html.

6. Ian Thomsen, "Oo-la-la Lenny," *Sports Illustrated*, December 6, 1993, http://sportsillustrated.cnn.com/vault/article/magazine/MAG1138703/index.htm.

Chapter 6

1. Ian Thomsen, "Oo-la-la, Lenny," *Sports Illustrated*, December 6, 1993, http://sportsillustrated.cnn.com/vault/article/magazine/MAG1138703/3/index.htm.

2. Chris Jones, "The Game," *Esquire*, March 1, 2003, http://www.esquire.com/features/the-game/ESQ0303-MAR_GAME.

3. Bill Madden, "Lenny Manages Eyes Headfirst Dive into Dugout," *New York Daily News*, February 29, 1997.

4. "Without Assurances, Dykstra Wants Release, "Associated Press, March 10, 1998, http://www.southcoasttoday.com/apps/pbcs.dll/article?AID=/19980310/NEWS/303109941.

5. Don Bostrom, "Francona Will Make Sure Spring Training Is Booked Solid," *Morning Call*, January 24, 1999.

6. Bill Madden, "Dykstra's Not Playing Games," *New York Daily News*, March 1, 2001.

Chapter 8

1. "Where Wall Street's Caviar Set Still Thrives," *New York Times*, March 24, 2008.

Chapter 13

1. We ended up pushing back the April 1 target date.

Chapter 14

1. The magazine was printed, complete with the masthead listing all of Doubledown's employees and writers.

Chapter 15

1. Lance Pugmire, "Fingering Nails," *Los Angeles Times*, April, 24, 2005.
2. WFAN interview with Mike Francesa, July 25, 2008.
3. Marilyn and Dennis, who died unexpectedly just a few years prior to the car wash fiasco, had divorced decades earlier. Marilyn then married Richard.
4. WFAN interview with Francesa.

Chapter 16

1. Keith Kelly, "Dykstra Swings Away," *New York Post*, May 2, 2008, http://m.nypost.com/p/news/business/item_i26EMPNDVKTLogfJA9I0ZJ.
2. Randall Lane later claimed the final figure was about $87,000.

Chapter 17

1. Joshua Lipton, "Piggyback," *Forbes*, June 30, 2008, http://www.forbes.com/forbes/2008/0630/052.html.

Chapter 18

1. Arash Markazi, "Cutter Dykstra Following Father's Baseball Path at Westlake High," *Sports Illustrated*, April 14, 2008, http://sportsillustrated.cnn.com/2008/writers/arash_markazi/04/14/dykstra.0411/index.html.
2. "Dykstra Following His Father's Basepath," *Ventura County Star*, April 11, 2007, http://www.vcstar.com/news/2007/apr/11/hes-a-diamond-cutter/?print=1.
3. Mike Scarr, "Young Dykstra Has More Than a Name," MLB.com, May 29, 2008, http://mlb.mlb.com/news/print.jsp?ymd=20080529&content_id=2792400&vkey=draft2008&fext=.jsp.
4. Randall Lane, "Jim Cramer Stock Touting Scandal," *The Daily Beast*, June 27, 2010, http://www.thedailybeast.com/articles/2010/06/28/jim-cramer-lenny-dykstra-stock-scandal-reports-the-zeroes.html.
5. Teri Buhl, "Penny Stock Company Sues Author Randall Lane on Alleged Lenny Dykstra Stock Pump Report," HedgeTracker.com, July 1, 2010, http://www.hedgetracker.com/article/Penny-Stock-Company-sues-author-Randall-Lane-on-alleged-Lenny-Dykstra-stock-pump-report.

Chapter 20

1. Christina Boyle, "Christie Brinkley, Peter Cook Divorce Ends with Settlement," *New York Daily News*, July 10, 2008, http://www.nydailynews.com/gossip/christie-brinkley-peter-cook-divorce-ends-settlement-article-1.347592.
2. Christina Boyle, "Shrink: Peter Cook Is Self-Absorbed Egotist with Sexual Compulsions," *New York Daily News*, July 9, 2008, http://www.nydailynews.com/gossip/shrink-peter-cook-self-absorbed-egotist-sexual-compulsions-article-1.348963.

Chapter 21

1. Josh Tyrangiel, "Lil Wayne: The Best Rapper Alive," *Time*, July 3, 2008, http://www.time.com/time/magazine/article/0,9171,1820148,00.html.

Chapter 22

1. Roger Ebert, "Wall Street," *Chicago Sun Times*, December 11, 1987, http://rogerebert.suntimes.com/apps/pbcs.dll/article?AID=/19871211/REVIEWS/712110302/1023.

2. Bruce Kelly, "Dykstra Down on Strikes," *Investment News*, May 3, 2009, http://www.investmentnews.com/article/20090503/REG/305039984.

Chapter 23

1. Keith Kelly, "Dykstra Nailed on Past Deals," *New York Post*, November 28, 2008, http://www.nypost.com/p/news/business/item_G4KKrKLYQWPrwY14FktaOI.

Chapter 25

1. Mike Fish, "Dykstra's Business: A Bed of 'Nails,'" ESPN, April 22, 2009, http://sports.espn.go.com/mlb/news/story?id=4084962.
2. "Living the American Dream," *Haute Living*, July 6, 2007, http://www.hauteliving.com/2007/07/living-the-american-dream/485/.

Chapter 27

1. "Nails in Jail," CNN/*Sports Illustrated*, October 14, 1999, http://sportsillustrated.cnn.com/baseball/mlb/news/1999/10/13/dykstra_arrested_ap.
2. Ibid.

Chapter 32

1. Brown offered to switch the full payments from TheStreet.com over to me until I was paid back. However, by the time of the suggestion, that was no longer possible.

Chapter 33

1. Dareh Gregorian, "Dykstra Whiffs on 7G Bill: Suit," *New York Post*, November 15, 2008, http://www.nypost.com/p/news/national/item_sNlD18eVfdjlHkpgcJKswM.
2. Thomas Zambito, "Ex-Met Lenny Dykstra Settles Bill with Accountants, Then Runs Mouth," *New York Daily News*, November 28, 2008.
3. Keith Kelly, "Dykstra Nailed on Past Deals," *New York Post*, November 28, 2008, http://www.nypost.com/p/news/business/item_G4KKrKLYQWPrwY14FktaOI.
4. Rich Scarcella, "Williams Has Harsh Words for Ex-Teammate Dykstra," *Reading Eagle*, January 16, 2009, http://readingeagle.com/article.aspx?id=121573.
5. Ibid.

Chapter 34

1. Dykstra promised me a $250,000 bonus once he sold his first airplane. Another time he offered me a rent-free apartment on Manhattan's West Side.

Chapter 36

1. Doubledown Media Letter, http://www.foliomag.com/pdf/Doubledown_Investor_Letter.pdf.
2. "Magazine Publisher Doubledown Media Closes," Reuters, February 3, 2009, http://www.reuters.com/article/2009/02/03/doubledown-idUSN0352987220090203.
3. Adam Warner, "Breaking News: More Tips from Lenny," *Daily Options Report*, January 24, 2009, http://205.164.56.138/feeds/Daily-Options-Report/110.
4. TheStreet.com declined comment for *Nailed!*

Chapter 37

1. "Stewart Slings Barbs Face-to-Face with Cramer," CNN Entertainment, March 13, 2009.
2. Stephanie Hoops, "Details of Dykstra Marriage Emerge from Divorce Papers," *Ventura County Star*, July 17, 2009, http://www.vcstar.com/news/2009/jul/17/details-of-dykstra-marriage-emerge-from-divorce.
3. Through a spokesman, Cutter declined an interview request for *Nailed!*

Chapter 40

1. "Lenny Dykstra Speaks Out," video, CNBC, August 11, 2009, http://video.cnbc.com/gallery/?video=1211884386.

2. Stephanie Hoops, "Dykstra Shut Out of Lake Sherwood," *Ventura County Star*, September 17, 2009, http://www.vcstar.com/news/2009/sep/17/guards-block-access-to-dykstras-lake-sherwood.

3. Ken Belson, "Dykstra's World Series Ring Tops $56,000 in Auction," *New York Times*, October 2, 2009, http://bats.blogs.nytimes.com/2009/10/02/dykstras-world-series-ring-tops-56000-in-auction.

4. "Dykstra's House 'Unshowable,' Court Papers Say," *Wall Street Journal*, December 30, 2009, http://blogs.wsj.com/bankruptcy/2009/12/30/dykstras-house-unshowable-court-papers-say.

5. Jane Wells, "Lenny Dykstra Strikes Out," CNBC, September 1, 2009, http://www.cnbc.com/id/32650256/site/14081545.

6. "Dykstra: A Lying, Deceitful Fraud," *The Smoking Gun*, June 30, 2010, http://www.thesmokinggun.com/documents/sports/dykstra-lying-deceitful-fraud.

7. "Dykstra Strikes Back at Bankruptcy Judge," *Wall Street Journal*, April 9, 2010, http://blogs.wsj.com/bankruptcy/2010/04/09/dykstra-strikes-back-at-bankruptcy-judge/.

8. Alison Gendar, "Ex-Met Lenny Dykstra Claims He Was Hoodwinked into Taking Out $20M in Loans He Couldn't Afford," *New York Daily News*, March 17, 2010, http://www.nydailynews.com/news/national/ex-met-lenny-dykstra-claims-hoodwinked-20m-loans-afford-article-1.177620.

9. "Dykstra Drops JPMorgan Suit, Foreclosure Looms," Reuters, March 29, 2010.

10. Jane Wells, "Dykstra: You Mess with Nails You Get the Hammer," CNBC, August 6, 2010, http://www.cnbc.com/id/38597125.

11. Ibid.

12. Alejandro Lazo, "Ex-Baseball Star and Bankrupt Financial 'Guru' Dykstra Envisions a Comeback," *Los Angeles Times*, October 5, 2010, http://articles.latimes.com/2010/oct/05/business/la-fi-lenny-dykstra-20101006.

13. Stephanie Hoops, "Dykstra Home Is Sold at Auction," *Ventura County Star*, November 20, 2010, http://www.vcstar.com/news/2010/nov/20/dykstra-home-is-sold-at-auction/.

Chapter 41

1. Alejandro Lazo, "Ex-Baseball Star and Bankrupt Financial 'Guru' Dykstra Envisions a Comeback," *Los Angeles Times*, October 5, 2010, http://articles.latimes.com/2010/oct/05/business/la-fi-lenny-dykstra-20101006.

2. Stephanie Hoops, "Foreclosure-Fighting Lawyer Faces Questions on His Ethics," *Ventura County Star*, October 29, 2010, http://www.vcstar.com/news/2010/oct/29/foreclosure-fighting-lawyer-faces-questions-on.

3. Ibid.

4. "Dykstra Investigated over Naked Massage Claim," *TMZ*, April, 22, 2011, http://www.tmz.com/2011/04/22/lenny-dykstra-lewd-conduct-investigation-housekeeper-naked-massage-allegations-lapd-cops-police.

5. "Woman Alleges Lenny Dykstra Stripped Naked, Asked for a Massage During Her Job Interview," *New York Daily News*, April 26, 2011, http://www.nydailynews.com/sports/baseball/mets/woman-alleges-lenny-dykstra-stripped-naked-asked-massage-job-interview-article-1.116200.

6. Robert Faturechi, "No Charges Against Lenny Dykstra in Alleged Sex Assault," *Los Angeles Times*, January 12, 2011.

Chapter 42

1. "Scorned Hooker Says Baseball Legend Lenny Dykstra 'Thinks He Can Treat People Like Crap,'" RadarOnline, December 31, 2010, http://www.radaronline.com/exclusives/2010/12/exclusive-interview-scorned-hooker-says-baseball-legend-lenny-dykstra-thinks-he.

2. "Ex Baseball Star Lenny Dykstra Rants: 'Black Wh*re Trying to Making Money Off Me,'" RadarOnline, January 18, 2011, http://www.radaronline.com/exclusives/2011/01/exclusive-interview-ex-baseball-star-lenny-dykstra-rants-black-whre-trying-making.

3. Ibid.

4. Bryan Alexander, "Inside Charlie Sheen's 'Major League' Bash," *Hollywood Reporter*, February 3, 2011, http://www.hollywoodreporter.com/news/inside-charlie-sheens-major-league-160813.

Chapter 43

1. "Lenny Dykstra Pleads Not Guilty," Associated Press, June 13, 2011, http://sports.espn.go.com/mlb/news/story?id=6657598.

2. Nancy Dillon, "Lenny Dykstra's Brother, Brian, Says Former Mets Hero Deserves to 'Pay for What He Did,'" *New York Daily News*, April 18, 2011.
3. "Charlie Sheen Bails Out Lenny Dykstra," *TMZ*, April 26, 2011.
4. Nancy Dillon, "Charlie Sheen Had 'Nothing to Do' with Paying Former New York Mets Star Lenny Dykstra's Bail: Lawyer," *New York Daily News*, April 26, 2011, http://www.nydailynews.com/sports/baseball/mets/charlie-sheen-paying-york-mets-star-lenny-dykstra-bail-lawyer-article-1.116429.
5. Lenny Dykstra, "Lenny: I'm Going to Come Out Swinging," *New York Post*, May 10, 2011, http://www.nypost.com/p/news/local/lenny_going_to_come_out_swinging_byB3LLKWTpe pfTMhetFXbK.
6. "How Lenny Dykstra Got Nailed," *Sports Illustrated*, March 12, 2012, http://sportsillustrated.cnn.com/vault/article/magazine/MAG1195702/index.htm.
7. Ibid.

Chapter 45

1. Bob Klapisch, "Dykstra's Downward Spiral Ongoing," Fox Sports, March 6, 2012, http://msn.foxsports.com/mlb/story/Lenny-Dykstra-New-York-Mets-jail-time-fall-from-grace-030612. Klapisch covers baseball for *The Record* in New Jersey and worked at the *New York Post* and *New York Daily News*. The author of five books, he was recently voted a top-five columnist in the country by the Associated Press sports editors.
2. Greg Risling, "Lenny Dykstra Sentenced to Three Years in Prison for Theft," Associated Press, March 5, 2012, http://www.vcstar.com/news/2012/mar/05/lenny-dykstra-sentenced-to-three-years-in-prison.
3. Nancy Dillon, "Ex-Met Dykstra Seeks to Withdraw Plea," *New York Daily News*, February 29, 2012.
4. Risling, "Lenny Dykstra Sentenced to Three Years in Prison for Theft."
5. Ibid.

Chapter 46

1. "Dykstra, Murray, Debarge: Jailbird Homies!" *TMZ*, May, 6, 2012, http://www.tmz.com/2012/05/06/lenny-dykstra-conrad-murray-james-debarge-la-county-jail.
2. Nancy Dillon, "Former New York Mets star Lenny Dykstra is sentenced to more than six months in prison for bankruptcy fraud after a judge accepted his request for leniency," *New York Daily News*, December 3, 2012, http://www.nydailynews.com/news/national/ex-met-lenny-dykstra-sentenced-prison-article-1.1212719.
3. Greg Risling, "Dykstra sentenced in bankruptcy fraud case," Associated Press, December 3, 2012, http://www.google.com/hostednews/ap/article/ALeqM5gnBTlVDf3gc8lJlogFFHfPvWB-wiA?docId=202dd30572b04c1999f110b8c3778eaa.
4. "Lenny Dykstra assaulted 2 L.A. jail officials, authorities say," *Los Angeles Times*, December 4, 2012, http://latimesblogs.latimes.com/lanow/2012/12/lenny-dykstra-assaulted-2-la-jail-officials-authorities-say.html.

Epilogue

1. Justin Tarranova, "Gooden Says Dykstra Tried to Bust Him Out of 'Celebrity Rehab,'" *New York Post*, March 24, 2011, http://www.nypost.com/p/blogs/backpage/gooden_says_dykstra_tried_rehab_Dwa8lnX2ZYvXsgCfNeNtUL.
2. Christian Red, "Lenny Dykstra Makes Bizarre House Call to Dwight Gooden During Doc's 'Celebrity Rehab' Stint," *New York Daily News*, May 25, 2011.
3. Bob Klapisch, "Dykstra's Downward Spiral Ongoing," Fox Sports, March 6, 2012, http://msn.foxsports.com/mlb/story/Lenny-Dykstra-New-York-Mets-jail-time-fall-from-grace-030612.